THE AMERICAN EXPLORATION AND TRAVEL SERIES

THE
CALIFORNIA
COAST

THE
CALIFORNIA
COAST

A Bilingual Edition of

DOCUMENTS
FROM THE
SUTRO COLLECTION

TRANSLATED AND EDITED IN 1891
BY GEORGE BUTLER GRIFFIN
RE-EDITED WITH AN EMENDED TRANS-
LATION, ANNOTATION, AND PREFACE BY

Donald C. Cutter

UNIVERSITY OF OKLAHOMA PRESS
NORMAN

By Donald C. Cutter

The Diary of Ensign Gabriel Moraga's Expedition of Discovery in the Sacramento Valley, 1808 (Los Angeles, 1957)
Malaspina in California (San Francisco, 1960)
Tadeo Haenke y el final de una vieja polémica (co-author) (Buenos Aires, 1966)
The California Coast: Documents from the Sutro Collection (editor) (Norman, 1969)

The paper on which this book is printed bears the watermark of the University of Oklahoma Press and has an intended effective life of at least three hundred years.

LIBRARY OF CONGRESS CATALOG CARD NUMBER: 69–16712

New edition copyright 1969 by the University of Oklahoma Press, Publishing Division of the University. Composed and printed at Norman, Oklahoma, U.S.A., by the University of Oklahoma Press. First edition.

PREFACE

Among the early annual *Publications of the Historical Society of Southern California,* the one to which recent Western historians have made frequent reference is Volume II, Part I, published in 1891. That publication is entitled *Documents from the Sutro Collection,* as translated, annotated, and edited by George Butler Griffin, president of the Society at that time. The collection contains nineteen documents which deal with the activities of the Spaniards in their early explorations of California and adjacent coastal waters; these accounts are of such lasting interest that they were re-edited, with additional notes, emended translations, and some corrections of the Spanish text made by comparison with existing copies of the documents.

The new notes include information about the uses subsequent scholars have made of these documents, as well as information about alternate translations and other places where the Spanish texts have appeared. Although several of the documents have been used by more recent scholars, this in no way diminishes desirability of reproducing this volume; on the contrary, it merely serves to illustrate the value of the original publication, which included many informative documents. Both Charles E. Chapman, in *A History of California: The Spanish Period,* and Henry R. Wagner, in *Spanish Voyages to the Northwest Coast of America in the Sixteenth Century,* made extensive use of the documents reproduced in this volume. In the former work, Chapters X and XI incorporate these materials with appropriate footnote acknowledgment on page 142. More recently, W. Michael Mathes reprinted versions of many of the sixteenth- and seventeenth-century documents in Spanish without annotations in the first volume of *Documentos para la historia de la demarcación comercial de California* (2 vols., Madrid, 1965).

In 1891, the date of publication of Griffin's work, Hubert Howe Bancroft had completed his monumental work on California's early history. In fact, George Butler Griffin had for some time worked in the preparation of that landmark of local history, the seven-volume

History of California. It is apparent from the copious remarks made by Griffin in his footnotes to the 1891 edition that he was not on friendly terms with Bancroft at the time of publication of the former's work. That Bancroft reciprocated this ill feeling seems evident from the index listing of Griffin in Bancroft's works, for Griffin's name does not appear on the designated text page; apparently it was removed from the text but not from the index. Such a practice was not unknown in the Bancroft works.

Research has disclosed an interesting sidelight on Sutro's acquisition of the documents presented here. This does not reflect upon the value of the selection of materials, but rather upon the activity of the San Francisco engineer's agents in Spain, who perhaps "took" Sutro for more money than the accomplished work merited. According to Griffin, "Mr. Sutro caused a search for documents relating to the history of California to be made in that great magazine of Spanish-American history, the India archives of Seville, and his agents succeeded in unearthing these buried treasures." This statement is ambiguous about the nature of the "treasures"; but upon investigation it is clear that they were not the original documents which Sutro acquired in Sevilla, but transcripts of the originals, probably made much as modern researchers acquire microfilm or photostatic copies of useful information. From various statements in the Griffin introduction, there is little doubt that Sutro's agents gave the impression of having made every effort to acquire these "buried treasures."

At the time probably neither Sutro nor President Griffin knew (though the latter perhaps suspected) that Sutro's agents had been at somewhat less than great pains to make their selection of materials in 1883 and 1884. Actually, fourteen of the first fifteen documents in the Griffin edition were printed in their Spanish version, almost exactly as they appeared in *Documents from the Sutro Collection,* in Francisco Carrasco y Guisasola, *Documentos referentes al reconocimiento de las costas de las Californias desde el cabo de San Lucas al de Mendocino, recopilados en el Archivo de Indias* (Madrid, 1882). Apparently Adolph Sutro's agents did nothing more "in unearthing these buried treasures" than to copy Carrasco's recently printed book. That Griffin might have had some inkling of this chicanery comes from his statement that these documents "have not been published heretofore—certainly not in this country."

Whatever the nature of the documents obtained by Sutro through his agents, whether transcripts, photographs, or originals, I had no opportunity to check these materials since the "Sutro Collection" was partly destroyed in the San Francisco fire and earthquake in 1906. According to the present director of the Sutro Library, Mr. Richard Dillon, the materials published in this volume were destroyed. In lieu of examining the "Sutro Collection" materials, therefore, I have checked the nineteen documents printed in 1891 against other available copies.

Because of uncertainties in such a procedure, and in an effort not to alter the Griffin manuscript any more than absolutely necessary, modifications have not been made in the Spanish version unless there was clearly a need for change. For example, the use of *x* for *j* and of *b* for *v*, and *vice versa*, was retained in accordance with the 1891 edition. Other comparable inconsistencies were left unchanged, and only slight alterations were made in Griffin's use of capital and small letters in the Spanish text.

In the English translations, changes of words and phrases have not been made unless it was felt that the new rendition materially clarified the earlier effort. However, accents have been added in the translations to conform to modern usage. The attempt has thus been to reproduce as completely as possible the earlier publication of the Historical Society of Southern California, to clarify various points in the introduction and footnotes, to improve the Spanish and English texts, and to make available once more this important information on *The California Coast*, with the term "California" here being used in its earlier and larger sense.

This edition, like the earlier Griffin edition, is bilingual, showing both the Spanish and its English translation. Unlike the earlier edition, however, this one runs concurrently, or approximately so, with the Spanish on left-hand pages and the English on facing right-hand pages. Griffin's annotation is placed on left-hand pages, facing the page of citation, with arabic numbers used for the footnote references. My annotation is placed on right-hand pages, with symbols (*, †, ‡, etc.) used for footnote references. This arrangement, it is hoped, will afford the reader with "immediate access" to the original Spanish, the English translation, the annotation of the Griffin edition, and my added annotation.

The 1891 editor, Griffin, suffered somewhat in not having optimal access to materials of a biographical nature concerning the subjects of the Sutro Collection documents. Time has remedied this, and the dramatis personae of the story unfolded in these documents have taken substantial form. Particularly worthy of extended notice are the men who were responsible for the greater number of documents or who were involved most prominently in the activity described. These outstanding explorers include Sebastián Vizcaíno, commander of the significant 1602–1603 reconnaissance of the California Coast; Father President of the California missions Fray Junípero Serra, renowned priest, author of documents 16 and 17, and founder of nine of California's missions; Franciscan Father Tomás de la Peña, chaplain and diarist on the *Santiago*, and author of document 18; Father Juan Crespi, chaplain and diarist aboard the same vessel and author of document 19; and Juan Pérez, pioneer naval officer and captain of the Spanish naval vessel *Santiago*.

Of the figures who appear fleetingly in the first six documents, little more is known today than was known to Griffin. In footnotes, attempts have been made to update bibliographical items of interest. But most of these persons were precursors to a more concerted effort, and the role of the precursor is always indistinct. Beginning with Sebastián Vizcaíno, however, we now have enough substantial information to make a few additional remarks. The role of the Estremaduran merchant-navigator Vizcaíno is discussed by W. Michael Mathes in his book, *Vizcaíno and Spanish Expansion in the Pacific Ocean, 1580–1630* (San Francisco, 1968). It is from this source that supplementary knowledge is drawn concerning Vizcaíno's notable career.

Vizcaíno was born in 1548 and began his military career early, serving in the Spanish invasion force which took Portugal in 1580. Three years later he was on his way to the New World with the Viceroyalty of New Spain as his destination. After three years in that area, Vizcaíno sailed from Acapulco to Manila, where he established himself as a merchant. After another three years, he returned to New Spain, where he married, became the father of two boys and a girl, and established himself as a merchant and investor. In 1593, he was a principal stockholder and participant in an exploitation corporation which obtained from the Viceroy fishing (particularly pearl hunting)

and mining rights along the Pacific Coast and in the Gulf of California. This project apparently never advanced to the execution stage.

In 1595, Vizcaíno established such good relationships with the Viceroy, the Count of Monterrey, that the merchant obtained a concession for exploitation of Lower California. Documents 7 through 12 of this volume are concerned with this contract and with modifications thereof. In total, these documents demonstrate some of the colonial problems of control and of favoritism in dealings between the crown or the viceroy and individual subjects. It is also obvious that the experienced Vizcaíno was a resourceful entrepreneur. Though no great success resulted from the activities chronicled in these documents, the clever Estremaduran was able to obtain command of the expedition which brought about his principal fame. While sailing northward in 1602–1603, Vizcaíno and his consort vessels ran the western coastline of North America, leaving on the map many permanent place names. Documents 13, 14, and 15 reflect various phases of this epic exploration, which is the most extensive and most famous for that area. Recommendations springing from Vizcaíno's exploratory reports prompted the Viceroy to consider permanent occupation of the key sites suggested by the commander of the 1602–1603 expedition—San Diego and Monterrey, as the latter was then spelled. Vizcaíno was the hero of the hour and was being primed to lead a colonizing expedition when a change in viceregal administration altered plans radically. The mariner was stripped of a well-earned honor, that of being named general of the lucrative Manila galleon ships for 1604. Plans for California's occupation were dropped, not to be revived for 165 years.

Vizcaíno, however, did not disappear with misfortune and dissolution of plans for occupation of San Diego and Monterey. He made a trip to Spain in 1607 and returned to Mexico in 1608 to find that interest in the Pacific had shifted to a search for two fabulous imaginary islands, Rica de Oro and Rica de Plata. In support of plans for more active participation in Pacific Ocean commerce, the Viceroy sent Sebastián Vizcaíno on an ambassadorial mission to open trade with Japan, and his mission had some short-lived success, but the era of Matthew Perry was still far off.

In 1615, the aging Vizcaíno, now sixty-eight, was called upon to defend New Spain's shores against impending pirate invasion. In that

year, a threat of destruction appeared in the form of the Dutch mariner Spilbergen, who had entered the Pacific. Little resulted from the invasion. After this episode, Vizcaíno's name was less important; doubtless he retired to his estates, his prize for earlier meritorious activity in the crown's service.

Fray Junípero Serra, author of documents 16 and 17 of this study, needs less introduction to those interested in the California Coast. His era is almost two centuries later. He is so important to the area's early development that his statue represents California in Statuary Hall in Washington, D.C. Few historical figures of the American West or of the Hispanic Northwest of New Spain have received the attention or honors bestowed on this son of humble, devout peasants of Mallorca. Petra, a small town toward the interior of this island, was the birth-place of Miguel Joseph Serra Ferrer, as he was christened in 1713. Having a youthful fondness for things religious, Serra decided quite early upon a clerical vocation. At the age of sixteen, he took the habit in the Franciscan Friary of Jesús, at the island capital of Palma. A year later he became a Franciscan friar and took the name Junípero, which seemed somewhat inappropriate in view of his seriousness. His aptitude for study led Serra to continue through to a doctorate in sacred theology at the Lullian University of Palma. Subsequently, Dr. Junípero taught as professor of philosophy and occupied the chair of Scotistic Theology in the same university from 1744 to 1749.

Rather suddenly, particularly for a man who had never left the restricted confines of the small Balearic island on which he had been born, Serra, intellectually accomplished professor and lecturer, de-cided to go as a missionary priest to the New World. He was then thirty-six years old. Upon arrival in New Spain, Serra and two com-panions received permission to go on foot to Mexico City, a fact which greatly enhanced the later legend of Fray Junípero's dedication to walking rather than riding.

Soon after he became associated with the College of San Fernando de México, Father Serra was at work in the mission field of Sierra Gorda among the Pame Indians. The small-statured Father Serra labored zealously and effectively. His name was considered for the job of re-establishing Mission San Sabá in central Texas, which had been ravished by Indian hostility. Though Serra was eager, ever courting the martyrdom which escaped him, circumstances did not

permit his going. Instead, duties around the college and activities in preaching missions to the Christian Spaniards occupied his time until the Jesuit expulsion of 1767 created a vacuum in the Lower California mission field.

Serra headed the missionaries sent to this new field for Franciscan labor. José de Gálvez' famous visitation to New Spain resulted in a determination to occupy the area of Upper California, neglected since the expedition of Sebastián Vizcaíno, 165 years previously. Lower California was to be the springboard, and Fray Junípero was selected as spiritual head of the Sacred Expedition organized for the purpose of extending Spanish Catholic Christianity to the great horde of unconverted Indians. Serra was to spend the rest of his life dedicated to the great tasks of selecting mission sites, founding religious centers of spiritual and temporal instruction of rude Indians, and stabilizing these institutions of Spanish frontier control. At the age of seventy, after more than fifteen years in service in California, Fray Junípero Serra died at his home mission, San Carlos Borromeo, in Carmel.

Serra was a devout, austere, dedicated, erudite Franciscan. His eloquent preaching and stern asceticism won him a large and respectful following. He was probably not very easy to get along with in any circumstance in which he felt that his position as spiritual leader was jeopardized or neglected. His difficulties with successive governors of Spanish California are too well known to detail here, but he was a man of strong faith and great virtue—he was a man for his own time.*

Author of the first of the Pérez voyage diaries of 1774, which is document 18, was Franciscan Father Tomás de la Peña y Saravia. The terminology which he used with considerable facility, like that of a man who knew the sea, probably resulted from the circumstances of his birth and youth at the tiny hamlet of Brizuela, some twenty-five miles from the Cantabrian north coast of Spain. Internal evidence both of his diary and of his clerical companion reveals Tomás de la Peña to have been a much better sailor, for in every case where only one of the two Franciscans said mass, it was always the Cantabrian Fray Tomás.

De la Peña was born in 1743 along the banks of the Río Nela in the

* Biographical information on Father Serra is based primarily on Maynard Geiger, O.F.M., *Palóu's Life of Fray Junípero Serra.*

xiii

extreme north of the province of Burgos, and at age nineteen received the habit in the Franciscan College of the province of Cantabria. Eight years later he left Spain in the company of a group of recruits for the Franciscan College of San Fernando de México. Leader of the group bound for Mexico City was Fray Rafael Verger. Subsequently, De la Peña was assigned to the Lower California mission field, where he served at Mission San José de Comondú. Less than a year later, in August of 1771, Father Tomás was transferred to Upper California as part of a general agreement between Dominicans and Franciscans concerning division of missionary responsibility, which placed Lower California under the former, while what is today the state of California was given to the Franciscans. Father Tomás de la Peña served at San Diego de Alcalá and San Luis Obispo, before going to San Carlos (Carmel) Mission. It was from San Carlos that he was detached to join Juan Pérez and the *Santiago* as chaplain and diarist. Although four separate accounts were kept of the 1774 voyage, it is probable that Father de la Peña's was the most accurate. Since he was a better sailor and therefore more capable of performing his duties as chaplain, a fact which is abundantly clear, it can be logically inferred that he was the better journalist. The repetition in the journals of Father Tomás and of Father Crespi stems from the fact that only one of them was truly fulfilling his duties. It is unlikely that it was the seasick Father Juan Crespi.

Following termination of the expedition, Father Tomás returned to San Carlos. In November, 1776, the Cantabrian Franciscan accompanied Captain Fernando de Rivera y Moncada on an overland journey to the newly founded San Francisco. Shortly thereafter, in January, 1777, he became one of the founding priests of what was "his mission," that of Santa Clara. For eighteen years he served there, and, under his administration, Santa Clara, out of the eleven extant missions, became statistically one of the most populous and prosperous. The veteran priest not only looked after approximately one thousand Indians but also was responsible, from time to time, for administering to the spiritual requirements of citizens of the nearby pueblo of San José de Guadalupe.

After long service in the California missions, Fray Tomás returned to the mother college in Mexico, where he served in various capacities

connected with the support of the frontier missions. In 1806, he died at the age of sixty-three.*

Fray Juan Crespi, the seasick companion of Fray Tomás de la Peña and author of the diary which is presented as document 19, is a well-known figure in early California history. As a Mallorcan, he was very much like many of the early important figures in that region—Serra, Pérez, and Palóu. As a historical figure, Crespi is particularly associated with Serra and Palóu. All three of these men were born on Mallorca in the Balearic Islands. Crespi was a pupil and favorite of Serra's and both a childhood playmate and a classmate of Francisco Palóu. Born in 1721, he was twenty-two years senior to Father de la Peña, his priestly companion aboard the *Santiago* in 1774. At the age of seventeen, he entered the Franciscan Order in the Convento de Jesús at Palma, and, as was customary, he made his profession a year later, in January, 1739. Most probably his date of ordination was 1746. Juan Crespi left for Mexico at the same time as Serra and Palóu but sailed aboard a different vessel. This Mallorcan priest, when reaching twenty-eight, embarked on a new phase of his life. A contemporary description of 1749 indicates that Fray Juan was "short in stature, of light complexion, pallid, though somewhat florid, with blue eyes and black hair."

In Mexico, Father Crespi became associated with the College of San Fernando. For seventeen years he served in Sierra Gorda's Franciscan missions in the area between Querétaro and San Luis Potosí, Tilaco being the main area of activity. When the Franciscans replaced the Jesuits in Lower California, Father Crespi was transferred there and placed in charge of Mission Purísima Concepción de Cadegomó.

Father Serra, his mentor, chose Crespi to accompany that land phase of the Sacred Expedition intended to establish permanent colonies in Upper California, which was under the command of Captain Rivera. Thus, at the age of fifty-eight, a subspecialty was launched which would later be described in his biography, *Fray Juan Crespi, Missionary Explorer of the Pacific Coast, 1768–1774*, published by Herbert E. Bolton. Bolton's evaluation of Crespi is that "among all the great diarists who recorded explorations in the New World, Juan Crespi

---

* Biographical information on Father Tomás de la Peña is taken principally from Maynard Geiger, *Palóu's Life of Fray Junípero Serra*, 411–12.

occupied a conspicuous place .... Gentle character, devout Christian, zealous missionary, faithful companion, his peculiar fame will be that of diarist. Of all the men of this half-decade, so prolific in frontier expansion ... Crespi alone participated in all the major path-breaking expeditions: from Velicatá to San Diego; from San Diego to San Francisco Bay; from Monterey to the San Joaquin Valley; from Monterey by sea to Alaska. In distance he out-traveled Coronado." The voyage on the *Santiago* was the last of these extensive travels.

From 1770 until his death on January 1, 1782, Father Juan Crespi made his headquarters at Mission San Carlos, at the founding of which he had been present. There he acted as assistant to Father Serra, performing some of his duties at nearby Monterey. In fairness to Crespi, it can be said that his land journals are more reliable than his sea diaries, but even in the latter, one can see evidence of frequent diary writing and a dedication to certain details that escaped the less experienced but more enthusiastic Father Tomás de la Peña.*

Of the important personages whose activities are reflected in the Sutro Collection documents, the least well known was the San Blas pilot, Juan Pérez. Generally reputed as one of the better naval officers of that department, he was "the foremost maritime figure in the early settlement of Alta California." Though not included in this documentary study, Captain Pérez fashioned his own journal of the 1774 expedition, as required by Spanish naval regulations and by established custom. This navigational diary, which awaits detailed study, is located in Mexico's Archivo General de la Nación, in volume 62 of the section entitled *Historia*.

Juan Pérez was alternately liked and disliked by the strong-willed Junípero Serra. The Father President spoke of the navigator as "our friend Juan Pérez," and as "our countryman from the banks of the Palma." Later, when Pérez did not follow Serra's wishes in supporting the contemplated occupation of San Francisco Bay by lending logistical support, Serra's opinion of the Mallorcan mariner was greatly lowered. Nonetheless, a reflection of Juan Pérez' popularity might be found in a harbor on the inboard (east) side of Queen Charlotte Island, designated on Spanish maps as *El Puerto de Juan Pérez*. In addition, a huge tree, forty feet tall and six feet in diameter, found on

---

* Biographical information on Father Juan Crespi is taken principally from Maynard Geiger, *Palóu's Life of Fray Junípero Serra*, 455–56.

the Plain of San Blas by the Spanish scientist José Longinos Martínez, was locally called the Juan Pérez tree, though classified by the natural scientist as *Pseudosmodigium perniciosum Engel.*

Very little is known about Pérez' youth, not even the year of his birth being recorded. He is credited with having seen "considerable service on the Manila galleon run as *piloto* or master," and in later years, admitted having "spent a great deal of time in China and the Philippines." Such information is evident from references contained in the journals of the 1774 expedition.

As the oldest and most experienced of the San Blas pilots, with connections dating back to his arrival there in 1767, he commanded the *San Antonio,* one of the three vessels involved in the Sacred Expedition to colonize California. Pérez distinguished himself by becoming the first Spanish officer of the eighteenth century to enter both San Diego and Monterey harbors from the sea. In 1770, he was credited with saving the northern settlements by his timely arrival with supplies, followed by his assistance in founding Monterey. When it came time to consider the problem of a prospective commander of an exploratory mission to extend Spanish claims to the extreme North Pacific, Viceroy Bucareli appointed the Mallorcan since he was "the only person with sufficient experience and service in the Department of San Blas to undertake the commission" on the *Santiago.*

Enough is said in documents 18 and 19 about Pérez' conduct while on that expedition. He made a notable reconnaissance but failed in two regards: he did not reach 60° as his instructions required, nor did he go ashore to perform that indispensable, symbolic act of possession, though it was not for lack of preparation—during this voyage and previous ones, Pérez was the victim of recurrent illness.

Pérez was later assigned to the Bruno Hezeta expedition of 1775, sailing again on the *Santiago,* this time as master, with the senior Hezeta as commanding officer. This expedition remedied the earlier lack of an act of sovereignty by taking formal possession several times. However, it did not reach the prescribed 60°; but the consort vessel, the *Sonora,* acting independently, reached two degrees short of that goal. The *Santiago* earlier had turned back somewhere along the coast off Vancouver Island. By August 29, the *Santiago* was back in Monterey for a prolonged stay. The return voyage to San Blas commenced on November 1, 1775, but after only two days out of port,

Pérez died. Amidst the ceremonial volley of muskets and the roar of cannon, he "was buried at sea almost within sight of the port which had been the locale of much of his service. News of his demise did not reach the mission of San Carlos at Monterey until 1776, at which time full funeral honors were accorded to his memory." Serra and his Franciscans were deeply grieved.*

In the present volume, some pictorial material pertinent to the California Coast has been added. The California Coast, as viewed by the Spaniards of the age of discovery, began with Cape San Lucas at the tip of Lower California and extended northward as far as Spain could lay claim. Consequently, items are included in the pictorial material which were distinctly a part of the California of yesteryear but would not be considered so today.

Spain's maximum claim, based on exploration and acts of possession, extended to Alaska, and certainly, on the basis of documents 18 and 19 presented here, extended as far north as 55° or at least 54° 40', as a result of Juan Pérez' voyage on the *Santiago*. Later Spanish explorations to the Pacific Northwest more clearly defined the geographical outlines, placed permanent names on the map, and made scientific or semiscientific investigations. Although little credit has been given to the Hispanic mariners of the eighteenth century, their intensive activity in the northern latitudes resulted in the establishment of two temporary bases in that area and in laying a claim so strong that attempts at settlement almost led to a general European conflict.

This book is not concerned with the struggle for power. But in the process of claims and counterclaims to the Pacific Northwest, a number of Spanish expeditions were sent, which carried competent artists and cartographers. In the field of cartography there was not only an interest in conventional maps but an equal preoccupation with the drawing of coastal profiles as an adjunct to maritime exploration. One of these maps depicts the Pacific Northwest Coast, and another depicts the Pacific Coast from just below Monterey to 58° N. latitude.

* Biographical information on Juan Pérez is based principally on James G. Caster, "The Last Days of Don Juan Pérez, the Mallorcan Mariner," *Journal of the West*, Vol. II, No. 1 (1963), 15–21, and Michael E. Thurman, *The Naval Department of San Blas, New Spain's Bastion for Alta California and Nootka, 1767 to 1798* (Glendale, 1967), 78–79ff.

The coastal profiles of San Lorenzo de Nutka with Tasis Peak in the background and of Cabo Frondoso (Woody Point) are also included.

Nine additional illustrations are included, none of which were made during the 1774 expedition but which are representative of items described by the journals thereof. Those from Nootka Sound are specifically of a group visited by the Pérez expedition on August 8 and 9. Although the remaining illustrations portray Indians living to the north of 54° 40', they do represent natives of a similar culture pattern.

Illustrative materials for this new edition can be found in the Museo Naval of Spain's Ministerio de Marina. I wish to express my gratitude to Admiral Julio Guillén, director of the Museo, for his aid and for permission to publish these unique records. During two early visits to Spain, in 1953 as fellow of the Del Amo Foundation of Los Angeles and Madrid, and in 1957–58 as Faculty Research Fellow of the Social Science Research Council, I had the opportunity to locate the materials added and to check the original manuscripts upon which the Sutro Documents published in 1891 were based. To these two organizations I wish to express my thanks for their support and interest in my research. I would also like to thank Mr. Lorrin Morrison, publisher of *The Journal of the West,* for his earlier participation on *The California Coast* and for making a copy of the 1891 edition available.

DONALD C. CUTTER

January 15, 1969
Albuquerque, New Mexico

CONTENTS

xxi

ILLUSTRATIONS

THE
CALIFORNIA
COAST

Tomada del original
Archivo General de Indias,
21 de Enero de 1884.
· P. El archivero
José Villaamil
y Castro

Con esta fecha digo al Jefe del Archivo de Yndias establecido en Sevilla lo que sigue:

"S. M. el Rey (q. D. g.) ha tenido a bien disponer que se conceda autorizacion a Mr Adolph Sutro para que examine y tome nota de los documentos que se custodian en ese Archivo; entendiendose esta autorizacion sujeta a las ordenanzas y demás disposiciones porque se rige esa dependencia. De Real órden comunicada por el Sr. Ministro de Ultramar lo digo a V. S. a los efectos indicados."

De la propia Real órden lo traslado a V. para su conocimiento.

Dios guarde a V. muchos años. Madrid 26 de Diciembre de 1883.

El Subsecretario

(rúbrica)   *Manuel de Eguélior*

Sor. Dn. Adolph Sutro   (rúbrica)

Under this date I say to the Chief of the Archive of the Indies established at Seville the following:

"His Majesty, the King—whom God guard—has seen fit to order that permission to examine and take notes from the documents kept in those archives be given to Mr. Adolph Sutro, it being understood that this authorization is given subject to the ordinances and other rules governing that bureau. By royal order communicated through the Overseas Minister I say this to Your Lordship for the end indicated."

By virtue of the same royal order I transmit this to you for your information.

God guard you many years.   Madrid, 26th December, 1883

Manuel de Eguélior

Under Secretary

(rubric of the Overseas Minister)   (rubric)

Mr. Adolph Sutro

INTRODUCTION

By GEO. BUTLER GRIFFIN

THE DOCUMENTS which the Historical Society of Southern California here offers to the public will be considered, the Society ventures to hope, welcome contributions to the treasure now laid up in the storehouse of students of the history of the Pacific coast, especially that of California, and of some interest to the general reader. It is believed that these documents, excepting only the last two, the diaries of Fathers Crespi and de la Peña, have not been published heretofore—certainly not in this country.

The privilege of publishing these documents the Society owes to the kindness of Mr. Adolph Sutro, of San Francisco. Mr. Sutro caused a search for documents relating to the history of California to be made in that great magazine of Spanish-American history, the India archives of Seville, and his agents succeeded in unearthing these buried treasures. They were submitted by Mr. Sutro to this society for examination and were found to be of such value that the generosity of the lender was taxed still further by a request that their publication by the Society should be sanctioned by him, a request which was granted at once. In addition to this, it is well to add, Mr. Sutro has aided otherwise and very materially in their publication.

The very voluminous series of books published, quite recently, by Mr. H. H. Bancroft, of San Francisco, contains a general summary of a very great part of the printed matter relating to the history of California, but it is evident that, at least so far as the early history of the Californian coast is concerned, only a very limited number of original manuscripts, and these easily accessible to the public, were examined. If any examination of the India archives at Seville was attempted, it must have been made very superficially, for a perusal of the books published by Mr. Bancroft will show that of the nineteen documents now printed the existence of all but two or three was unknown to the writers employed by that gentleman; and, possibly because the outlying province of California was of such little importance to the earlier historians of cisatlantic Spain, these documents

7

escaped the notice of Torquemada and other Spanish authors beyond whose researches the writers referred to apparently have not cared to venture. A perusal of these Spanish historians will enable the student to verify this latter assertion; that Mr. Bancroft's writers were equally careless will appear more fully in footnotes appended to the documents now published.

Three of the documents now put in type are printed from photo-lithographic copies of the originals, even the color to which the ink of these originals has faded being reproduced carefully, made for Mr. Sutro, in 1883 and 1884, by express permission of the King of Spain, and certified by the signature and official seal of the keeper of the *Archivo General de Indias* at Seville. These three documents are the letter which Sebastián Vizcaíno wrote at Monterey Bay on the 28th December, 1602, and the two letters of President Junípero Serra to the Viceroy of Mexico. A facsimile of President Serra's letter, of 7th October, 1774, is given as a frontispiece to this publication. [The Serra facsimile is shown on page 130 of this edition.] The authenticity of the other sixteen documents is unquestionable also.

It has been thought proper to print the Spanish *verbatim et literatim*, the capitalization and punctuation also being carefully adhered to, for in this way the documents can not but be of more value to the scholar. Translations are appended for the use of the general reader; and, although at times the meaning of the original is much obscured by the singularly involved and otherwise ungrammatical style of the writer, it is believed that in the translation, in every instance, the statements of the writer have been presented with accuracy.

It has been thought advisable to print all the documents relating to the same subject together and in the order of their dates, the repetition of matter contained in the footnotes thus being avoided.

GEO. BUTLER GRIFFIN
President of the Historical Society of Southern California

LOS ANGELES, 1st November, 1891

8

Document No. 1

Letter of Fray Andrés de Aguirre to the Archbishop of Mexico, giving an account of some rich islands inhabited by civilized people, discovered by a Portuguese trader, and situated in latitude 35° to 40° north—written in 1584–85

CARTA de Fray Andres Aguirre al Ylmo. Sor Arzobispo de Mexico participandole la conveniencia de reconocer y descubrir la costa N. O. de la Nueva España y dando noticias de unas islas ricas y de gente civilizada a donde aportó una nave portuguesa y se hallan de los 35 a 40 grados de latitud norte.*

Ylustrisimo Señor—El spiritu Santo more siempre en la anima de vuestra señoria ilustrisima. el descubrimiento que vuestra señoria manda hacer assi para entender la disposicion de la costa, puertos y calidades de la tierra y gente della, que hasta agora está descubierta al poniente de esta Nueva España en la mar del sur, como para proseguir el descubrimiento de aquella costa y tierra desde cuarenta y un grado de latitud adelante es de mucha ymportancia y muy necesario assi para la buelta de las naos de las yslas filipinas y de todas las partes del poniente como para entender y saver la disposicion y calidad de la tierra y gente de ella y yslas que se entiende ay de mucha ymportancia cercana a aquella costa. aunque las naos que vienen de poniente cada año al puerto de acapulco rreconoscen aquella costa y a vista de ella navegan mas de quinientas leguas, no se save hasta agora que puertos ó reparos tiene ymporta mucho saverse para que las naos que vienen necesitadas de rreparar por haver navegado hasta aquella costa de dos mill leguas sin hazer escala en tierra alguna puedan rreparar y proveer sus necesidades.

no es de menor ymportancia proseguirse el descubrimiento de aquella costa de los cuarenta y un grados de latitud adelante para entender los secretos della, porque tiene por cierto que es continente con la costa de la China sino las divide un angosto estrecho que llaman de Anian que segun se tiene noticia, esta es lo último descubierto de la costa de la China en cinquenta y dos grados de latitud.

en aquel parage y en el que ay de las yslas de Japon hasta lo último descubierto de nuestra costa segun el Padre Fray Andres de Urdaneta tuvo relacion de un capitan portugues ay yslas muy ricas muy pobladas

LETTER of Fray Andrés de Aguirre to the Most Illustrious Lord Archbishop of Mexico, bringing to his notice the usefulness of exploring the northwest coast of New Spain and giving information of some rich islands, inhabited by civilized people, where a Portuguese ship touched, and which are in from 35 to 40 degrees of north latitude.*

Most Illustrious Lord: May the Holy Spirit ever dwell in the soul of your most illustrious lordship. The voyage of discovery which your lordship orders to be made, as well for the purpose of gaining a knowledge of the coast and harbors, and the quality of the land and condition of its people, to the present time discovered to the westward of this New Spain in the South Sea, as for the further prosecution of the exploration of that coast and region beyond the forty-first degree of latitude, is of great importance and very necessary both in connection with the return voyage of vessels from the Philippines and all parts of the west, and for the purpose of understanding and knowing the lay of the land and its qualities and those of its people and of the islands of great importance which are understood to lie near that coast. Although the ships which come every year from the west to the port of Acapulco make a landfall on that coast and sail within sight of it for more than five hundred leagues, to the present time it is not known what harbors or stopping places it has. It is very important to know this, so that ships which come needing to stop, after reaching that coast from a distance of two thousand leagues, without touching anywhere, may stop and provide for their needs.

Nor is it of less importance that the exploration of that coast be continued beyond forty-one degrees of latitude in order that its secrets may be revealed, for it is held as certain that it is a portion of the coast

* Original document in Archivo General de Indias, Mexico 27. Hereinafter this archive will be cited as AGI. Spanish version of this document is to be found in Francisco Carrasco y Guisasola, *Documentos referentes al reconocimiento de las costas de las Californias desde el cabo de San Lucas al de Mendocino, recopilados en el Archivo de Indias*, 9–12. Hereinafter cited as Carrasco, *Documentos de las Californias*. This work ascribes a date of 1584 to the document. A slightly variant version appears in W. Michael Mathes (ed.), *Documentos para la historia de la demarcación comercial de California* (2 vols., Madrid, 1965), I, 6–10. This second version is from the manuscript copy found in the Museo Naval, Colección Navarrete, Tomo XVIII. The Mathes study is henceforth cited as *Docs. para la demarcación de California*.

An alternate translation of most of this document appears in Henry R. Wagner, *Spanish Voyages to the Northwest Coast of America in the Sixteenth Century*, 136–37. Hereinafter cited as Wagner, *Spanish Voyages*. Most of Griffin's 1891 translation is reproduced in Charles E. Chapman, *A History of California: The Spanish Period*, 140–41.

de gente de mucha policia, la qual rrelacion yo bi y ley y yendo el y yo a España a dar quenta a su magestad del subceso de la primera jornada que por su mandado hizimos en la qual se descubrieron y poblaron las yslas Philipinas y se descubrió la navegacion y buelta de ellas a esta nueva españa, el dicho padre dió esta relacion a su magestad y yo tomé copia della y la guardé hasta que partiendo de españa en esta flota se perdió la nao en que yo venia y en ella se me perdió la rrelacion y todo lo que traia y su magestad me havia hecho merced y limosna. Lo que en rresolucion contenia es lo siguente.

"una nao portuguesa salió de malaca para las yslas de Japon y cargó

¹ At this time all navigators believed in the existence of a strait by which communication could be had between the Atlantic and the Pacific. It was the hope of finding this means of escape with his booty-laden ship that brought Francis Drake to the Californian coast in 1579. Lorenzo Ferrer de Maldonado claimed that, in 1588, he entered the strait on the coast of Labrador and emerged at the Pacific end in latitude sixty. Juan de Fuca asserted that, in 1592, he entered the strait from the Pacific in latitude forty-seven, and that he sailed through it to the Atlantic. But this elusive strait was pushed farther and farther to the northward until at length it has become Bering's strait and the northwest passage.

² In his youth and early manhood Andrés de Urdaneta had been a soldier, and was famous as a navigator and cosmographer, and he had sailed in this capacity in one of the ships which, under the command of García de Loaisa, had visited the Philippines and other islands of the South Sea. In 1563 the King of Spain ordered Viceroy Velasco, of New Spain, to send colonists for the settlement of the Philippines. Meanwhile Captain Urdaneta had entered the order of Augustinian friars at the city of Mexico. He and five of his brethren, among whom Andrés de Aguirre, the writer of this letter, were selected to go on the expedition as missionaries. The command was given to Miguel López de Legazpi, a resident of the city of Mexico; and on the 21st November, 1564, a fleet of four vessels sailed from the port of Navidad, in Colima for the islands. This was the expedition which founded Manila. Orders had been given to López de Legazpi for the determination, if possible, of a practicable return route from the islands to New Spain. On the 1st June, 1565, the flagship, the San Pedro, under command of Felipe Salcedo, a youth of sixteen years of age and grandson of the commander, was dispatched from Cebú for that purpose, and Fathers Urdaneta and Aguirre sailed in her. The course of the San Pedro was eastward to the Ladrones [Marianas], thence northward to latitude 38° north, and thence, with a favoring slant of wind, eastward to the American coast, the ship making a landfall somewhere to the northward of what is now Monterey Bay. The voyage was long and disastrous. The ship had sailed with a crew very limited in number; during the voyage Salcedo, the navigating officer and fourteen others died; and, when at length she arrived at Acapulco, there were not sufficient able-bodied men on board to bring her to an anchor. The two friars had tended the sick and shriven the dying, had navigated and steered the ship and had prepared from day to day the chart which was used, for many years afterwards, by the navigating officers of Manila galleons.

³ Friar Andrés is in error here, for the Philippines were discovered by Magelhaens (Magellan) in 1521, in the course of his famous voyage, and it was on one of these islands that he lost his life in a skirmish with the natives. Probably it was some error similar to this which led a writer employed by Mr. H. H. Bancroft to assert that the Philippines were discovered by the expedition under Ruy López de Villalobos, which sailed from Navidad in New Spain, in *November, 1541!* See *History of the Pacific States*, x. p. 130 (table of contents of cap. VI) and the text on p. 137.

of China, unless it be that they are separated by a narrow strait called Anian,[1] which, according to notices had, is in that part of the coast of China lately explored, in fifty-two degrees of latitude.* In that region, and on that lying between the Japanese islands and that portion of our coast recently discovered, according to the account that Father Andrés de Urdaneta[2]† obtained from a Portuguese captain, there are very rich islands very thickly populated by people of urbane customs. This narrative I saw and read while he and I were going to Spain in order to give to His Majesty an account of the outcome of the first voyage we made by his order, during which the Philippine islands were discovered and settled[3] and the manner of navigating thither and of making the return voyage thence to New Spain was determined.‡

The said father gave this narrative to His Majesty and I made a copy of it, which I kept until, leaving Spain in this fleet, the ship in which I came was lost, and in it the narrative and all I was bringing with me, on which account His Majesty gave me a reward and alms. What in effect the narrative contained is as follows:

"A Portuguese ship sailed from Malacca for the islands of Japan and at the city of Canton took on board Chinese goods. Arriving within sight of Japan she encountered a storm coming from the west, so severe that it was impossible to reach those islands and she ran before it under very little sail for eight days, the weather being very thick and no land having been seen. On the ninth day the weather abated and cleared, and they sighted two large islands. They reached one of these at a good port, well peopled, there being a great city surrounded by a good stone wall. There were many large and medium sized vessels in port. Immediately on their entering the harbor there flocked to the ship a great number of persons of that land, well-dressed and cared for and manifesting much affection for the people of the ship. The lord of that island and city, learning that

---

* See Martín Fernández de Navarrete, "Examen histórico-crítico de los viajes y descubrimientos apócrifos del Capitán Lorenzo Ferrer Maldonado, de Juan de Fuca y del Almirante Bartolomé de Fonte," in *Colección de documentos inéditos para la historia de España,* Tomo XV.

† For additional information on Urdaneta see Mariano Cuevas, *Monje y marino: La vida y los tiempos de Fray Andrés de Urdaneta.* A shorter account of Urdaneta's career is in Lesley Byrd Simpson, *Many Mexicos,* 61–62.

‡ In footnote three, editor Griffin takes both Aguirre and California historian Bancroft to task, and, in each case, needlessly. *Descubrir* in Spanish does not necessarily imply initial discovery but embraces the concept of exploration as well, nor does the term have such limited meaning in English.

en la ciudad de Canton las mercaderias de China y llegando a vista de Japon le dió un temporal poniente tan recio que no pudo tomar aquellas yslas y corrió con poca vela ocho dias el tiempo muy cerrado sin haver rreconocido tierra alguna; al noveno dia abonanzó el tiempo y aclaró y tuvieron vista de dos yslas grandes, arribaron a una dellas en un buen puerto poblado con una gran ciudad cercada de buen muro de piedra, estavan en el puerto muchos navios grandes y medianos, luego que entraron en el puerto acudió a la nao mucha gente de la tierra bien vestidos y tratados y mostrando a los de la nao mucho amor y sabiendo que eran mercaderes ymvió el señor de aquella ysla y ciudad a dezir al capitan de la nao que saliese y los que quisiese de su gente en tierra y sin recelo alguno de que se les hiciese agravio, antes se ofrecia todo buen acojimiento y llevase memoria de las mercaderías que traia en su nao porque se las tomarian rrescatarian a su contento, el capitan comunicó con su gente esto y se determinó inviar a la ciudad al escribano de la nao con la memoria de las mercaderias y dos mercaderes uno portugues y otro armenio vecinos de Malaca. El Señor de la tierra los rrescivió en su casa que era grande y bien edificada y los trató con mucho amor y rregalo y entendiendose por señas y que la tierra era muy abundante y rrica de plata y otras cosas, seda y ropa volvieron el escribano y el mercader portugues a la nao para sacar las mercaderias en una cassa que le dieron para ello y el armenio quedó con el Señor de la tierra y fué tratado con mucho rregalo, hasta que sacadas las mercaderias en tierra y acudiendo gran numero de gente a rrescatar con plata en gran cantidad en treynta y tantos dias vendieron todas sus mercaderias haciendo grande y rrica ganancia conque quedaron todos muy rricos y cargaron su nao de plata; el tiempo que en esta ysla estuvieron y entendieron que el señor della lo era de la otra que estava a vista quatro leguas y de otras que cerca dellas avia todas ellas rricas de plata y muy pobladas. La gente blanca y bien dispuesta bien tratada y vestida de seda y rropa fina de algodon, gente amorosa y muy afable. La lengua diferente de los chinos y japones y facil de tomar porque en menos de quarenta dias que los portugueses estuvieron en aquella ysla se entendian con los naturales. Son aquellas yslas abundantes de buenos mantenimientos, arroz que es el pan que usan, aves como las nuestras en gran abundancia, patos mansos y muchos puercos, cabras, bufanos y mucha caza de venados y jabalies en gran abundancia, de diversas aves y volateria y

they were merchants, sent to the captain of the ship to say that he and those of his people he might select should come ashore without any fear that they would do them harm. On the contrary, he assured them, they should be received well, and he requested that they should bring with them the manifest of the goods the ship brought, for they would take them and trade for them to their content. The captain communicated this to his people, and it was resolved that the notary of the ship should be sent ashore with the manifest of merchandise and two merchants, one a Portuguese and the other an Armenian, residents of Malacca. The lord of the land received them in his house, which was large and well built, and treated them with affection, making them presents, they understanding one another by signs. The land was very rich in silver and other things, silk and clothing. The notary and the Portuguese merchant returned to the ship in order to land merchandise and store it in a building which was assigned to them for that purpose, while the Armenian remained with the lord of the land and was treated very hospitably. The merchandise having been taken ashore, and a vast number of persons coming to purchase it with a great quantity of silver, in some thirty days they sold all the goods, making great gains, so that all became very rich, and they loaded the ship with silver. During the time that they were on the island they learned that the lord was suzerain of the other island also, which was within sight, four leagues away, and of others which were near to these, all being rich in silver and very populous. These people are white and well-formed, well cared for and clothed in silk and fine clothing of cotton; an affectionate and very affable people. The language differs from that of the Chinese as well as that of the Japanese, and is readily learned, for, in less than forty days that the Portuguese passed on the island, they were able to converse with the natives. These islands abound in the means of maintaining life well— rice, which is the bread they use; fowls like ours in great number; tame ducks and many hogs; goats; buffaloes* and much game with deer and wild boars in great abundance; various birds and fowls and fishes, both many and good, and a great plenty of many kinds of fruit. The climate of the land is very good and healthful. These islands are in from thirty-five to forty degrees of latitude. The difference in

---

* Mathes reads this "Rufano," while the Sutro documents have "bufano," but the sense would require "bufalo."

muchos pescados y buenos y grande abundancia de frutas de muchas diferencias: el temple de la tierra muy bueno y sano. estan aquellas yslas de treynta y cinco grados a quarenta de latitud no se puede entender la longitud del japon a ellas por aver corrido con tormentas y el tiempo muy cerrado y oscuro. Corrieron de japon a levante y hecho su rrescate volvieron a Malaca pusieron por nombre a estas yslas por respeto del mercader armenio que entre la gente de la nao era muy respetado, yslas de harmenio." Esto es lo que de la rrelacion tengo de memoria assi para descubrir estas yslas como otras en aquel parage y golfo. Como para lo demas de aquella costa es de mucha importancia hacerse este descubrimiento para lo hacer seran muy acomodadas las dos acabras del porte y fabrica que don Juan de Guzman dixere, como quien tambien lo entiende en lo qual y en todo lo demas tocante a esta jornada pueda vuestra señoria ilustrisima seguir su parecer suplique a nuestro señor sea para gran servicio sullo y de su Magestad. Ylustrisimo Señor. De vuestra señoria ilustrisima menor capelan.

Fray Andrés de Aguirre

4 This letter is not dated. It is addressed to the Archbishop of Mexico, and Father Aguirre mentions that his lordship ordered a voyage to be made to the northwest coast. On the 25th September, 1584, Pedro de Moya y Contreras, who had succeeded Alonso de Montúfar in the archepiscopal see, became sixth viceroy of New Spain and governed as such until the 18th October, 1585. I am inclined to think, therefore, that this letter must have been written during the twelvemonth indicated. After the latter date no prelate became viceroy until Archbishop García Guerra succeeded Don Luis de Velasco, and he ruled from the month of June, 1611, until his death in February, 1612. He gave no orders for a voyage to the northwest coast; and Father Aguirre, if he were still living in 1611, must have been quite aged. Moreover it is not probable that Father Aguirre would have allowed so many years to pass before making the narrative of the Portuguese captain known to the viceroy of New Spain. In fact, an allusion in one of the documents contained in this volume indicates that the story of the "Isles of the Armenian" was known to the authorities of New Spain shortly after the time of Moya y Contreras. The narrative itself appears to be just such a yarn as navigators have been given to spinning for several thousand years. Possibly the story was told to the Spaniards by one of a rival nation for the purpose of putting them on a false scent, for in those days all sailors, and landsmen as well, believed firmly that the seas were full of undiscovered islands inhabited by people rich beyond compare. As a matter of fact there are no such islands as those of which the sailor gives a description. A ship sailing from Canton to within sight of Japan and thence running before a gale from the west for eight days, on the ninth would not be in the neighborhood of any islands. There is an island called "Rica de Plata," in latitude thirty-three north, but it is in longitude on hundred and seventy-one east of Greenwich, more than forty degrees to the eastward of the Portuguese captain's landfall in Japan. It is not probable that a ship of that period could have run that distance in the time mentioned; nor are any such people or beasts as those described by Father Aguirre to be found on "Rica de Plata."

longitude between them and Japan cannot be arrived at, because they had run before the gale and the weather was very thick and obscure. They ran from Japan to the eastward; and, having disposed of their merchandise, they returned to Malacca. They named these islands, out of regard for the Armenian merchant, who was greatly respected by the people of the ship, 'Isles of the Armenian.' " This is as much of the narrative, as I remember it, as will serve for the discovery of these islands as well as others in that region and corner of the sea. As regards the rest of that coast, it is very important that this exploration should be made; and for this purpose two coasting vessels of the burden and build which Don Juan de Guzmán may determine will serve. With regard to who should take part in the decision of this matter, as well as in all things concerning this exploration, your most illustrious lordship will follow his own judgment. I pray Our Lord that this may be for His great service and that of His Majesty. Most Illustrious Lord: From the least chaplain of your most illustrious lordship.

Fray Andrés de Aguirre[4]

Document No. 2

Paragraph of a letter from the Marqués de Villamanrique, Viceroy of New Spain, to His Majesty the King of Spain, making suggestions concerning the exploration of the coast of the South Sea, and giving notice of a vessel sailing for that purpose—dated 10th May, 1585

Capitulo de una carta del Virey de la Nueva España el Marques de Villamanrique a S. M. esponiendo lo que considera oportuno referente al descubrimiento de las costas de la mar del sur y dando noticia de una embarcacion que sale con este intento, su fecha de 10 de Mayo de 1585.*

14. Dice vuestra magestad en la misma carta, en el capitulo segundo della que ansi mismo escribió el arzobispo que los navios que vienen de las Filipinas reconocen la costa de esta tierra setecientas leguas y mas y menos antes de llegar al puerto de gapulco [sic] y vienen ansi a vista de tierra y que como no saven los puertos de toda esta costa aunque tienen necesidad de tomar tierra para rreparar los navios y proveerse de agua y otras cosas no lo pueden hacer ni tienen donde ampararse de tiempos contrarios que de ordinario corren por aquellas partes y que lo mismo sucede a los navios que antes de llegar a la costa padecen temporal ú otras necesidades que por no tener puerto en ella buelven arribar a las yslas de donde salieron y que para que esto cesase y vuestra magestad tuviese noticia de toda aquella costa que algunos dicen corre hasta confinar con la tierra firme de la china y otros que acava en el estrecho que llaman de anian que va a salir al parage de irlanda, havia mandado hazer dos fragatas para que saliesen a reconocer buscar y descubrir todos los puertos é yslas rrios, montes é

---

1 Gali sailed on a voyage from Acapulco for the Philippines in March, 1582, and sailed from Macao on his return voyage in July, 1584. The Archbishop of Mexico, Pedro de Moya y Contreras, became *visitador* of New Spain in 1583 and sixth viceroy in September, 1584. On the 18th October, 1585, Don Alonso Manrique de Zúñiga, Marqués de Villamanrique, succeeded him. These are the dates given by Mr. H. H. Bancroft's writers. Yet here we have a letter from the Marqués—as viceroy—dated in *May 1585*, before his arrival in New Spain, probably before his departure from Spain. Can it be possible that Mr. Bancroft's writers are in error in this matter of dates? It is evident, however, that Gali had returned from his voyage to the Philippines, and that the Archbishop dispatched him, or was about to dispatch him, (the Spanish is *sale*—"sails") on another voyage. Of this second voyage no mention is made in the books published by Mr. H. H. Bancroft.

2 Archbishop de Moya y Contreras, the same to whom Fray Andrés de Aguirre addressed the letter containing the yarn about the "islands of the Armenian."

PARAGRAPH of a letter from the viceroy of New Spain, the Marqués de Villamanrique, to His Majesty, setting forth what he deems timely with regard to the exploration of the coasts of the South Sea and giving notice of a vessel about to sail[1]† for that purpose—dated 10th May, 1585.‡

14. Your Majesty says in the same letter, in the second paragraph thereof: Furthermore, also, the Archbishop[2] wrote that the ships which come from the Philippines run along the coast of this land for seven hundred leagues, more or less, before arriving at the port of Acapulco, and come in this way with the land in sight, and that, as the harbors of this coast are not known, although there is need of landing, in order for the ships to stop and to obtain water and other things, this cannot be done; that there are no places for shelter from the contrary winds which ordinarily prevail in those parts; that the same is true with regard to ships which, before making the coast, encounter storms or which suffer other needs, and having no harbor there, they return to the islands whence they came; that this condition of things should cease and, in order that Your Majesty might gain information concerning all that coast, which some say joins on to the main land of China while others hold that it ends at the strait called Anian which leads to Ireland, he had ordered to be built two ships to be sent out for the exploration, investigation and discovery of all the harbors and islands, rivers, mountains and inhabited places there are there, and what languages are spoken and what peoples live there, what their manner of life may be, what fruits they produce and what degree of civilization they may enjoy—all to be explored and investigated—and that for this purpose he had engaged a good navigator and cosmographer; that in addition to this, by this route, and at

* Original document in AGI, Mexico 20. Spanish version appears in Carrasco, *Documentos de las Californias*, pp. 12–14. An extremely variant version of this is found in *Docs. para la demarcación de California*, I, 11–13, and is taken from Museo Naval, Colección Navarrete, XIX.

† Griffin again takes Bancroft to task needlessly. The problem lies in improper reading of the original document. Proper dating is May 10, 1586, rather than 1585. See Wagner, *Spanish Voyages*, 367.

‡ A partial translation appears in Wagner, *Spanish Voyages*, 151. A second document containing the substance of paragraph 14 is in Pedro de Moya y Contreras to the King, a letter dated January 22, 1585, in AGI, Mexico 336, and is partially translated in Wagner, *Spanish Voyages*, 367. The document is also found in Museo Naval, Colección Navarrete, XIX.

avitaciones que ay e de que lenguas é gentes era abitada é poblada e de su modo de vivir y que frutos y aprovechamientos tienen graduandolo y descubriendolo todo y que para ello tenia piloto y cosmografo muy bueno y que demas de lo sobredicho por esta via y a menos costa que por tierra se podria comunicar el nuevo megico en estando poblado como se colige de la relacion que de aquello avia dado Antonio despejo y si quando yo llegase huviesen salido estas fragatas que esperase el suceso y avisase a vuestra magestad y que no siendo ydas provea lo necesario y que para lo de adelante en cosas semejantes quando sucediere no me resuelva en ejecutarlas sin dar primero avisso a vuestra magestad si ya no fuese tan forzoso que ubiere peligros en la tardanza. Lo que en esto pasa segun lo que yo entiendo de que puedo dar quenta a vuestra magestad es que la costa de la nueva españa se suve por la parte del sur hasta quarenta y dos grados porque viniendo de las yslas philipinas las naos de vuestra magestad an tomado la tierra en aquella altura y hasta agora desde alli hasta el puerto de gapulco por toda la costa no ha parecido conveniente hacerse poblaciones ni por no las haver avido ni a tenido riesgo ningun navio y como vuestra magestad tiene relacion por el viaje que hizo el marques del valle a las Californias y Francisco Vazquez Coronado a las ciudades de cibolas, la mas de aquella gente y costa es de gente brava, prove y que se mantiene de pescar y como el poblar por agora podria tener inconveniente y de no lo aver hecho no parece ninguno, si vuestra magestad por agora fuere servido no habrá para que tratar de ello y quando las naos que salen de las yslas philipinas arriban escerca del puerto de manila de donde salen y antes que tomen altura porque en tomando alguna los vendavales que acerca del puerto los hacen arrivar, essos les son vientos frescos y buenos para venir a estos reynos y en quanto aquel descubrimiento del nuevo mexico se puede comunicar por aquella mar y costa parece segun la demarcion que es parte mediterrana y asta agora no se save que le corresponda la mar del norte, ó sur tan cerca que se pueda hacer lo que a vuestra magestad le an ynformado.

3 The voyage of Cortés in 1535.

4 Vásquez Coronado's expedition of 1540 to the Zuñi and Moqui countries.

5 Meaning that, after sailing northward to the latitude of Manila on the return voyage to New Spain, they sailed still farther northward—in fact, to a point some three hundred miles to the northward and eastward of the southern end of Japan—before striking the current flowing to the eastward and a favorable slant of wind.

a less cost than by land, communication might be had with New Mexico, on its being settled, as may be understood from the statement on this subject that had been made by Antonio de Espejo;* and that, if on my arrival these ships had sailed, I should await the result of the voyage and advise Your Majesty of the same, but, if they had not sailed, I should proceed as might be necessary in the case, while in future, under similar circumstances that might arise, I should not resolve on the execution of anything before consulting Your Majesty, provided the matter was not so urgent that there might be danger in delay. What there is in this matter—as I understand the facts—of which I can give an account to Your Majesty is this: On the south coast New Spain reaches to forty-two degrees,† for Your Majesty's ships, coming from the Philippine islands, make a landfall in that latitude; and, until now, from that point to the port of Acapulco, along the whole coast it has not seemed convenient to make settlements, and even without having had them, no ship has suffered any peril. From the reports of the voyage to the Californias made by the Marqués del Valle³ and the expedition of Francisco Vázquez Coronado⁴‡ to the cities of Cíbola, Your Majesty has learned that the greater part of the people on that coast is a savage people eking out a scanty living by fishing; and, as it might be inconvenient to make settlements there just now, while from not having done so no inconvenience has arisen, there is no need, for the present service of Your Majesty, to treat of that matter. When the ships which sail from the Philippine islands reach the neighborhood of the port of Manila, whence they sail, before getting their northing,⁵ the southeasterly winds which aid them in arriving there are also favorable and good for coming to these kingdoms. And as to the exploration of New Mexico, and whether communication can be had by that sea and coast, it appears from the demarcation of the same that it is an intermediate region, and it is yet unknown whether it be nearer to the southern sea or to the northern sea for the purposes of that concerning which Your Majesty has been informed.

* On Espejo see Herbert E. Bolton, *Spanish Exploration in the Southwest, 1542–1706,* 163–94.

† By the "South coast" the writer meant the coast of the Mar del Sur; that is, the Pacific Coast.

‡ On Vásquez de Coronado see Herbert E. Bolton, *Coronado, Knight of Pueblo and Plains.*

El arzobispo no hizo las fragatas que escrivió que pensaba hacer y para conseguir lo pretendia aviendo llegado de las yslas philipinas y de marcar que es la tierra firme de la gran china el capitan Francisco gali que es piloto y cosmografo que refiere tenia le tornó a despachar en un navio que llaman Sant Juan que es de vuestra magestad y en el que avia navegado y le dió officiales de la nao y marineros y diez mill pesos para que si por ser viejo el navio en que yba no pudiese seguir la derrota que le avia mandado en las yslas philipinas hiziese otro y comprase lo necesario y demarcase la tierra firme del xapon, yslas de armenio y todas las demas que tuviese rrazon y noticia en aquel mar del sur y de alli su viage en la mayor altura que el tiempo le diese lugar hasta tomar la costa de la nueva españa y que tomada viniese por ella viendo la tierra y puertos y demarcandolo todo para que se tenga de ello entera noticia venido que sea si traxera alguna relacion y entendido lo que ubiere hecho, informaré a vuestra magestad de lo que me pareciere que conviene a su real servicio.

Marqués de Villamanrique

[6] Fray Andrés de Aguirre's yarn, which was told to Urdaneta by the Portuguese captain, and by him to the King of Spain, seems to have been considered credible.

The Archbishop did not build the ships which he wrote he thought of building; and, for the purpose of carrying his plan into effect, Captain Francisco Gali,* the navigator and cosmographer to whom he referred, having arrived from the Philippines and the demarcation of the main land of Great China, he determined upon dispatching him in a ship called *San Juan* belonging to Your Majesty, accompanied by that in which he had come, and he furnished to him naval officers and sailors and ten thousand dollars, so that, if the ship in which he went, because it was so old, could not make the voyage ordered to be made, he might build another at the Philippine islands and purchase what might be necessary in order that he might make the demarcation of the mainland of Japan, the islands of the Armenian[6] and all others in that part of the South Sea of which he might have information, and then make his way as far to the northward as the weather would permit and until he made the coast of New Spain; and, this landfall being made, that he should come homeward along this coast, examining the land and harbors, mapping and noting all—so that there be a complete account of it. When he arrives, should he bring any report, and on my learning what he may have accomplished, I shall inform Your Majesty of what may seem to me proper for your royal service.

Marqués de Villamanrique

* For a brief account of Gali, sometimes spelled Gualle and Hualde, see Chapman, *op. cit.*, 113–15. On the trip of Gali, see: *The Third and Last Volume of the Voyages, Navigations, Trafiques, and Discoveries of the English Nation*, collected by Richard Hakluyt (London, 1600), 442–47, and *Apuntamientos sobre los actos de poseción en el mar del sur por la corona de España por Juan Bautista Muñoz*, Madrid, June 11, 1790, in Archivo Histórico Nacional, Estado, 4291[1].

Document No. 3

Paragraph of a letter from the Conde de Santiago, Viceroy of New Spain, to the King of Spain, referring to the commissioning of Sebastián Rodríguez Cermeño for a survey of the coast of the South Sea—dated 6th April, 1594

Cᴀᴘɪᴛᴜʟᴏ de una carta del Virey de la Nueva España Don Luis de Velazco a S. M. fecha en Mexico a 6 Abril de 1594 referente a cargar a Sebastian Rodriguez Cermeño el reconocimiento de las costas de la mar del sur segun lo dispuesto por su magestad.*

Por un capitulo de carta que vuestra magestad mandó escrivirme en 17 de henero de 1593 manda que se descubran y demarquen los puertos del viaje destas yslas para la seguridad de las naos que ban y bienen y supuesto que para hacerlo hera menester navio y dinero, ó a lo menos permitir a la gente alguna inteligencia ó negociacion de las que vuestra magestad tiene prohibidas en que pudiesen ser aprovechados conforme a su trabajo, y se compró el navio San Pedro con que hiciesen el descubrimiento de tornaviaje en caso que los navios que el año pasado fueron ó alguno dellos haya faltado, y ordene al piloto que agora ba en la capitana que se llama Sebastian Rodriguez Cermeño, y es hombre platico en la carrera, seguro y que tiene posible, aunque portugues porque no los ay deste officio castellanos, que haga el descubrimiento y demarcacion y le ofresi que como lo hiciese assi lo haria la gratificacion de mercancias, que escribí al gobernador le permitiese cargar en el navio algunas toneladas de ropa para que se aproveche de los fletes y le hiciese dar todo lo que oviese menester para el efecto, de lo que hiciere daré aviso a vuestra magestad a su tiempo.

1 The Philippines.
2 The governor of the Philippines is the official referred to.

PARAGRAPH of a letter of the Viceroy of New Spain, Don Luis de Velasco, to His Majesty, dated at Mexico, 6th April, 1594, with regard to putting Sebastián Rodríguez Cermeño in charge of the survey of the coasts of the South Sea, according to the disposition made by His Majesty.*

In a paragraph of the letter which, on the 17th of January, 1593, Your Majesty ordered to be written to me, it is ordered that a survey and demarcation of the harbors to be found on the voyage to and from these islands[1] be made, with a view to the safety of the ships which come and go; and, a ship and money being necessary for this purpose, or, at least permission to engage in ventures now prohibited by Your Majesty, in such manner that the gain would compensate the labor, the ship *San Pedro*† was bought, in which the exploration might be made on the return voyage, provided that the ships which sailed last year, or some one of them, had failed to do this; and I ordered the navigator who at present sails in the flagship, who is named Sebastián Rodríguez Cermeño and who is a man of experience in his calling, one who can be depended upon and who has means of his own—although he is a Portuguese, there being no Spaniards of his profession whose services are available—that he should make the exploration and demarcation, and I offered, if he would do this, to give him his remuneration in the way of taking on board merchandise; and I wrote to the governor[2] that he should allow him to put on board the ship some tons of cloth in order that he might have the benefit of the freight money, and I caused him to be given all that might be needed for the purpose, and concerning what he may do I shall advise Your Majesty in due season.

* Original document in AGI, Mexico 22. Spanish version appears in Carrasco, *Documentos de las Californias*, p. 16. Wagner merely mentions this document in *Spanish Voyages*. *Docs. para la demarcación de California*, I, 118–19 has a nearly identical document.

† The vessel *San Pedro* was taken to the Philippine Islands, where Rodríguez Cermeño picked up the *San Agustín* for the return voyage.

Document No. 4

Paragraph of a letter from the royal officials of Acapulco to the Conde de Monterrey, Viceroy of New Spain, giving tidings of the loss of the ship *San Agustín*—dated 1st February, 1596

CAPITULO de carta de los oficiales reales de Acapulco, al Virey de Nueva España, fecha en Acapulco a 1° de Febrero de 1596 dando noticia de la perdida de la nao San Agustin.*

El miercoles 31 de henero de este año entró en este puerto un barco que llaman en Philipinas Viroco y en él Joan de Morgana piloto, quatro españoles marineros, cinco yndios y un negro, que dieron nueva de que el navio San Agustin del descubrimiento se ha perdido en una costa donde dió y se hizo pedazos, y que se haogo un fraile descalzo y otra persona de las que en el venian y de setenta hombres ó mas que se metieron en este barco solo vinieron estos porque el capitan y piloto del dicho navio Sebastian Rodriguez Cermeño con los demas desembarcaron en el puerto de la Navidad y entienden estarán ya en esa ciudad el subceso y discurso de su viaje y perdida del navio y en la parte que consta por declaracion que con juramento hizo el dicho piloto Joan de Morgana que es con esta y el varco visitamos y en el no venian ningun genero de mercaderias, los hombres casi desnudos a causa de ser tan chico que por milagro parece haver llegado a esta tierra con tanta gente.

1 This was the ninth viceroy, Gaspar de Zúñiga y Acevedo, Conde de Monterrey.

2 A *viroco* was a small vessel without a deck, having one or two square sails and propelled by sweeps. Its hull was formed from a single tree, hollowed out and having the sides built up with planks.

3 Probably an Augustinian friar. The spiritual care of all things connected with the Philippines had been assigned to the Augustinians.

4 The city of Mexico.

5 The *San Agustín* was cast away in what is now called Drake's Bay. It was a hazardous undertaking to sail from that place to Acapulco in a vessel so small and so overcrowded.

PARAGRAPH of a letter from the royal officers at Acapulco to the Viceroy of New Spain,[1] dated at Acapulco, 1st February, 1596, giving tidings of the loss of the ship *San Agustín*.*

On Wednesday, the 31st of January of this year, there entered this harbor a vessel of the kind called in the Philippines a *viroco*,[2]† having on board Juan de Morgana, navigating officer, four Spanish sailors, five Indians and a Negro, who brought tidings that the ship *San Agustín*, of the exploring expedition, had been lost on a coast where she struck and went to pieces,‡ and that a barefooted frair[3] and another person of those on board had been drowned, and that, of the seventy men, or more, who embarked in this small vessel, only these came in her, because the captain and pilot of said ship, Sebastián Rodríguez Cermeño, and others, went ashore at the port of Navidad and, as they understand, have already arrived in that city.[4] The outcome and account of the voyage and of the loss of the ship, together with the statement made under oath by said navigating officer, Juan de Morgana, accompany this. We visited the vessel, finding no kind of merchandise on board, and that the men were almost naked. The vessel being so small it seems miraculous that she should have reached this country with so many people on board.[5]

* Original document in AGI, Mexico 22. *Docs. para la demarcación de California*, I, 156–57 contains this document but ascribes it to AGI, Mexico 23. Spanish version also in Carrasco, *Documentos de las Californias*, 24. This contains extracts from Viceroy Velasco's letters of October 8, 1593 and of April 6, 1594, both of which appear in AGI, Mexico 22.

† The *viroco* was a pre-fabricated vessel brought from the Philippines aboard the *San Agustín* to be assembled on the California coast and subsequently employed in surveying the shallow waters anticipated along the coast. It was given the name *San Buenaventura*.

‡ In 1940 and 1941, two archaeological expeditions sponsored by the University of California uncovered artifacts clearly resulting from the wreck of the *San Agustín* at Drake's Bay. See Robert F. Heizer, "Archaeological Evidence of Sebastián Rodríguez Cermeño's California Visit in 1595," in California Historical Society *Quarterly*, Vol. XX, December 1941, 315–28 and Museo Naval, Colección Guillen, California (MN 1509) for Rodríguez Cermeño's account.

Document No. 5

Paragraph of a letter from the Conde de Monterrey, Viceroy of New Spain, to the King of Spain, giving notice of the loss of the ship *San Agustín* and of discoveries made in her—dated 19th April, 1596

Capitulo de una carta a Su Magestad del Virey de la Nueva España Conde de Monterrey fechada en Mexico a 19 de Abril de 1596 con noticias de la perdida de la nao San Agustin y lo que se consiguió descubrir con ella.*

Sobre la perdida del navio S. Agustin que venia de las yslas de poniente hacer el descubrimiento de las costas de la mar del sur, como vuestra magestad fué servido de mandar al Virrey Don Luis de Velazco escribí a vuestra magestad en el segundo de aviso lo que acaba duplicado, despues de llegado, alguna gente que se salvó de la que venia en el navio y entre ellos los oficiales del que se pretenden culpar unos a otros como siempre acontece en semejantes subcesos, enviome y remitiome la audiencia de Guadalajara ciertos auctos que por su horden se hicieron entre ellos, habiendo tomado tierra en aquel distrito, quedanse mirando y que en caso que resulte culpado alguno y parece conveniente castigarle, se hará. Aunque es arta compasion de lo que an padecido despues que dió al traves el navio, de la mucha perdida de hacienda que hicieron en él; de lo que fuere necesario avisar a vuestra magestad se dará quenta y por ahora solo se me ofrece decir que en el descubrimiento de los puertos dice el piloto que procuró cumplir con su obligacion en la lancha con que vinieron despues de la perdida del navio y trae escripta una relacion cuya copia será con esta. Pero yo lo é examinado en presencia del cómitre y contramaestre que ambos son platicos y aunque conforman en algunas cosas difieren en otras y me parece que se convence y colige claro que algunas bayas de las principales y donde mas se podia esperar de hallar puerto las atravesaron de punta a punta y de noche y en otras entraron poco, a todo debió dar ocasion forzosa la hambre y enfermedad con que dicen que venian que los haria apresurar el viaje. Y asi entiendo que no está en

1 The Philippines.
2 The second mail-packet which had sailed for Spain that year.
3 The *viroco* of which mention is made in the communication of the officials of Acapulco.

PARAGRAPH of a letter to His Majesty from the Viceroy of New Spain, the Conde de Monterrey, dated at Mexico, 19th April, 1596, giving tidings of the loss of the ship *San Agustín*, and of the discoveries they were able to make with her.*†

Touching the loss of the ship *San Agustín*, which was on its way from the islands of the west[1] for the purpose of making the exploration of the coasts of the South Sea, in accordance with Your Majesty's orders to Viceroy Don Luis de Velasco, I wrote to Your Majesty by the second packet[2] what I send as a duplicate with this letter. After the arrival here of some of those who went in the ship and were saved, among them the officers, who tried to inculpate one another—as always happens under similar circumstances—the *audiencia*‡ of Guadalajara remitted to me certain documents relating to proceedings had in the matter by its order, for they landed in that district. These are under consideration; and, in case any one be found culpable, and it seem fitting to punish him, this will be done. While the sufferings they underwent after the ship was cast away elicit compassion, concerning the great loss of the property on board her caused by them I will give an account of so much as it may be necessary to make known to Your Majesty. At present, all that occurs to me as necessary to say is that, in the matter of the survey of harbors, the navigating officer says he endeavored to comply with his obligation in the *lancha*[3] in which they travelled after the ship was lost, and he has brought with him a report in writing, of which a copy accompanies this letter. But I have examined him in the presence of the second-in-command and the boatswain, who are both experienced and, although they agree in some particulars, they differ in others. To me there seems to be convincing proof, resting on clear inference, that some of the principal bays, where with greater reason it might be expected harbors would be found, they crossed from point to point and by night, while others they entered but a little way. For all this a strong incentive

---

* Original in AGI, Mexico 23. Spanish version is in Carrasco, *Documentos de las Californias*, 17–18, and reproduced in *Docs. para la demarcación de California*, I, 161–62. The document is mentioned but not quoted in Wagner, *Spanish Voyages*, 167.

† Cermeño's activity along the California coast is treated in Chapman, *op. cit.*, 116–23.

‡ The Audiencia de Guadalajara was the administrative court of that city and served as headquarters for a major subdivision of the extensive Viceroyalty of New Spain. The Guadalajara jurisdiction included the surrounding area and the extension of land claimed by Spain to the northward of the settled area of Mexico.

cuanto a este descubrimiento cumplido el intento de vuestra magestad y todos convienen en que esta diligencia no se habia de intentar de tornaviaje de las yslas y con navio cargado sino de esta costa yendo siempre por ella adelante.

4 It is very evident that these two last documents were unknown to the writers of Mr. H. H. Bancroft's books, as well as to the authors of the printed works consulted with reference to Rodríguez Cermeño's disastrous voyage. What little Bancroftian historians have to say about the loss of the San Agustín, is this: "Of the result we know only that his vessel, the San Agustín, ran ashore in what was named at the time San Francisco Port, since known as Drake Bay. Whether the ship escaped after being lightened of her cargo or was accompanied by a tender on which the crew escaped is not recorded; but Cermeño's pilot Bolaños lived to visit the port again with Vizcaíno in 1603, and his statement is extant on the voyage. It is not impossible that some additional results of the expedition were intentionally kept secret by the government; at any rate, no record has ever come to light in the archives." History of the Pacific States, X, 147—and this: "Of Cermeño's adventures we know only that his vessel ran aground on a lee-shore behind what was later called Point Reyes. . . . It is possible that the San Agustín was accompanied by another vessel on which the officers and men escaped; but much more probable I think that the expression 'was lost' in the record is an error, and that the ship escaped with the loss of her cargo. One of the men, Francisco Bolaños, was piloto mayor, or sailing-master, under Vizcaíno in 1603, when he anchored in the same port to see if any trace of the cargo remained, but without landing. The statement of Bolaños as reported incidentally by Ascensión and Torquemada is, so far as I can learn, the only record extant of this voyage." Id., XIII, 96. In this case, certainly, comment on the accuracy of the work quoted does not seem to be called for. Mr. Bancroft's writer misspells the name Cermeño, but errors of that kind are frequent in Mr. Bancroft's publication. It appears, from these documents, that the name of the chief navigating officer of the San Agustín was not Bolaños.

must have existed, because of the hunger and illness they say they experienced, which would cause them to hasten on their voyage. Thus, I take it, as to this exploration the intention of Your Majesty has not been carried into effect. It is the general opinion that this enterprise should not be attempted on the return voyage from the islands and with a laden ship, but from this coast and by constantly following along it.[4]

Document No. 6

Paragraph of a letter from the Conde de Santiago, Viceroy of New Spain, to the King of Spain, informing him that money is lacking for the survey of the mainland coast, but that there are persons who will undertake to do this if certain concessions be made to them—dated 8th October, 1593

Cᴀᴘɪᴛᴜʟᴏ de una carta del Virey de Nueva España Don Luis de Velazco, a S. M. diciendole que para hacer el descubrimiento de los puertos de la tierra firme hay falta de dinero; pero que existen personas que lo hagan por su cuenta mediante ciertas concesiones, fecha en Mejico a 8 de Octubre de 1593.*

Para hazer el descubrimiento ó demarcacion de los puertos de esta tierra firme hasta las yslas philipinas como vuestra magestad lo manda, ay falta de dinero y si no es de la caxa real no se puede suplir porque penas de camera, gastos de justicia quitre y vacaciones estan tan apuradas que deven de tiempo atras muchos dineros a la real hacienda, avido otra persona que trate de hazerlo debaxo de algunas condiciones y lo de mas momento es que se le dé facultad para llevar dinero con que tratar y contratar en los puertos que descubriere y como este es negocio oscuro y de que podrian resultar inconveniente no he tomado resolucion en ello, parece que limitandole cantidad y prohibicion que no tratase en puerto descubierto aunque arribase a algunos con tiempos contrarios y haciendo otras prevensiones que al asentarlo ocurrieran se podrá tratar dello. Vuestra magestad mandará lo que fuese servido.

(Al margen se encuentra el siguiente acuerdo del Consejo: "hagase la cedula que en tiempo se ha dado.")

PARAGRAPH of a letter from the Viceroy of New Spain, Don Luis de Velasco, to His Majesty, informing him that for the purpose of making the survey of the ports of the mainland money is lacking; but that there are individuals who will do this at their own expense, provided certain concessions be made. Dated at Mexico, 8th October, 1593.*

In order to make the exploration or demarcation of the harbors of this mainland as far as the Philippine Islands, as Your Majesty orders, money is lacking; and, if it be not taken from the royal treasury, it cannot be supplied, as for some time past a great deal of money has been owing to the royal treasury on account of fines forfeited to it, legal costs, and the like. But there is another person who desires to make it under certain conditions, the most important being that he be given permission to take money with which to trade and transact business at the harbors which he may discover. As such a proceeding is little understood and something untoward might result therefrom, I have come to no determination in the matter. It would seem that by limiting the amount of business, and prohibiting trade at ports already discovered—although the ship might touch there under stress of weather—and by taking other precautions which might suggest themselves at the time of making the contract, the matter could be arranged. Your Majesty will order what you may please.

(In the margin is noted the following resolution of the Council: "Let a decree be prepared in accordance with what has been agreed on.")

* Original in AGI, Mexico 22. Spanish version in Carrasco, *Documentos de las Californias*, 15–16.

Document No. 7

Paragraph of a letter from the Conde de Monterrey, Viceroy of New Spain, to the King of Spain, concerning the expedition to New Mexico and the concession to Sebastián Vizcaíno—dated 20th December, 1595

CAPITULO de una carta a su Magestad del Virey de la Nueva España Conde de Monterey sobre entrada en el Nuevo Mexico y concesion a Sebastian Vizcaino.*

Sobre la entrada del Nuevo Mexico tomó el Virey Don Luis de Velazco cietro asiento con Don Juan de Oñate quando yo venia caminando desde el puerto para aqui; y poco antes hizo cierta concesion a un Sebastian Vizcaino sobre la entrada de las Californias adonde por asiento havia de yr a pescar perlas; yo he visto los papeles de este último negocio para lo que tocaba a dar órden en la execucion, y los otros porque el Virrey a instado en que yo los vea antes de la entrada y dificulte en lo que me pareciere y se olgara de no embarazar el tiempo con nueva deliberacion, pero haviendo de hacerlo es forzoso que sea con atencion y consexo para tomar resolucion de la materia y asi no me he resuelto sobre las dudas que se me ofrecen que son algunas y por no tener estado estos negocios para escribir mas largo sobre ellos, lo dexo para el segundo navio de havisso contentandome con darle a vuestra magestad del que voy haciendo y de que muy presto me determinare para que si algo se huviese de reformar se haga y lo demas se ponga en execucion brevemente, será vuestra magestad servido de yr aguardando mis cartas aunque las partes pidan alguna confirmacion ó cedula porque assi conviene a su servicio hasta que yo escriba.

¹ The Conde de Monterey landed at Vera Cruz on the 18th September, 1595, and, on the 5th October following, entered the city of Mexico and took charge of the government. This letter was written, undoubtedly, shortly after the latter date, probably being that referred to in the document next following this as having been written on the 20th December, 1595. And this is another document which must have escaped the research of Mr. H. H. Bancroft, as his writers refer to it nowhere in any of the volumes in which Vizcaíno's voyages and Oñate's conquest are related—for in those ingeniously contrived tomes what is said on any subject is cut up and distributed through several volumes. These writers say—*History of the Pacific States*, V, 781—that Viceroy Velasco and Don Juan de Oñate completed the arrangements for the conquest of New Mexico on the 24th August, 1595. In this letter of Viceroy Monterey he says that the contract was entered into while he was on his way from Vera Cruz to the capital, viz.: after the 18th September of that year.

PARAGRAPH of a letter to His Majesty from the Viceroy of New Spain, the Conde de Monterey, concerning the entry into New Mexico and the concession to Sebastián Vizcaíno.*

Touching the entry into New Mexico, Viceroy Don Luis de Velasco entered into a certain contract with Don Juan de Oñate† while I was on my way from the port to this place; and, a short time before this, he made a certain concession to one Sebastián Vizcaíno‡ concerning an expedition to the Californias, whither, by the terms of the agreement, he was to go for the purpose of fishing for pearls. I have seen the papers relating to the latter matter, for purposes connected with giving orders for the execution thereof, and those relating to the former, because the Viceroy insisted that I should see them before the departure of the expedition, and I made such strictures as seemed good to me. The matter should be properly adjusted without wasting time in renewed deliberation thereon; but, since this is necessary, it is necessary also that it be done with care and after counsel thereon, in order that a fitting resolution be taken. Therefore, I have come to no conclusion respecting the doubts which suggested themselves to me, for there are such; and, because these matters are not in a sufficiently advanced state for writing about them at greater length, I postpone doing so until the departure of the next dispatch ship, contenting myself with giving to Your Majesty an account of what I am doing and what I may very soon determine upon, so that, if there be anything requiring alteration, it may be changed, while the rest may be done promptly. May Your Majesty be pleased to continue awaiting the arrival of my letters, although interested persons may ask for some concession or royal decree—for, until I shall write, this will be more fitting for your service.[1]

* Original in AGI, Mexico 23. Spanish version in Carrasco, *Documentos de las Californias*, 18–19.

† See George P. Hammond, *Don Juan de Oñate and the Founding of New Mexico.*

‡ On Vizcaíno see Chapman, *op. cit.*, 124–42 and Bolton, *Spanish Exploration in the Southwest, 1542–1706*, 43–134. Alvaro del Portillo y Diez de Sollano, *Descubrimientos y exploraciones en las costas de California*, 161–208, 292–435, contains the story of Vizcaíno's activities supported by a documentary section. Hereinafter this work will be cited as Portillo, *Descubrimientos y exploraciones.*

Document No. 8

Letter of the Conde de Monterrey, Viceroy of New Spain, to the King of Spain, on the propriety of not sending expeditions undertaken by individuals to discover and take possession of the provinces to the northward of New Spain, and of precautions to be observed concerning what Sebastián Vizcaíno is doing with regard to an enterprise of this kind—dated 29th February, 1596

Carta a su Magestad del Virey de la Nueva España sobre conveniencia de no enviar espediciones particulares a tomar posesion y descubrir las provincias al norte de la Nueva España y tomando precausiones para lo que hace en este sentido Sebastian Vizcaino.*

En carta de veinte de diciembre cuyo duplicado yrá con esta havisé a vuestra magestad de la jornada que hallé cometida por cierta capitulacion y patentes del Virey Don Luis de Velasco mi antecesor, a Sebastian Vizcaino para que por su cuenta y de ciertos mercaderes de aquí fuese a las Californias y que yendo é procediendo a la execucion me habia resultado ciertas dubdas de que daria cuenta a vuestra magestad quando pudiese decir juntamente la resolucion y asi lo haré en esta carta. Haviendo hecho asiento los años pasados con ciertos particulares que se ofrecieron de yr a las Californias a pescar perlas y tomar noticia de aquella tierra y comenzada la jornada no llegó a efecto por cierta quistion y deshavio que havia habido entre la gente que yba y su caudillo, el qual murió en esta ciudad pendiente cierto pleito criminal, ante los alcaldes, y por incidente el que se trató sobre el cumplimiento del asiento este se determinó y fué condenado Sebastian Vizcaino y otros que eran compañeros suyos a instancia del fiscal de vuestra magestad a que en conformidad del asiento hiciese dentro de tres meses la jornada y movido el virey Don Luis de Velasco por algunas causas que a ello le devieron inclinar por via de gracia, le concedió a peticion suia la entrada y pacificacion de las dichas Californias en conformidad de las ordenanzas que ay de vuestra magestad con todas las onrras, gracias excepcion que se acostumbran hacer a los pacificadores y pobladores de nuevas provincias: en su ultima se trató commigo de este negocio en general por el virrey y por la parte como de resolucion tomada por asiento antiguo y confirmada por carta de executoria de la sala del crimen a pedimiento del fiscal y asi me pareció que no devia haver necesidad ni aun lugar de parar cosa alguna desta materia para mas que tratar de executar lo acordado y asi

A LETTER to His Majesty from the Viceroy of New Spain on the propriety of not sending private expeditions to take possession and make discoveries in the provinces to the northward of New Spain, and taking precautions against what Sebastián Vizcaíno is doing in this respect.*

In a letter of the 20th December, of which a duplicate will accompany this, I advised Your Majesty of the expedition which I found had been entrusted by virtue of the agreement made by my predecessor, Don Luis de Velasco, to Sebastián Vizcaíno, and a permit to the effect that, on his account and that of certain traders of these parts, he might go to the Californias, and that in proceeding to the execution of the contract there had occurred to me certain doubts of which I would give account to Your Majesty when I should be able to mention them in connection with my resolution in the matter; this I shall do in this letter. In years past an agreement was made with certain individuals who offered to go to the Californias for the purpose of fishing for pearls and obtaining information concerning that country, and preparations for the expedition were made; but the undertaking resulted in nothing, because of a certain question and falling out arising between those who were about to take part in the expedition and their leader, who died in this city during the pendency before the judges of a certain criminal cause, in which the question of carrying out said agreement was involved incidentally. The matter was determined, and Sebastián Vizcaíno, and others who were his partners, were required, at the instance of Your Majesty's prosecuting attorney, to begin the journey, in accordance with the agreement, within three months; and the Viceroy, Don Luis de Velasco, influenced by certain motives inducing him to lean toward leniency, at his petition granted a concession for the entry and pacification of the said Californias, in conformity with existing ordinances of Your Majesty, with all the honors, favors and exemption usually given to the pacifiers and settlers of new provinces. In his last letter, the Viceroy took up with me this matter generally; and, seeing that there had been a former agreement which was confirmed by decree of the criminal court at the instance of the prosecuting officer, it seemed to me for this reason

---

* Original in AGI, Mexico 23. Spanish versions in Carrasco, *Documentos de las Californias*, 19–22 and in *Docs. para la demarcación de California*, I, 151–55.

venido aqui se comenzó a levantar la gente y queriendo ver los papeles hallé que el auto y executoria caian solamente sobre lo que tocaba a la pesqueria de las perlas y de ninguna manera sobre la entrada y pacificacion y reparar en ello, por parecerme que el sugeto de la persona, su calidad y caudal no es suficiente para una cosa que puede venir a ser tan grande y que requiere diferentes fuerzas y modo de proceder de lo que aora se presupone y juzga, pues aunque en materia de utilidad; haciendose el viage a su costa y sin gasto alguno de vuestra magestad parece que se va a ganar y no a perder la esperanza de buen suceso por medio tan flaco es poco y mucho lo que se aventura no solo en la reputacion que se perderia con estas naciones de yndios si a este hombre y su gente deshiciesen los naturales de aquella tierra, pero en lo principal que es la conciencia y autoridad de la real persona de vuestra magestad, me parece que se arriesga mucho en que una jornada que licitamente no puede ser de derecha conquista, sino de predicacion del evangelio y pacificacion y reduccion se encomiende por caudillo y cabo a un hombre de poca estofa y menos brio y capacidad para tan grande negocio, esta dificultad me pareció comunicar al virrey Don Luis de Velasco y por lo que me escrivió, que fué con la prudencia que entiende y trata todas las cosas, no cesaron las rrazones del temor que yo tenia de los desordenes desta gente, y hallando perplexidad en el caso por los peligros que se descubrian en esto para la reputacion y para la consciencia y por las dificultades que tambien se representaban conforme a justicia y conciencia en alterar lo tratado y quitarle a este hombre su jornada, en especial teniendo ya hechos gastos, lo hice ver a un teologo y jurista, de los que mejor parecer podian tener en esta dubda y habiendoles juntado fueron de acuerdo en que la concession del virrey para esta pacificacion de las Californias conforme a las hordenanzas de Viceroy Monterey tiene fuerza de asiento y contrato y que siendo al principio gracia, hera ya de justicia y no padeciendo el capitan manifiesta incapacidad ó haviendo hecho delito no podia variarse; la audiencia a quien di cuenta desto sintió lo mismo. Y visto esto y que aun mandarle por instruccion que solo descubriese y que suspendiese la entrada hasta dar cuenta les pareció contra justicia, segun el estado que el negocio tenia me resolví a no desvaratarle ni desaviar su jornada a Sebastian Vizcaino teniendo por cierto que lo que en esta parte fuera de justicia será de conciencia y que no puede ser de buen gobierno lo que vá contra ella; y porque

that there should be no necessity, or even room, for any decision holding up anything in this matter, but rather trying to carry out what had been agreed upon. So, this conclusion having been reached, recruiting for the expedition began; but I, on an examination of the papers in the case, found that the proceedings and decree had reference to the pearl fishery only and not at all to the entry and pacification and living in the land; for, it seemed to me, with regard to the person, his quality and capital are not sufficient in connection with an enterprise which may come to be of such vast importance, and one requiring greater backing and a method of proceeding other than what is now thought and deemed sufficient; for, even looking at the matter from the utilitarian point of view, although he make the journey at his own cost and without any expense to Your Majesty, it seems to be of little moment whether he goes for gain and in order not to lose the chance of good fortune, but of great importance the hazarding of not only the repute which would be lost among these nations of Indians if the natives of that country should repel this man and his people, but—this is the principal thing involved—that of the conscience and authority of the royal person of Your Majesty. It appeared to me to be risking much if an expedition which cannot lawfully be one of direct conquest, but one of preaching the gospel and pacification, and of bringing the people into subjection to the crown, were entrusted to a man as leader and chief whose position is obscure and who has not, even in less degree, the resolution and capacity necessary for so great an enterprise. It seemed to me proper to communicate my opinion of these difficulties to Viceroy Don Luis de Velasco; and, judging from what he wrote to me on the subject, and he did so with the prudence marking his investigation and treatment of all things, the motives that I had for fearing some mishap occurring to these people did not fail to work upon his mind also. Being greatly perplexed in the consideration of this matter, because of the perils to repute and conscience which might result, as well as by the difficulty presenting itself as to conformity with justice and conscience in the alteration of a compact and taking away from this man his right to make the expedition especially as he had been already at expense in the matter, he submitted the question to a theologian and jurist, of those whose opinions are entitled to greater consideration in doubtful cases of this nature; and these gentlemen, having taken counsel to-

he juzgado convenir al servicio de nuestro señor y de vuestra magestad
que puesto havia de pasar adelante por hallarse ya hecha y encaminada le execucion de ello y no padecer este hombre defectos notorios
que en derecho pueden escusar a vuestra magestad de cumplir con él
se le ayudase y diese calor para que la gente que a levantado y pretende embarcar que es muy razonable en número y calidad le estime
y respecte a él, lo he procurado quanto me ha sido posible y prevenido
desde aora con honrrarle yo aqui y darle autoridad al mayor peligro
que anteveo y temo por donde yo no le digiera que es algun menospre-
cio y atrevimiento de parte de los soldados que lleva y que por este
camino le venga a desobedecer y a seguirse dello mucha desorden, he
apretado como puedo y debo hacer a que me dé memoria y satisfaccion
acerca de los navios y lanchas que lleva y de los aparejos dellos y de la
gente y vastimentos que para sustentarla a de embarcar y de las
armas y municiones y otras cosas todo ello por sus generos y cantidades
lo que a dado he mandado ver a personas platicas y les parece suficiente; pero en el cumplimiento de lo que dice que embarcará consiste
el llevar recado suficiente para que los religiosos que lleva franciscos
puedan estar seguros a la conversion y pacificacion y para poblar su
gente aquella tierra sin que por evidente necesidad de comida ó otras
cosas vayan a peligro notorio y claro de hacer violencias y robos a los
naturales, asi he mandado a los oficiales reales de Acapulco que hagan
registro muy puntual y riguroso de lo que a ofrecido llevar y no le
consienta embarcar sin que vaya todo ello y para que se haga otro
tanto en el puerto de Salagua de la provincia de Colima a donde
endereza otra parte de su gente y de los generos que lleva me a parecido poner buen recado por no haver alli oficiales reales y ser tierra
desviada y muy conveniente que no se fie esto y aun lo que en los
primeros havisos podria saberse desta gente por aquella parte de
qualesquiera personas y ministros de los nacidos aqui que por ventura
seran obligados a los mercaderes que tienen a cargo esta jornada y a
los que van en ella, y asi he enviado persona particular de confianza
y de platica que a sido soldado y podra dar buena cuenta de lo que alli
se ha de hacer y de la conducion de los soldados y castigo de los
desordenes que hicieren por aquel camino en los pueblos de los yndios
que como no acostumbrados al transito de la gente de guerra que suele

gether, concurred in considering that the concession of the Viceroy for this pacification of the Californias according to the orders of Your Majesty had the force of an agreement and contract; that what was at first a favor had become his just due; and that, as the captain manifested no incapacity and had been guilty of no offense, the compact could not be changed. The *audiencia*, to which I gave an account of this matter, was of like opinion. This being determined, and it appearing to that body to be contrary to justice even to give him instructions to make discoveries only and not to take possession before reporting those discoveries, I, in view of the length to which the affair had gone, resolved not to annul the contract nor to interfere with the expedition of Sebastián Vizcaíno, holding it for certain that in this thing that which is justice is also a matter of good conscience, and that what contravenes this is not an indication of good government. And, because I have deemed it appropriate for the service of Our Lord and that of Your Majesty, inasmuch as it was necessary to go on with the affair since it had begun and as this man does not possess notorious defects which can rightfully excuse Your Majesty from aiding and fomenting his undertaking, in order that the persons he has enlisted and intends to put on board ship, and who in number and condition make a reasonably good showing, may esteem and respect him, I have done all that lay in my power to show him honor while here and to clothe him with authority in view of the greater danger I foresee and fear on his account, though I would not say it to him—which is some lack of respect and an overbold bearing on the part of the soldiers whom he takes with him, so that in this way they may come to disobey his orders, all this giving rise to great disorder. I have insisted, as far as I could and ought to insist, that he should furnish me with a satisfactory memorandum concerning the ships and *lanchas* he intends to take with him, and the tackle and rigging, and the people and the necessary provisions for them that he intends embarking, and the arms and ammunition, and other matters, all being inventoried in kind and by quantities. He has furnished this memorandum; I have caused it to be examined by persons understanding such matters, and what has been provided appears to them to be sufficient. But, in order to carry out fully what he says he intends to do, it is essential that he take with him a complete provision of all things necessary, so that the

yr a filipinas podran padecer y sentir mas travajo. Dios guarde a vuestra magestad Mexico 29 de hebrero de 1596.

El Conde de Monte Rey.

(Decreto del Consejo). Vista en 27 de Mayo de 1596 escribasele al Virrey que quite a este Sebastian Vizcaino esta conquista y descubrimiento y que avise a que otra persona se puede encomendar que la pueda hazer con mas satisfaccion y esperanza de buen suceso.

[1] In volume X of the historical works published by Mr. H. H. Bancroft a good deal of what is said in those volumes about the first and second voyages of Sebastián Vizcaíno is related. Chap. VI of this volume treats of "Voyages to the Northwest," and the writer remarks: "These voyages treated in this chapter have already been put before the public many times in many forms, often with accuracy and completeness. Both individually and collectively they were in former years the subject of much more research than the inland annals of the same period, and later researches in the Spanish and Mexican archives have brought to light comparatively little new material." *History of the Pacific States*, X, 132. It seems to be apparent that, in the matter of Vizcaíno's first voyage, no attempt was made to bring to light any new material to be found in the archives at Seville. Mr. Bancroft's writer says merely: "In 1594 Viceroy Velasco, probably by royal instructions, contracted with Sebastián Vizcaíno to explore anew and occupy for Spain the Islas Californias. Velasco's successor, the Count of Monterey, ratified the contract and dispatched the expedition in 1597." *Id.*, X, 147. That the letter here published was unknown to that writer is sufficiently evident from the contents of the foot-note to be found on that same page:—". . . . Torquemada, followed apparently by all other writers, states that in 1596 the King ordered Viceroy Monterey to send Vizcaíno to California, and that the expedition was made the same year. All the evidence I have to the contrary is a royal cédula of Aug. 2, 1628, [*sic*] in Doc. Hist. Mex., series ii, iii, 442–3, in which the King states the facts as I have given them, adding that Monterey ordered Vizcaíno to fulfill his contract, 'no embargante que en la sustancia y capacidad de su persona, halló algunos inconvenientes.' " Mr. Bancroft's writers always are content with what Torquemada tells. In fact, in a foot-note at the end of this same Chap. VI, it is said that "the standard authority for Vizcaíno's voyage is Torquemada, *Mon. Ind.*"

Franciscan friars who will accompany him may undertake the conversion and pacification of those lands in safety, and that the lands be settled, without there being unavoidable lack of food and other things and consequent very great danger of doing violence to and robbing the natives, and I have ordered the royal officials at Acapulco to make a very exact and rigorously careful listing of all that he has offered to take, and not to consent to his departure unless he take all with him. And I have ordered that the same thing be done at the port of Salagua,* in the province of Colima, where he will meet some of his people and a part of the things he is to take with him. It seemed to me well to take these precautions because there are no royal officials there and it is an out of the way place, and it is very proper that in this particular nothing be taken on trust, while it might even happen that the first tidings had of these people in that region would come from persons of no standing and agents of persons born here who may chance to be under obligations to the traders who have undertaken this expedition and to those actually taking part in it. Wherefore I have sent a private individual who is of my confidence, a man of experience who has been a soldier, and he will be able to give good account of what may be done there, and of the conduct of the soldiers, and the punishment inflicted upon them for any disorder of which they should be guilty along the road in the towns of the Indians, who, not being used to the transit through their country of troops such as are generally sent to the Philippines, might be subjected to suffering and injury. God guard Your Majesty. Mexico, 29th February, 1596.

The Conde de Monterey

(Decree of the Council). This communication having been taken under consideration on the 27th of May, 1596, let it be written to the Viceroy that he take from Sebastián Vizcaíno the right to make this conquest and discovery, and that he report to what other person they can be entrusted, who may conduct the same more satisfactorily and with the hope of success.[1]

* Salagua or Calagua is modern Manzanillo, Colima.

Document No. 9

Letter of Sebastián Vizcaíno to the King of Spain, announcing his return from the expedition to the Californias—dated 27th February, 1597

CARTA a S. M. de Sebastian Vizcaino fecha en Mexico a 27 de Febrero de 1597, participando haber vuelto de su espedicion a las Californias.*

Del puerto de Salagua escrivi a vuestra magestad dandole aviso de la jornada y descubrimiento que iba a hazer de la California y de los navios y gente que a ella llevaba y del buen despacho quel Conde de Monte Rey me mando dar para todo lo a ella nessesario; y aora aviso a vuestra magestad de lo sucedicho en el dicho viaje que es lo contenido en la relacion que el dicho Conde de Monte Rey envia a vuestra magestad. Yo me holgara fueran las nuevas conformes a mi deseo, mas como todo está sujeto a la voluntad de Dios que es el que guia semejantes negocios, conformandonos con ella le damos gracia por todo lo sucedido. Quedo con el sentimiento que es razon por no haber tenido ventura de llegar al cabo un negocio en que tanto servicio de Dios y de vuestra magestad se interesaba y con grandisima lastima de considerar la infinidad de almas que se pierden en aquella tierra. De manera que ni la perdida de mi hacienda ni el peligro de mi persona y travajos que en ello he padecido me duelen tanto como el no haberle podido dar buen fin a este negocio y descubierto toda la ensenada de la California de que entiendo resultaran cosas de grandissima importancia, pero como aquella mar no hera conoscida salimos en tiempo tan contrario que eso solo fué la causa principal de nuestra desgracia que habiendo de salir a principio de Marzo emboque por el golfo de la California a mediado de Agosto en tiempo de nortes y norueste tan furioso que estuvo todo el daño donde pensamos que estuviera nuestro buen suceso, segun nos enseñó la esperiencia. Lo que es pesqueria de perlas creo que es infinita por el grandissimo numero de conchas de ella que ay a la ribera; no pude hazer diligencia en pescarlas porque el tiempo era tan rigoroso que apenas nos daba lugar para repararnos y assi nos ubimos de volver con los navios rrotos sin ser posible pasar adelante. Reciba vuestra magestad mi buen deseo que

LETTER TO His Majesty from Sebastián Vizcaíno, dated at Mexico, 27th February, 1597, announcing his return from the expedition to the Californias.*

From the port of Salagua I wrote to Your Majesty, giving notice of the voyage of discovery which I was about to make to California, and of the ships and people I was taking with me, and of the prompt dispatch of everything necessary, which the Conde de Monterey ordered to be given to me; and I now advise Your Majesty of what occurred on said voyage—which is what is contained in the report which the said Conde de Monterey sends to Your Majesty. I should congratulate myself were the tidings in conformity with my desire; yet, as everything is subject to the will of God, it being He who guides in similar undertakings, let us, conforming ourselves to this, give Him thanks for all that happened. It grieves me, as stands to reason, not to have had the good fortune to carry out fully an undertaking in which the service of God and Your Majesty was so deeply concerned, and it gives me the greatest pain when I consider the infinite number of souls going to destruction in that land. To such an extent is this the case that neither loss of property, nor personal peril encountered, nor the labors which have been mine in this connection, give me so much sorrow as does my not having been able to accomplish successfully this undertaking—in not having explored the whole gulf of California, an enterprise from which, I understand, things of the greatest importance will result. But, as that sea was unknown, we set forth at a season so inopportune that this alone was the principal cause of our misfortune. Being obliged to sail early in March, I entered the gulf of California about the middle of August, during the season of north and northwest winds so furious that, as experience has shown to us, where we thought to achieve success defeat resulted. As to the fishing for pearls, I believe that to be without limit, for the number of shells on the shore is very great. I was not able to do anything in the way of fishing for them because the weather was so bad that we had not time even to stop and were obliged to return with the ships damaged and without having been able to pursue the voyage farther. May your

* Original in AGI, Mexico 116. Spanish versions are to be found in Carrasco, *Documentos de las Californias*, 34–35, and in *Docs. para la demarcación de California*, I, 284–85.

aunque de vasallo pobre, con lo que me sobra de animo se puede suplir lo que las fuerzas no alcanzaron y de nuevo me ofrezco a servir a vuestra magestad como a mi rey y señor con lo que me queda de hacienda y vida, que quisiera fuera en mucha mas cantidad para emplearlo todo en su real servicio con las veras que debo y deseo. Guarde nuestro señor a vuestra magestad muchos años como la cristiandad ha menester y sus criados y vasallos deseamos de Mexico a veinte y siete de febrero de mil quinientos noventa y siete. Criado de vuestra magestad.

Sebastián Vizcaíno

Majesty take into consideration the good intentions which animated me, though but a poor vassal; let my super-abundant good-will be weighed against what my energy failed to accomplish. I offer myself again for the service of Your Majesty, as my king and lord, myself and what remains to me of fortune and life; and I would that these were greater, so that I might dedicate all to your royal service with the earnestness that is due, and as I wish. May Our Lord guard Your Majesty many years, as is necessary for the sake of christendom and as your servants and vassals desire. Mexico, twenty-seventh of February, one thousand five hundred and ninety-seven.

The servant of Your Majesty,

Sebastián Vizcaíno

Document No. 10

Report which Sebastián Vizcaíno makes for the information of the King of Spain concerning his expedition to the Gulf of California—written early in 1597

Relacion que Sebastian Vizcaino a cuyo cargo fué la jornada de las Californias, da para el Rey nuestro Señor, dando a entender lo que vido en la dicha jornada desde el puerto de Acapulco hasta paraje de veinte y nueve grados dentro de la ensenada de las Californias a la parte de norueste que es de donde se bolvió por no poder pasar adelante por el tiempo ser contrario y aversele quebrado los hierros del timon con una tormenta y lo que vió en la tierra y mar y entiende de la jornada es lo siguiente.*

Primeramente advierte que desde el puerto de Acapulco que es donde salió hasta el de Calagua ay cien leguas por mar costa a costa.

Desde el puerto de Calagua al cabo de corrientes ay sesenta leguas siempre por la costa.

Desde este cabo de corrientes a las yslas de San Juan de Mazatlan ay setenta leguas, yendo ya por la ensenada de las Californias governando al norte.

Desde estas yslas al puerto de Culiacan ay cuarenta leguas governando al norte.

Desde este puerto a balde hermoso paraje de Sinaloa ay cincuenta leguas.

Desde este paraje atrabesé la ensenada y boca de las Californias que podra tener de atravesia ochenta leguas.

Tomé tierra de la otra banda en altura de veinte y quatro grados en una baya muy grande que de la parte de la mar la cercan dos yslas muy grandes en baya capaz para mucha cantidad de navios y puerto limpio.

En este paraje me salieron mucha cantidad de yndios a resibir de paz y en ella estubieron el tiempo que en el dicho paraje estube y lo que en el me sucedió fué que queriendo decir los religiosos misa, hecho un altar en tierra saqué del navio la ymagen de nuestra señora para

---

1 The distances given here by Vizcaíno are very much out of the way. The same thing may be said of all the distances given by him in this report. When we consider the imperfection of the instruments used by navigators of those days it is a matter of wonder that disasters at sea were not more frequent.

NARRATION THAT Sebastián Vizcaíno, under whose command the expedition to the Californias was sent out, gives for the information of the King our Lord—giving account of what he saw during the said expedition from the port of Acapulco to a place in twenty-nine degrees of latitude, within the gulf of California, to the north-westward, from which place he returned, not being able to go on farther because the weather was unfavorable and the rudder-irons had been broken in a storm. What he saw by land and sea and learned during the expedition is as follows:*

First: he says that from the port of Acapulco, whence he sailed, to that of Calagua it is a distance of one hundred leagues, not losing sight of land.

From the port of Calagua to Cape Corrientes it is a distance of sixty leagues, still along the coast line.

From Cape Corrientes to the islands of San Juan de Mazatlan it is a distance of seventy leagues, the course being north and within the gulf of California.

From these islands to the port of Culiacán it is a distance of forty leagues, the course being north.

From this port to Balde Hermoso, a place in Sinaloa, it is fifty leagues.

From this place I stood across the gulf of California; the distance may be eighty leagues.[1]

I made a landfall on the other coast in latitude twenty-four, in a very large bay, which to seaward is shut in by two very large islands, a bay which is of capacity sufficient for a great number of ships, the harbor being free from obstructions.

At this place there came to me a great number of Indians, who received me peacefully, and who remained at that place while I was there. What happened there is this: The clergy being desirous of celebrating mass, and an altar having been erected on shore, I caused the image of Our Lady to be taken out of the ship for the purpose of placing it on the altar, and it was carried in procession from the

---

* Original in AGI, Guadalajara 133. Spanish versions are to be located in Carrasco, *Documentos de las Californias*, 25–34; *Docs. para la demarcacíon de California*, I, 316–27; and Portillo, *Descubrimientos y exploraciones*, 293–99. Charles E. Chapman, *Catalogue of Materials in the Archivo General de Indias for the History of the Pacific Coast and the Spanish Southwest*, 70, lists this as Document No. 1 and dates it 1597. This work hereinafter cited as Chapman, *Catalogue of AGI*.

ponella en el dicho altar llevandola en procesion desde la playa al paraje donde estaba dicho altar, en este tiempo llegó un yndio principal con mas de ochocientos yndios con arcos y flechas y los salí a resibir y ellos se me binieron de paz y llegando ante la ymagen de nuestra señora hincandome de rodillas besando sus pies y al frayle que la tenia las manos, visto esto el dicho yndio echó de si el arco y flechas que traya y se humilló delante de la dicha ymagen besandole sus pies y mirando al cielo y al sol, decia por señas que si aquella ymagen avia venido del y dandosele a entender por señas dió grandes voces a los demas yndios sus compañeros los quales acudieron a hacer lo que el dicho principal avia hecho de que todos los españoles que alli ybamos sentimos el contento que hera razon y llevando la dicha ymagen en prosesion a poner en el altar siempre fué el dicho yndio principal danzando a su usanza delante della.

En este paraje tomé posesion de la tierra ante los dichos yndios quieta y pacificamente y los dichos yndios dandoselo a entender por señas lo tuvieron por bien; puse por nombre a la provincia la Nueva Andalucia; al puerto San Felipe; y a las dos yslas a la una la ysla de San Francisco y a la otra San Sebastian.

En este paraje estube cinco dias y no pude detenerme mas respecto de ser la tierra muy fragosa y no aber aguaduce que poder beber.

Deste paraje pasé a otro que está mas al norueste como quince leguas de que hace una gran ensenada con muchos baxios y al entrar en él me calmó el viento y como las corrientes son muchas y la nao que hera de mas de seiscientas toneladas, me llevó a un baxo donde estuve quatro dias en seco de que fué necesario alijar y cortar los arboles y sacar los bastimentos a tierra en planchadas de que se me mojaron muchos y perdieron y al cabo de los dichos quatro dias con la creciente me sacó la dicha corriente del baxo y entré en esta dicha ensenada, la qual puse por nombre la de la Paz porque en ella me salieron a rescibir muchos yndios dandonos lo que tenian como hera pescado muchas frutas de la tierra caza de conejos, liebres, benados.

En este paraje hice alto fortificandome en un fuerte que hice de

---

2 It is impossible for me to give with certainty the modern names of this port and the two islands, for lack of reliable maps of Lower California. Yet, if the given latitude be anywhere near correct, San Felipe was to the southward and eastward of the bay which Vizcaíno called La Paz, the islands being Ceralbo and Espíritu Santo. The bay of La Paz still retains its name. But the points at which Vizcaíno touched cannot be located very accurately.

beach to the place where the altar was. At this time there appeared an Indian chief, accompanied by more than eight hundred Indians armed with bows and arrows. I went forth to meet them and they came to me in peace. Going to where the image of Our Lady was, I fell upon my knees, kissing its feet, and also the friar who held it in his hands. Seeing this, the said Indian threw aside the bow and arrow he was grasping and humbled himself before that image, kissing its feet; looking toward the sky and the sun, he asked by gestures whether that image had come thence. Making himself understood by signs, he shouted to the other Indians, his companions, who drew near in order to do as this Indian had done—whereat all of us Spaniards who were there were content, as it was fitting we should be. And, while carrying the image in procession to place it on the altar, the Indian chief went always before it, dancing after the manner of his people.

At this place I took possession of the land, in the presence of these Indians, quietly and peacefully, the Indians by signs giving it to be understood that this seemed good to them. I named the province Nueva Andalucía; the port San Felipe; the two islands, one San Francisco and the other San Sebastián.[2]

At this place I remained five days, but could not stay longer because the land was very uninviting and there was no drinkable water.

From this place I went on to another, some fifteen leagues farther on to the northwest, where there is a great bay with many shoals. On my entering there the wind died away; and, as the currents are many and the ship of more than six hundred tons burden, I was carried upon a shoal where the ship remained aground for four days—in consequence of which it was necessary to lighten her and to cut away the masts and to carry the provisions ashore on planks and the like, so that a great part of them was wetted and lost. After the four days had passed, with the flood tide, the current carried me away from the shoal and I entered the bay, which I named La Paz, for there a great many Indians came forth to receive me, giving to us what provisions they had, such as fish, many fruits of the earth, rabbits, hares and deer.

At this place I halted, fortifying myself in a fort which I constructed of a stockade and fascines, as I could go no farther with the flagship, which was dismantled, for in that country the winter begins in the month of October, the season when I was at that place.

But, being desirous of exploring all the gulf, I determined to enter

estacada y faxina por no poder pasar mas adelante con la nao capitana por estar desaparejada y comenzar en aquella tierra el ynvierno por el mes de Octubre que es quando estuve en este paraje.

Y deseoso de descubrir toda la ensenada me determiné de con el navio pequeño y lancha entrar la boca dentro a descubrilla dexando en este paraje la nao capitana y la gente casada y mas embarazosa llevando conmigo ochenta ombres y asi lo hice dexando al capitan Rodrigo de Figueroa por mi teniente en este paraje.

Salí deste puerto que está en veinte y cinco grados escasos a tres de Octubre y yendo navegando por la dicha ensenada tuve una gran tormenta de viento norte, durome quatro dias y al cabo dellos me dió un huracan de viento sur de que estube muy a pique de perderme que me duró dos dias y al cabo dellos cesó y me hallé en paraje de veinte y siete grados metido entre seis yslas y muchos baxos que Dios por su misericordia me libró y siendo de dia me salierron de tierra cinco piraguas de yndios haciendo señas que fuese a su tierra prometiendo cosas de comer y agua que llevaba falta; y ansi arribe al paraje que los yndios señalaban y salté en tierra con quarenta y cinco ombres y en ella me rescibieron mucha suma de yndios dandome pescado fruta y mostrando gran contento en avernos visto y en este paraje uno de mis soldados desconsideradamente dió a uno de los dichos yndios sin yo bello con el cabo del arcabuz en los pechos de que se enojaron los dichos yndios y nos tiraron algunas flechas aunque no de mucha consideracion y visto el atrevimiento de los yndios mandé disparar quatro arcabuces por alto para asombrallos y no ofendellos, al ruydo de la polvora cayeron todos en el suelo y pasado el humo della se levantaron y visto que no se les avia hecho daño con mas ympetu volvieron a flechar de que mandé abaxar a los mios la mano y a la primera rociada cayeron no se quantos de que los demas comenzaron a huir por una serrania arriba, y visto que en este paraje no avia que hacer me embarqué para pasar adelante y siendo la chalupa que llevaba pequeña no nos pudimos embarcar todos dexando al sargento mayor en tierra con la mitad a quien envié luego la chalupa y entre los dichos soldados tuvieron diferencias sobre quien lo avia hecho mejor de que no se embarcaron quando se les mandó de que se hizo gran diligencia y vista la determinacion que tenia de castigar algunos desobedientes se envarcaron y viniendo para el navio ya desviados de tierra llegaron por una playa gran golpe de yndios tirando flechas por alto de que

it for the purpose of discovery with the small ship and the *lancha*, leaving at this place the flagship and the people who were married and most burdensome, taking with me eighty men. This I did, leaving Captain Rodrigo de Figueroa as my lieutenant at this place.

I left this port, which is in a little less than twenty-five degrees of latitude, on the 3d of October. While I was navigating said gulf I encountered a storm from the north, which lasted four days, at the end of which time we were struck by a hurricane from the south, during the continuance of which we came near foundering. This storm lasted two days, and, on its cessation, I found myself at a point in latitude twenty-seven, and in the midst of six islands and many shoals, from which it pleased God in his mercy to deliver me; and, being daytime, there came from land five canoes full of Indians making signs that we should go ashore and promising things to eat and water, of which there was lack. So I came to a place which the Indians showed to me and went ashore with forty-five men. There a great number of Indians met me, giving me fish and fruit and manifesting great content in seeing us. At this place one of my soldiers, unseen by me, inconsiderately struck one of the Indians in the breast with the butt of his arquebus, at which the Indians were angered and discharged some arrows at us, though not very many. Seeing the boldness of the Indians, I ordered four arquebuses to be discharged in the air, in order to frighten without injuring them. At the noise of the discharge they all fell to the ground; but, the smoke having cleared away, they rose up, and, seeing that no harm had been done to them, with greater earnestness they fell to shooting arrows again. On this I ordered my people to lower their fire, and at the first discharge there fell I do not know how many of them, upon which the rest of them began to run away, up the slopes of the mountain. Seeing that nothing could be accomplished here, I set about embarking in order to pursue my journey; but, the long-boat which I had being small, all could not embark at once. So I left the sergeant major with half of the people on shore, sending the long-boat back for them at once. Among these soldiers presently there arose differences, concerning who had carried himself the better in the fray, so that they did not embark, when ordered to do so, without some delay; but, seeing that the punishment of the disobedient was determined upon, they embarked. While the boat was making for the ship, and already at some distance from the

una dellas dió en la nariz a uno de los marineros que venian bogando y como se sintió herido lo dexo de hacer y el otro haciendo su oficio tomó la chalupa por abante y a este alboroto los soldados que venian en ella comenzaron a menearse de que se hicieron a la banda y con el peso se sosobró la dicha chalupa y los cogió debajo y como estaban armados se fueron a pique y de veinte y cinco se escaparon seis a nado, por ser las armas que llevaban de cuero y con tablas que fueron socorridos.

Vista la desgracia que en este paraje se nos sucedió y quedar sin chalupa ni servicio con que poder saltar en tierra ni tomar agua y que la lancha con la tormenta pasada no parecia con acuerdo de todos torné a arribar al puerto de la Paz donde avia dejado los demas compañeros. Llegado a este dicho puerto y entendido por los demas lo que avia sucedido de las grandes tormentas que aviamos pasado y la perdida de los compañeros desmayaron muchos dellos y mas la gente de la mar que conocido el ynvierno y tiempo forzoso no se atrevian a navegar de que me pidieron los volviese a la nueva españa pues no podian pasar adelante y envernar allí no podia ser porque la tierra hera falta de bastimentos y grandes serranias que no se podia entrar por ellas y los bastimentos que aviamos llevado avia ya pocos porque con la perdida del navio San Francisco avian benido a menos y los que se avian gastado y para poder ynvernar no avia hartos y para que no pereciesemos les di licencia para que en el navio San Francisco y lancha se volviesen a esta nueva españa quedandome con el navio San Jusepe y con quarenta hombres de mar y guerra los mas bien yntencionados para entrar por la dicha ensenada a descubrilla del todo.

Deste paraje sali a veinte y ocho de Octubre del dicho año de noventa y siete yo para descubrir la dicha ensenada y los demas para la nueva españa.

Siguiendo mi viage tuve muchas tormentas, tiempos contrarios de norte y noruestes que son los mas contrarios que como la boca está de norte a sur y mi navegacion es al norte me fueron contrarios de tal manera que en sesenta y siete dias que estuve dentro de la dicha boca despues de venida la demas gente no pude subir mas de hasta veinte y nueve grados y esto forcejando con el navio de tal manera que se me quebraron los hierros del timon y visto y conoscido el ynvierno y que no podiamos pasar adelante con el navio por requerimiento de todos

shore, there came upon the scene a great number of Indians shooting arrows aloft. One of these hit one of the oarsmen on the nose, who ceased rowing when he felt himself wounded; the man on the other side continuing his work, the long-boat took a sheer and in consequence the soldiers on board were thrown into disorder. They commenced to attempt to regain their positions; and, while this was being accomplished, the long-boat took a list to one side, and owing to the weight, upset on top of them; and, as they were fully armed, their defensive arms being of leather, they went under, and six out of twenty-five escaped by swimming and were rescued with boards.

In view of the misfortune that befell us at this place, and as we were without a long-boat or any means of going ashore or of obtaining water, and as the *lancha* had not appeared since the storm, all being in accord, I turned backward for the port of La Paz, where I had left the other comrades. Having reached the said port, and what had occurred being learned by these others, because of the severe storms we had experienced and the loss of our comrades, many of them lost heart, especially the mariners, who, having a knowledge of the winter and the inclement weather, were afraid to continue the navigation. So they requested me to take them back to New Spain, since it was impossible to go on; while to winter in that place was equally impossible because of the lack of food in the land and the great mountainous wilds which it was impossible to penetrate, and as the stock of provisions we had brought was very greatly reduced by the disaster to the ship *San Francisco* as well as by the amount consumed, so that there remained not enough for wintering there. So, that we might not perish, I gave permission that they might return to New Spain with the ship *San Francisco* and the *lancha*, while I would remain in the ship *San Jusepe*, with forty men, between sailors and soldiers, of those best disposed to push on into the said gulf with intent to discover the whole of it.

We left this place on the twenty-eighth of October of the year ninety-seven—I for the discovery of said gulf and the others for New Spain.

Following my route, I encountered many storms and contrary winds from the north and northwest, these being the most contrary as the gulf stretches from north to south and my course was northward. So contrary were they that, during the sixty-six days I re-

arribé al puerto de las yslas de Mazatlan governando con las escotas trayendonos Dios de misericordia.

Lo que entiendo desta jornada por descargo de mi conciencia y lo que debo a cristiano y leal vasallo advierto lo siguiente.

Primeramente me parece conviene baya adelante y se buelva a ella por muchas razones; la primera por el mucho servicio que a Dios nuestro señor se hará en la conversion de tantas almas como alli ay y de tan buena gana dieron muestras de rescibir el evangelio que en esto confio en Dios se hará con mucha facilidad.

Ansi mismo advierto que la tierra es mas dos veces questa nueva españa y mejor altura y paraje porque desde veinte y un grados que comienza el cabo de San Lucas yendo a la parte dol norueste ay mas de mill leguas de tierra firme y esto lo he visto.

Ansi mismo advierto que lo que es perlas ay gran suma y ricas porque en los parajes donde yo estuve heran todos comederos dellas y quando el navio San Francisco estuvo encallado echandose un marinero al agua en unas hostras que sacó en una dellas hallaron trece granos de aljofar bueno y los yndios por señas me dixeron que dexase pasar el ynvierno que la mar estaria sosegada y que ellos entrarian y sacarian mucha cantidad y para muestra de ques verdad esto envio dos perlas de las que los yndios me dieron porque vuestra Magestad las vea.

Ansi mismo advierto que en la mar ay la mayor cantidad de pescado de toda suerte que ay en mar descubierta.

Ansi mismo advierto en las marinas ay gran cantidad de salinas y tantas criadas de naturaleza que se pueden cargar mill flotas y en esto no ay que aver duda ninguna porque lo vide.

Ansi mismo advierto que por relacion que tuve de los dichos yndios naturales por señas que en la tierra dentro a la parte del norueste veinte dias de camino avia muchas poblaciones gente vestida y que trayan en las orejas y narices oro, y que avia plata, muchas mantas de algodon, maiz y bastimentos y gallinas de la tierra y de castilla y tomando arena en sus manos la echaban por alto dando a entender que como arena avia gente adelante y esto me dixeron los dichos yndios no

---

[3] This is a very wild statement on the part of Vizcaíno. His distances are given very inaccurately, and, by his own showing, he explored but eight degrees of latitude along a coast trending to the northward of northwest.

mained in the gulf after the rest of the people had left, I could not ascend it farther than latitude twenty-nine, and this only by dint of driving the ship in such a manner that the rudder-irons broke. This taking place, and the winter having set in, and as we were unable to make farther progress in the ship, in accordance with the request of all hands I arrived at the port of the isles of Mazatlan, steering by means of the sheets of the sails, God in pity conducting us.

From what I have come to know during the expedition, for the discharge of my conscience and in pursuance of my duty as a Christian and a loyal vassal, I report as follows:

First: It seems advisable to me that the work be continued and that this exploration be undertaken anew, for many reasons. Of these the principal is the great service which will be rendered unto God our Lord by the conversion of so many souls as there are in that land, of those who so willingly gave proofs of a desire to receive the holy gospel; and I trust in God that will be effected very easily.

I note also that the land is of twice the extent of this New Spain, and is preferable for its latitude and situation; because, commencing at Cape San Lucas, which is in latitude twenty-one, and going towards the northwest, there are more than a thousand leagues of mainland; and this I have seen.[3]

So also I note that as to pearls they are abundant and of excellent quality; for at the places I visited all were eaters of the oyster. And, when the ship *San Francisco* was aground, a sailor entering the water brought up some oysters and in one of them were found thirteen grains of good, but misshapen pearls and the Indians by signs told me that, letting the winter pass so that the sea should be smooth, they would enter the water and bring out a great quantity. As a token that this is the truth I send two of the pearls the Indians gave to me, that Your Majesty may see them.

I note, further, that in the sea there is a greater quantity of fish of all kinds than there is in any other discovered sea.

I note, also, that in those waters there is a great number of salt deposits, so abundantly supplied by nature that a thousand fleets can be laden. Of this it is not possible to have any doubt, for I have seen them.

I note, further, that, from the statement I had from the Indians, made by signs, in the interior of the land, at a distance of twenty days' journey towards the northwest, there are towns of people

en un paraje solo sino en muchos y aunque mi voluntad fué pasar adelante no pude por las razones dichas.

Y siendo vuestra Magestad servido de que esta jornada se consiga ahora que ya se a entendido los tiempos de la navegacion y lo que se a de llevar se asertará y será servido Dios nuestro señor y vuestra Magestad y su real corona acrecentada y atento a que de la jornada pasada he quedado disposibilitado de posible para que yo la pueda hacer a mi costa al presente aventuraré mi persona y poco posible que me ha quedado en vuestro real servico ques lo que deve un buen vasallo y bien yntencionado por su señor ayudandome é haciendome merced a mi y a los que volvieren a la jornada; pido por esta relacion que en ella pediré como criado haciendonos vuestra Magestad merced como nuestro Rey y Señor.

Lo que yo Sebastian Vizcaino pido a vuestra real Magestad ansi para ayuda de costa como mercedes para que la jornada se consiga con el bien que se pretende.

Primeramente se me ha de dar de la real caxa para ayuda de costa para bastimentos y navios socorro de gente y otras cosas necesarias para el dicho avio treinta y cinco mill pesos en moneda y estos no han de entrar en mi poder sino en la persona que su Magestad nombrare ó el Virrey en su nombre para que dellos compre las cosas necesarias para la dicha jornada.

Yten he de ser despachado de parte de vuestra Magestad en el puerto de Acapulco los navios de carena carpenteria, xarcia, velas y las demas cosas necesarias hasta poner los dichos navios a la vela.

Yten se me ha de dar en el dicho puerto de los reales almacenes cincuenta quintales de xarcia menuda para llevar de respeto.

Yten se me ha de dar ochenta arrobas de polvora.

Yten cincuenta quintales de brea.

Yten treinta quintales de estopa.

---

⁴ Fowls of the country were turkies; fowls of Castile, chickens. The Californian Indians had neither turkies nor chickens.

⁵ Subsequent discoveries show that Vizcaíno did not fully understand the sign-language in use among the Indians of the peninsula, or—and this was probably the case —he, like most of the explorers of his time, allowed the information he obtained to be fashioned in the reporting by his wishes as to the effect to be produced on the King's mind. It was Vizcaíno's laudable ambition to prevail on the monarch to consent to his making another exploration.

wearing clothes and who have golden ornaments in the ears and nose, and they have silver, many cloaks of cotton, maize and provisions, and fowls of the country and of Castile;[4] and, taking some sand in their hands, they threw it into the air—thus giving it to be understood that even as the sands were in quantity so were the people of those parts. This the Indians told me, not only at one place but in many. And, although it was my wish to go on farther, for the reasons set forth I could not do so.[5]

And should it please Your Majesty that the expedition be undertaken, now that the season for navigation be understood and what it is necessary to take known, it will be done in a proper manner, and God our Lord will be served as well as Your Majesty, and your royal dominion increased. And, in view of the fact that after the late expedition I have remained deprived of means to undertake it at my own cost just now, I will risk my person and the little that remains to me in your royal service, as a good and well-intentioned vassal should do for his lord, I being aided to do so and receiving favors for myself and for those who may return with me to take part in the expedition. I ask for this on the showing of this report and will ask for it as a servant, Your Majesty showing us favor as our king and lord.

That which I, Sebastián Vizcaíno, ask of Your Royal Majesty, as well in the way of aid for the cost thereof as in the matter of favors, so that the expedition result in the achievement of the end sought, is this:

First: There shall be given to me from the royal treasury, in aid of the cost of provisions and ships, pay of the people, and other things necessary in fitting out, the sum of thirty-five thousand dollars in money. This need not be placed in my hands, but in those of some person named by Your Majesty, or by the Viceroy in your name, that he may purchase the things necessary for the expedition.

Item: There is to be made available to me by Your Majesty at the port of Acapulco the ships for fitting out, the carpentry, rigging, sails, and other things necessary for putting the ships under sail.

Item: I am to be given, at the said port, from the royal stores, fifty quintals of small tackle as spares.

Item: I am to be given eighty *arrobas* of powder.

Item: Fifty quintals of pitch.

Yten treinta quintales de clavazon de toda suerte.

Veinte y cinco quintales de plomo.

Veinte quintales de cuerda para alcabuces.

Veinte piezas de lona.

Quarenta pipas vacias hechas en quarto para la aguada.

Quatro mill estoperoles y veinte mill tachuelas de bomba.

Yten se ma han de dar seis calabrotes para marras de los dichos navios.

Todo lo qual se me ha de dar con las condiciones siguientes.

Primeramente que en mi poder no ha de entrar ninguna cosa de lo aqui contenido sino en poder del tenedor de bastimentos que fuere nombrado por el Virrey para que del dinero compre lo necesario conforme a las memorias que se le dieren y de lo demas lo tenga en su poder para lo que fuere necesario en el descurso de la jornada.

Yten es declaracion que todo lo que montare ansi del dinero como de la carena y despacho de los navios como de lo que valiere las demas cosas que pido han de ser apreciadas en el puerto de Acapulco de que haré escritura de volvello a su Magestad de lo primero que Dios me diere en el descurso de la dicha jornada con declaracion que si por algun caso fortuyto no se consiguiere lo que se pretende a de correr el riesgo la parte de su Magestad de lo que ansi me diere con que buelto que sea al puerto de Acapulco ó otro de la costa de la Nueva España lo que oviere quedado en especie se entregará a la parte de su Magestad sin que el dicho Sebastian Vizcaino quede obligado a pagar en caso fortuyto cosa alguna.

Demas desto a de concederme vuestra Magestad y hacer merced a los que hubieren de yr a la dicha jornada las cosas siguientes.

Primeramente para animar a la dicha gente se les a de conceder que puestos en la real corona puertos de mar cabeceras y ciudades los demas pueblos se les ha de encomendar a la dicha gente por la hórden

---

⁶ A *cédula* was a decree signed by the king, with the formal "*Yo el rey*" (I the King) used in such cases by Spanish monarchs. All of the decrees referred to in this document were *cédulas*—the word *decree* being used in translation. The system of *encomiendas*, which was introduced into Hispaniola as far back as the time when Columbus himself governed that island, was a transplanting of the feudal system to America. The Indians simply became vassals of Spanish lords. As a rule, *encomiendas* were given for three lives only; and in this case the document has been annotated in the margin, undoubtedly in the India Council, in accordance with the rules—"*está concedida esta merced por tres vidas*"—this boon is granted for three lives.

Item: Thirty quintals of oakum.

Item: Thirty quintals of spikes and nails of all sorts.

Twenty-five quintals of lead.

Twenty quintals of slow-match for arquebuses.

Twenty bolts of canvas.

Forty empty pipes, in one-quarter size, for water.

Four thousand round-headed spikes and twenty thousand of a smaller size.

Item: I am to be given six spare cables for mooring said ships.

All of this is to be given to me subject to the following conditions.

First: None of the above mentioned articles are to be given into my possession, but are to be given in charge to the store-keeper who may be appointed by the Viceroy, in order that he may buy with the money what is necessary, in conformity with requisitions made upon him, and that he keep all other things in his possession, to be served out during the expedition, as they may be needed.

Item: It is declared that the total to which all shall amount, the money and the outfitting and dispatch of the ships, as well as the value of the other things I ask for, is to be appraised at the port of Acapulco, and I will give an undertaking in writing to return the value of the same to His Majesty from the first gain which God may give to me during the expedition, subject to a stipulation that, if by any mischance the end sought be not gained, the loss shall be His Majesty's, and that on return to Acapulco, or any other port of New Spain, what may remain of that which may be given to me shall be returned to His Majesty—so that, in case of mischance, the said Sebastián Vizcaíno shall not be obliged to pay for anything.

Besides this, Your Majesty is to grant to me and to those who shall go on the said expedition the following things:

First: In order to encourage said persons, it shall be conceded to them that, the sea-ports, capitals of departments and cities being brought into subjection to the royal crown, the other districts are to be given to said persons in *encomienda*, in the same way that other districts in the Indies are given, and this for five lives; and concerning this a special *cedula* shall be sent.[6]

Item: It is to be granted to said persons, in order to encourage them more to go to serve Your Majesty, spending of their means and risking their persons, as an honor to themselves and their descendants, that

que los demas pueblos de las yndias estan encomendados y esto por cinco vidas de que se a de enviar cedula particular.

Yten se a de conceder a la dicha gente para que mas se animen y vayan a servir a vuestra magestad y gasten su hacienda y aventuren sus personas, para honrrallos a ellos y a sus descendientes haciendolos caballeros hijosdalgo, y que desta merced gozen ansi en las tierras que poblaren como en las demas provincias de las yndias, reynos de Castilla y con un treslado de la cedula que para esto se a de dar y certificacion de que fué a la dicha jornada y estuvo en ella dos años y pobló y el santo evangelio en las provincias fué rescibido que el tal ayudó a ello se le de ejecutoria dello la qual le sea guardada en todos los dichos reynos con las mercedes franquezas y libertades que gozan los demas caballeros hijosdalgo conforme a los fueros de Castilla de Leon.

Yten se ha de dar cedula para que por treinta años no paguen alcabala y almoxarifasgo de lo que llevaren ni enviaren de la dicha jornada para el sustento y honrramiento de sus personas y siendo por via de granjeria lo pague como se acostumbra en la Nueva España.

Ase de dar cedula para que ninguna justicia deste reyno se pueda entremeter ni conocer de causa dependiente de la dicha jornada ni con la gente della si no fuere el Virrey della como capitan general a quien siempre se an destar sujetos.

Ase de dar cedula para que por los precios que los bastimentos se venden entre los naturales desta nueva españa se tomen para esta jornada pagandoselo ansi para lo que de presente fuere menester como para lo que se enviare a pedir de socorros y para llevallos a los puertos se puedan tomar requas pagandoles sus fletes como se acostumbran pagar en los que se llevan al Puerto de Acapulco para el despacho de los naos de china.

<hr />

[7] This patent gave the person so favored the right to entitle himself *"Don."* In some cases the right to heraldic arms accompanied the privilege. At a period later than Vizcaíno's day the title came to mean nothing; today the word signifies as little as our *esquire* written after a man's name. In Spanish-America the custom died hard; and, here in California, for instance, many persons who had no sort of claim to the title, made a point of insisting on being called *Don*. The word *fuero* has been rendered by *law of privilege*. There were all sorts of privileges, possessed by cities and provinces, as well as by individuals, classes and callings—from the necessity for the king's obtaining permission to raise recruits for the army (as was the case in the Biscayan provinces) to the right of a *grande* to wear his hat in the royal presence, the privilege of a soldier to be tried by soldiers, a clergyman by an ecclesiastical court, and so forth. This demand was also annotated in the India Council—*"está concedida esta merced en todas las yndias"*—this privilege is granted throughout all the Indies.

[8] Also annotated in the India Council—*"está concedida por el asiento"*—it is conceded in the agreement.

they be made *hidalgos*, and that this privilege they shall enjoy both in the lands in which they may settle and in the other provinces of the Indies, kingdoms of Castile—this to be accompanied by a copy of the decree given for this purpose and a certificate that the person so favored took part in the said expedition and remained in such service for two years and settled in the land, and that the holy gospel was received in such provinces and that this said person aided to bring this about. Such person shall be given the customary patent of nobility and the same shall have effect in all of said countries, and he shall enjoy the favors, exemptions and liberties that other *hidalgos* enjoy according to the laws of privilege of Castile and Leon.[7]

Item: A decree shall be given to the effect that for thirty years there are to be paid no excise duties nor customs duties on what shall be taken on the expedition or sent for afterwards by such persons for their sustenance and the honoring of their persons; but, if such things be for purposes of gain, then duties shall be paid as is customary in New Spain.[8]

Also; a decree shall be given to the effect that no judicial officer of this realm shall intervene in or take cognizance of a cause arising out of matters connected with said expedition, or in which a person taking part therein is interested, except it be the Viceroy, to whom, as captain-general, they are always subject.

Also; a decree shall be given to the effect that provisions for this expedition shall be taken at the prices at which they are sold among the natives of this New Spain, as well what is at present requisite as what may be sent for afterwards; and that, for transportation to the ports, the same rates shall be paid as are paid for carrying goods to Acapulco for the depot of the China vessels.

And these privileges and aid in the matter of cost being given and granted, I offer to take on said expedition the following:

First: I will take five ships, with such artillery of the proper calibre as may be necessary.

Item: I will take one hundred and fifty men—soldiers and sailors—and among them divers, carpenters and other artisans.

Item: I will take sufficient arms for these one hundred and fifty men, and the ammunition which may be necessary.

Item: I will take provision sufficient for one year for these one hundred and fifty men—and, in the way biscuit, maize, flour, bacon,

Y consediendose las mercedes y ayudas de costa que pido me ofresco a llevar a la dicha jornada para avio della lo siguiente.

Primeramente llevaré cinco navios con el artilleria suficiente que fuere menester.

Yten llevaré ciento y cinquenta hombres de mar y guerra y entre ellos algunos buzos oficiales de carpinteria y otros oficios.

Yten llevaré armas suficientes para estos ciento y cinquenta hombres y con las municiones que fueren menester.

Yten llevaré bastimento suficiente para un año para estos ciento y cinquenta hombres y antes mas de biscochos, maiz, harina, tocino, aceyte, vinagre, habas, garvanzos, cecinas y otras legumbres que se llevan a semejantes jornadas.

Yten llevaré rastros para la pesqueria de perlas chincoros para el pescado, mineros para descubrir minas y aderezo para fundir metales.

Yten llevaré hornamentos para los religiosos para celebrar el culto divino.

Yten llevaré quatro pipas de vino para la misa y frayles enfermos.

Yten llevaré para dar a los yndios naturales dos mill pesos empleados para dalles de vestidos y otras menudencias que ellos apetecen para traellos de paz que resciban el santo evangelio.

Yten llevaré la gente a mi costa a los puertos donde ovieren de embarcarse, sin que a los naturales desta nueva españa se les haga vejacion sino que se les pague lo que dieren como corre entre ellos.

Demas desto pagaré a vuestra Magestad el quinto de todo el oro,

[9] The payment of a fifth part to the crown was always obligatory, and Vizcaíno need not have promised; that he knew this his concluding words indicate.

[10] This letter must have been written early in 1597, shortly after Vizcaíno's return from his voyage. It is a very important and interesting document. As the report of the commander of the expedition it must be taken as the most accurate and best account of the occurences of the voyage. The document is of value because we are enabled to judge of the character and aims of explorers of that day; we learn something of their treatment of the Indians; and we can form an excellent idea of the outfit the explorers of the sixteenth century took with them, in all essential details, as well as of the rewards they claimed and received. The account of this voyage given in the Bancroftian series of historical works will be found chiefly at pp. 148–50 of vol. X of the *History of the Pacific States*. It will be interesting for the curious to compare this account with the official report of the commander of the expedition, now before us. The Bancroftian author cites authorities only at second and third-hand. He even gives our Californian Taylor— whom elsewhere, in a bibliographical note, he berates roundly—as authority for Vizcaíno's return to Acapulco in October! He does not mention the names of the ships, and knows nothing about Vizcaíno's proposition to the King. Errors which occur in the Bancroftian account are corrected in this report.

oil, vinegar, beans, peas, dried meat, and other like things, a greater quantity than it is customary to take on such expeditions.

Item: I will take rakes for the pearl fishery and fishing-nets, miners to search for mines and an apparatus for reducing ores.

Item: I will take vestments and the like for the clergy, that they may conduct divine worship.

Item: I will take four pipes of wine for the mass and sick friars.

Item: I will take, to be given to the Indians, two thousand dollars, to be invested in clothing and the trifles of which they are fond—for the purpose of attracting them peaceably to receive the holy gospel.

Item: At my own cost and charges I will take the people to the ports where they are to embark, without oppressing the natives of this New Spain but, paying for what these may furnish that which is customary among them.

Besides this, I will pay to Your Majesty the fifth part of all the gold, silver, pearls, precious stones and other valuable mineral substances which may be obtained on said expedition, and this in perpetuity.[9]

Item: I will pay the tenth part of the fish that may be taken, cleaned and in barrels as the rest shall be sent, and I will deliver them, at my cost, at the port of Acapulco, to the officers of your royal treasury.

Item: I will pay the twentieth part of all the salt obtained during said expedition, and I will send it to the ports of New Spain; this I will do at my own cost without putting Your Majesty to any expense.

So, also, I will undertake to make the discovery of the whole inlet and gulf of California; and of all I will take possession for Your Majesty, turning over to the royal crown sea-ports, heads of departments and cities—all this in the most quiet way and without working any wrong to the natives, but by kind means and gifts attracting them to the service of God and Your Majesty.

Item: I will make settlements in the most proper places I may find in said land; I will build forts, and I will explore to a distance of one hundred leagues toward the interior; and in all I will do the best I can, and what I should do as a loyal vassal of Your Majesty.[10]

Sebastián Vizcaíno

plata, perlas, piedras preciosas y otros metales de valor que se hallaren en el dicho descubrimiento y esto siempre.

Yten pagaré el diezmo del pescado que se pescare aderezado y enbarillado como se enviare lo demas y a mi costa se entregará en el puerto de Acapulco a los oficiales de vuestra real hacienda.

Yten pagaré la veintena parte de toda la sal que de la dicha jornada se sacare y enviare a los puertos de la nueva españa y esto lo despacharé a mi costa sin que de parte de vuestra Magestad se gaste ninguna cosa.

Ansi mismo me obligaré de descubrir toda la ensenada y boca de las Californias y de toda ella tomaré posesion por vuestra Magestad poniendo puertos de mar, cabeceras y ciudades en la real corona todo lo mas quietamente é sin hacer agravio a los naturales della sino con buenos modos y dadivas para atraellos al servicio de Dios y de vuestra Magestad.

Yten que poblaré en la parte mas conveniente que hallare en la dicha tierra y haré fuertes y descubriré cien leguas la tierra adentro y en todo haré lo que pudiere y lo que devo a leal vasallo de vuestra Magestad.

Sebastián Vizcaíno

Document No. 11

Paragraph of a letter from the Conde de Monterrey, Viceroy of New Spain, to the King of Spain, giving his reasons for not making use of the decree taking from Sebastián Vizcaíno his commission for the expedition to the Californias—dated 28th July, 1597

CAPITULO de una carta a S. M. del Virey de Nueva España el Conde de Monte-Rey, fecha en Mexico a 28 de Julio de 1597, dando cuenta de la razon porque no se usó de la cedula para quitar los titulos y despachos que se dieron a Sebastian Vizcaino sobre el descubrimiento de las Californias.*

Entre estos despachos que tuve con los galeones rescibi cedula de vuestra magestad en que fué servido mandarme que impida la jornada de las Californias y quite los titulos y despachos que tenia para ella a Sebastian Vizcayno a quien esto estaba cometido por el Virrey Don Luis de Velazco, dias a que volvió de la jornada el dicho Sebastian Vizayno como dello y del subceso que tuvo e dado aviso a vuestra magestad y asi por haverse retardado tanto esta horden paresce que no es a razon hazer con Vizcayno la demostracion que se va quitarle los despachos mayormente haviendo él gastado hazienda en la jornada y ydo ya y buelto ella y procedido con mas cordura y ser que se podia esperar del aunque con subceso siniestro y desacreditado, vuestra magested será servido mandarme lo que en esto é de hazer.

PARAGRAPH of a letter to His Majesty from the Viceroy of New Spain, the Conde de Monterey, dated at Mexico, 28th July, 1597, giving an account of the reason why no use was made of the decree taking from Sebastián Vizcaíno the commission and orders given to him for the voyage of discovery to the Californias.*

Among these dispatches which came to me in the galleons, I received a decree of Your Majesty, in which you were pleased to order me to suspend proceedings in connection with the expedition to the Californias, and to take away the commission and orders concerning the same from Sebastián Vizcaíno, to whom they had been given by the Viceroy, Don Luis de Velasco. It is some time since the said Sebastián Vizcaíno returned from the expedition, of which fact, as well as of what he accomplished, I advised Your Majesty. And, therefore, inasmuch as this order has been so delayed, it does not seem reasonable to make an attempt to take away his commission from Vizcaíno; the more so since he has been at expense in the expedition and has gone and returned already; and as he has acted with greater skill and judgment than could have been expected of him, although with poor success and loss of reputation. May Your Majesty be pleased to give me orders regarding what I am to do in the matter.

* Spanish versions appear in Carrasco, *Documentos de las Californias*, 36, and in *Docs. para la demarcación de California*, I, 286–87. Original in AGI, Mexico 23.

Document No. 12

Paragraphs of a letter from the Conde de Monterrey, Viceroy of New Spain, to the King of Spain, concerning the expedition to the Californias and some new matters which have come to light touching the same—dated 26th November, 1597

Cᴀᴘɪᴛᴜʟᴏs de carta a S. M. del Virey de Nueva España de 26 de Noviembre de 1597 en que hace relacion del discurso y estado tocante al descubrimiento de las Californias y de algunas particularidades que de nuevo se han entendido.*

Porque vuestra magestad me manda en las cartas que rescebi este año, que de relacion del subceso que tuvo el viaje de las Californias y porque pueda venir en la flota horden de lo que cerca de este negocio se deva hazer de nuevo será necesario decir en particular el estado que tiene y las dubdas que se ofrecen en este negocio. En el segundo aviso que partió por marzo y en el despacho general di quenta a vuestra magestad del subceso que tuvo la jornada y señaladamente de la esperiencia que havia dado Sebastian Vizcaino de que junto de ser platico en esta mar del sur y hombre sosegado y de muy sano pecho y yntencion, tenia algun mediano y vastante caudal en lo que yo no esperava del ninguno ques en la capacidad para regir su gente y brio para hazerse respetar della, cossa que rrares veces se halla faltando autoridad en el sugeto. Dixe por esto a vuestra magestad en el capitulo de la carta que escrivi este año sobre materias de guerra, que por este concepto que forme por la esperiencia de lo pasado contra el que antes havia hecho por discursso y por ser acabada la ocasion con su buelta no usava de la cedula en que vuestra magestad vistas mis cartas me envió a mandar que quitase los despachos a este hombre; despues con motivo que dió para ello el haver otros que hablasen en hacer asiento escluyendo yo del todo a Vizcayno, communique el acuerdo de esta real audiencia el estado del negocio y presente el fiscal que tambien vió en su casa los papeles, y haviendolo conferido todo paresció que aunque este descubrimiento no se temiera de ynutil como he escripto a vuestra magestad otras veces, yo no podria ejecutarle por medio de

---

¹ The Conde de Monterrey.

² The royal *audiencia* was the Viceroy's council and the supreme tribunal of the viceroyal government. The *fiscal* was the king's procurator.

PARAGRAPHS of a letter to His Majesty from the Viceroy of New Spain,[1] dated 26th November, 1597, in which he makes a report on the discussion concerning the discovery of the Californias, and its condition, and of some related particulars which have recently come to light.*

Because Your Majesty orders me, in the letters which I have received during the year, to make a report of the result attending the voyage to the Californias, and as there may come by the fleet orders touching that which should be done in this matter, it will be necessary to particularize concerning the condition of the affair and the doubts which arise in connection therewith. By the second packet, which sailed in March, as well as in the general dispatch, I gave to Your Majesty an account of the result of the expedition and, especially, of the evidence which Sebastián Vizcaíno had given that, in addition to possessing a practical knowledge of the South Sea and being a man of even disposition, upright of good intentions, he is of medium yet sufficient ability, although I had feared it was otherwise, for governing his people, and this coupled with energy enough to make himself respected by them, a thing rarely accomplished when the faculty of making authority regarded is lacking. It was on this account I said to Your Majesty, in that paragraph of the letter I wrote this year which treats of matters concerning war, that, because of this opinion which I was led to form from a knowledge of what had occurred, contrary to that which I had arrived at from previous reasoning, and because in view of his return the occasion had passed, I have made no use of the decree by which Your Majesty, after a consideration of my letters, ordered me to take away his commission from this man. Afterwards, being influenced by the fact that others were talking of a desire to make a contract, and this without my taking Vizcaíno into consideration at all, I submitted the matter to this royal *audiencia* for a resolution, the *fiscal*,[2] who had also examined the documents at his office, being present; and, everything in relation thereto having been discussed, it was concluded that, although it might not be feared this expedition would be made uselessly, as I wrote to Your Majesty on other occasions, I could not have it undertaken by Vizcaíno, or any other person, without Your Majesty's order and the approval of the

---

* Original in AGI, Mexico 23. Spanish version in Carrasco, *Documentos de las Californias*, 36–41. The Sutro transcript portion is found within a larger document reproduced in *Docs. para la demarcación de California*, I, 304–15.

Vizcayno ni de otra persona sin horden de vuestra magestad y
aprovacion que fuese servido hazer del asiento como tampoco dicen
propuso el Virrey Don Luis de Velazco dar patentes y rrecados a
Vizcaino para la ejecucion de lo pasado sin enviar primero a vuestra
magestad el asiento y tomar orden suya porque ansi está dispuesto en
un capitulo de las hordenanzas de nuevos descubrimientos que en el
principio. Paresció ansi mismo que aun capitular ni hacer asiento para
enviarle al consejo no se podria aora porque con Vizcaino no era razon
aviendo cedula de vuestra magestad para quitarle los despachos
pasados sin haver ynformado a vuestra magestad de lo que de nuevo
se a entendido quanto a la mediana capacidad del subjeto y con otro
no se podia contratar en derogacion del asiento primero de Vizcaino
por la pretension quel tiene de que no es acabado el tiempo y fuerza
del y porque luego lo havia de poner en justicia en la audiencia donde
avia de ser oydo sin embargo de la cedula de vuestra magestad en que
se le mandan quitar los despachos respecto de no estar ya el negocio
en el principio come alla se figuraba sino metidas muchas prendas
del gasto grande que Vizcaino y sus compañeros hicieron en la
jornada pasada, de mas de que fundandose la cedula en mi relacion
de la yncapacidad y dignidad del subjeto para el govierno y para
hazerse respetar en el, pudiera alegar y ofrecerse a provar las esper-
iencias que a hecho en contrario para que el cumplimiento de la
cedula, se suspendiese hasta que vuestra magestad fuese nuevamente
ynformado, visto todo esto he tenido por lo mas acertado consultar a
vuestra magestad este negocio en el estado que tiene. La vez pasada
solo di relacion a vuestra magestad de como avia hallado encaminada
por el virrey la ejecucion de aquella jornada y que por desconfianza
que yo tenia del subjeto avia comunicado con la audiencia y con algun
theologo de los de mas opinion de aqui la dubda en que estava de
impedirle al Vizcaino su viaje y que a todos parescio contra justicia y
conciencia y que por esto lo dexe proseguir y quedava con mucho
cuidado del subceso, y lo que ahora se consulta a vuestra magestad es
que el subceso ynfeliz del viaje no rresulta por las rrelaciones aber
nascido de incapacidad de Vizcaino que antes mostró mediano talento
y brio mas que de un mercader tan hordinario se podria esperar en
semejante jornada, sino ignorancia de aquellos mares y haver dis-

---

[3] Mere matters of the civil law were submitted to the *audiencia*; the professor of
canon law gave an opinion in those pertaining to the equity side of the tribunal.

contract you might be pleased to make; for it is said that Viceroy Don Luis de Velasco did not issue the commission and give orders to Vizcaíno for the performance of what has been done without first having sent the contract to Your Majesty and receiving your orders— as such is the routine called for by the first part of the ordinances relating to new discoveries. It was concluded, moreover, that even to enter into an agreement and submit the same to the Council could not now be done, since it was not right to do this so far as Vizcaíno is concerned, there being a decree of Your Majesty that the authorization given to him in the past should be taken away, without first informing Your Majesty of that which has been learned of late concerning the medium capacity of this person; while a contract could not be entered into with any one else in derogation of the previous agreement made with Vizcaíno, by reason of the claim he makes that, in the matter of time and the binding effect of his contract, it is operative still, and because immediately he would throw the matter into litigation in the *audiencia*, where it would be necessary to give him a hearing notwithstanding the decree of Your Majesty taking away his commission, the matter not being in its inception, as was thought, but the question of the great expense incurred by Vizcaíno and his companions in the voyage which was made now forming part of it. It was considered, in addition, that, the decree being founded on my report concerning the incapacity of that person and his lack of worthiness for command and ability to make himself respected in its exercise, he could allege and offer to prove deeds of his which show the contrary, so that a compliance with the decree should be suspended until Your Majesty might be further informed. In view of all this, I have thought it better to consult Your Majesty concerning this matter in its present condition. In my last communication I gave Your Majesty an account only of the manner in which the execution of that enterprise had been commenced by the Viceroy, and of how, because of the lack of confidence in the individual which I entertained, I had conferred with the *audiencia*, and consulted a theologian of those held in greatest repute here, concerning the doubt which suggested itself to me in the matter of preventing Vizcaíno's voyage, and that to all it appeared to be contrary to justice and conscience to do so,[3] and for this reason I permitted the prosecution of the enterprise, my mind being filled with misgiving touching the result. What I now desire to lay before

puesto su jornada desalumbradamente en quanto al porte de los navios, multitud de la gente y cortedad de provision en algunos vastimentos y que Vizcaino pretende bolver conforme a su asiento de que envio copia con esta carta y con el ahinco y deseo que tiene de proseguir encarece mucho la largueza y ymportancia de aquella tierra contra lo que al principio escribieron y comunmente se entiende y significa grande prosperidad en la pesqueria de perlas, y en esto parece que concuerdan otras relaciones.

Esto presupuesto será vuestra magestad servido de mandar si este descubrimiento se a de proseguir, ó no, que para mas luz en ello y de su pretencion pedi a Sebastian Vizcaino el papel que aqui va, y a Don Gabriel Maldonado, hijo de Melchior Maldonado veintiquatro de Sevilla otra que tambien envio de su pretension. Mi parecer es de que por aora no se intentase entrada en aquella tierra para a ver de pacificarla y poblarla y que solamente para tomar buen tino y con fundamento de lo que ella es y entera seguridad de la sustancia de la pesqueria de perlas y para mayor luz de lo que toca a la defensa y seguridad de estos reynos y naos que andan en la carrera de la china se rreconociese bien la pesqueria y los puertos y costas de aquella ensenada y en algunas partes la tierra de las mismas Californias y que esto fuese con poca gente en embarcaciones pequeñas y para hacerlo tengo por bastante medio el de Vizcaino porque aviendolo reconocido ya en mucha parte y esperimentado lo que ubo de yerro la vez pasada lo podria enmendar mas facilmente; pero no tiene fuerzas para hacer el viaje sin costa de vuestra magestad y haviendo de ser con ella parece que seria mejor compralle a el los aparejos que tiene aunque el gasto creciese y nombrar vuestra magestad para ello a él y a otra persona que sin quedar prendada vuestra magestad por contrato lo hiciese si a esto da lugar el derecho que este hombre pretende que le resulta del asiento pasado por tiempo de algunos años. Aunque dando lugar a esto mas aprovechado medio seria cometerse a Don Gabriel Maldonado dando seguridad pues sin gasto de vuestra magestad se ofrece a hacerlo y podria llevar consigo algunos soldados ó marineros de los que llevó Vizcaino; este pide que sucediendo vien lo que ahora se hiciese fuese preferida su persona para el asiento de la pasificacion y entrada de la tierra tiene calidad y buena opinion, de cuerdo y honrado trato y quando vuestra magestad fuese servido desto podria en caso de no tener fuerzas y caudal bastante de hacienda Don Gabriel, ni poder

Your Majesty is that, as appears from the reports, the unfortunate ending of the voyage was not due to incapacity on the part of Vizcaíno, who, on the contrary, gave evidence of some ability and greater spirit than could have been expected from a mere trader engaged in an enterprise of this kind, but to his lack of acquaintance with those seas and his having planned the expedition mistakenly as to the burden of the ships, the excessive number of his crews and a scantiness in the matter of certain kinds of stores; that Vizcaíno asserts his intention of going on another voyage in conformity with the provisions of his undertaking, a copy of which I send with this letter; and that, owing to the earnestness and desire shown by him for the prosecution of the enterprise, he enhances the extent and importance of that region, although it is in opposition to what was written at first and is commonly understood and indicates that great prosperity will grow out of the pearl fishery; and this, it appears, other reports confirm.

This, of course, Your Majesty will be pleased to order: Whether or not this enterprise be continued. In order to throw more light on this and on the claim of Sebastián Vizcaíno, I exacted from him the accompanying document, and from Don Gabriel Maldonado,* son of Melchior Maldonado, member of the municipal council of Sevilla, another concerning his claim, which also I send. My opinion is that for the present no expedition to that region, with intent to subject and settle it, should be attempted, but one for the purpose merely of ascertaining definitely what there is there, in order that complete assurance be had concerning the value of the pearl fishery, and that greater light may be thrown on what relates to the defense and security of these realms and the ships which make the China voyage. The condition of the fishing grounds should be well examined and the harbors and coast of that gulf and, in some places, even the interior country of the Californias, should be thoroughly explored, and this should be done with crews few in number in vessels of little burden. For this I think that this Vizcaíno will serve sufficiently well; for, having explored already a great part of that region, and possessing a knowledge of the mistakes of the last voyage, he will the more readily avoid similar errors. But he has not means to make the voyage without aid in the cost thereof from Your Majesty; and, this aid being

---

* Gabriel Maldonado, son of Melchor Maldonado, is mentioned in Chapman, *Catalogue of AGI*, 70, as author of a document in AGI, Guadalajara 138, on pearl fishing and colonization in Baja California. Additional documentation is in AGI, Indiferente 745.

cumplir lo que ofrece, venir desde luego proveido otro medio que tomase y en qualquiera que no aya de ser en continuacion del asiento primero de Vizcaino seria necesario para que tuviese execucion el intento enviar cedula para que la Audiencia a su pedimento y contradicion no ympidiese la jornada aunque fuese oydo en via hordinaria. (Al margen de este capitulo se encuentra el siguiente acuerdo del consejo.)

"Que se le rresponda que por lo que aqui dize y lo que se inclina al cumplimiento del asiento de Sebastian Vizcaino y por la aprobacion que hace de su capacidad y persona, parece que conviene que él continue la jornada que ha comenzado en ejecucion de su asiento y que esto conviene sea con la brevedad posible y que le ayude para ello con lo que pide en el segundo memorial que dió, ó con lo menos de aquello que pudiere concertar y encaminar y que enbie con él religiosos de mucha aprovacion y los mas que pudiese y algunas personas cuerdas y de satisfaccion que le ayuden y que le advierta por ser ejemplo de la prudencia, consideracion y buen termino con que deve proceder, y le reprehenda las imprudencias que en el viaje pasado tuvo y particularmente el haber muerto a los yndios que en su relacion haze y haber dexado de castigar al soldado que dió con el cuento del arcabuz al yndio y que trate a los yndios con mucho amor y caricia y regalo para atraerlos de su voluntad al evangelio y no permita se les haga agravio y del que hiziere y resultase de la jornada aviese y del objeto se consulte a su magestad y que el principal intento que ha de llevar sea la conversion de los yndios."

A me parecido acordar a vuestra magestad con proposito de la materia que contiene el capitulo antes deste, la perdida del navio San Agustin que aviese en las primeras cartas despues que vine a este reyno y que con ella cesó el descubrimiento que venia haciendo por mandado de vuestra magestad y horden del Virrey don Luis, de toda esta costa en que tocan las naos que vienen de las Philipinas. El intento era ymportante por el fin que se llevaba en reconocer algun puerto acomodado que en caso de necesidad les pudiese ser a las naos de rreparo y abrigo. El modo de hacerse el descubrimiento pareció a todos los hombres platicos que se hubiera acertado mejor saliendo el navio de aca y siguiendo luego la misma costa: yo tendria por muy conveniente que vuestra magestad mandase que se hiciese con efecto en embarcaciones pequeñas y sin hacer caudal de lo que traxeron escripto

necessary, it seems to be the better plan to buy from him the outfit he has, although in so doing the outlay be augmented, and that Your Majesty appoint him and some other person for the arrangement of the matter in such a way that, while Your Majesty be not bound by a contract, it might be made, were it feasible, under the right which this man claims as resulting from the agreement made with him and still binding for a term of years. Although this be taken under consideration, the better plan would be to entrust the enterprise to Don Gabriel Maldonado, he giving security; for he offers to undertake it without expense to Your Majesty, and he could take with him some of the soldiers and sailors who accompanied Vizcaíno. He asks that, if success should attend what were done now, he may be preferred in the contract for the exploration and pacification of the land. He has a good position in society and is held in good repute; is of good judgment and honorable conduct. When Your Majesty shall be pleased to give your orders respecting this matter, in case it were found that Don Gabriel had not resources and means sufficient and could not comply with what he offers to do, some other way of which advantage could be taken might then be provided for. Whatever plan be adopted, except it be for the continuation of the prior agreement made with Vizcaíno, it would be necessary, in order that the intention be carried out, to send a decree, so that the *audiencia*, in case of his demand and opposition thereto, would not prevent the expedition being made, although the ordinary legal method of determining the matter were adopted.

(In the margin the following resolution of the council appears:)

"Let him be answered that, from what he says here, and as he is inclined to comply with the agreement made with Sebastián Vizcaíno and as he approves his sufficiency and his person, it is fitting that he go on with the work of the expedition which he has begun, in execution of his contract, which is confirmed; that he do this with all possible speed, and that he be aided in accordance with what he asks in the second memorial presented by him, or, at least, with so much of his demand as may be agreed upon and made operative; that there be sent with him religious of well approved character, and as many of them as possible, as well as some judicious persons of satisfactory reputation to assist him, and that he be admonished to regard them as examples of the prudence and consideration he should observe and the tact with which he should proceed; that he be reproved for the

entonces y yo envié a vuestra magestad porque no quede con satisfacion de las relaciones que tube y advierto que si esto huviese de mandarse hazer se podia incluir en ello reconocer la costa y puertos de la ensenada de la California, y tambien la pesqueria llevando algunos buzos para ella y encargandolo todo a una misma persona si en este mar y en el tiempo que se ha de hazer pareciese que lo puede cumplir y sino dividiendo este cuidado entre dos navichuelos con cabezas y aparejo conveniente y con dos barcos de conserva para lo que puede ofrecerse.

(Al margen se encuentra el siguiente acuerdo.) "Que haga executar lo del navichuelo que aqui dize se podria enbiar de Acapulco a reconocer la costa sin embarcarse en lo de las Californias sino fuere de passo, y que esta diligencia se haga luego con la prevencion que conviene."

lack of prudence shown on his last voyage, particularly in having killed the Indians as he relates in his report and in having allowed the soldier who struck the Indian with the butt of his arquebus to go unpunished, and that he treat the Indians with great love and tenderness, making gifts to them in order to attract them voluntarily to the holy gospel, not permitting injury to be done to them; that he report what he may do and what the result of the expedition may be; that His Majesty be consulted in the matter, the main end he is to accomplish being the conversion of the Indians."

It seems proper that, in connection with the matters treated of in the paragraph immediately preceding this, I should recall to the attention of Your Majesty the loss of the ship *San Agustín*, which I reported in the first letters written after my arrival in this realm, and to the fact that with this event the exploration of all the coast, which is of interest in connection with the ships that come from the Philippines, and which was being carried on by command of Your Majesty and order of the Viceroy Don Luis, came to an end. The object was of importance, for the end sought was the survey and location of some commodious harbor which, in case of necessity, should serve these ships as a place where shelter might be had and a stop made. To all practical men it seemed that in making this exploration the better method would have been for the ship to sail from here and along the coast. I should deem it to be very fitting for Your Majesty to order that this should be done in vessels of light burden, without considering what at that time had been written on the subject to be of importance. I sent this information to Your Majesty because I was not satisfied with the reports I had received; and I suggest that, if the order for the undertaking be given, in it may be included the matter of the exploration of the Gulf of California as well as an examination of the fishing-grounds, for which purpose some divers should be taken on the ships; and that the whole be entrusted to one and the same person, if it be thought that he can do what is to be done in these waters and in the time in which it has to be done; or, if not, that the work be divided between two chiefs with two small ships properly fitted out, with staunch vessels in convoy for whatever may occur.

(In the margin appears the following resolution:)

"Let that which is said here concerning the ship of light burden, which could be sent from Acapulco to explore the coast, be done; and

this without complicating the matter with what relates to the expedition to the Californias, unless this be attended to on the way; and let this be undertaken at once with circumspection that is proper."[4]

[4] This letter, and the comments thereon made in the India Council, had they been known to Mr. H. H. Bancroft's writers, would have shed considerable light on certain matters connected with Vizcaíno's voyage, which those writers understood very imperfectly.

Document No. 13

Letter of Sebastián Vizcaíno to the King of Spain, announcing his departure from Acapulco on the expedition for the exploration of the coast from Cape San Lucas to Cape Mendocino—dated 5th May, 1602

Carta a S. M. de Sebastian Vizcayno, fecha en Acapulco a 5 de Mayo de 1602 manifestando que sale con las naos al descubrimiento y demarcacion de la costa desde el cabo de San Lucas a el de Mendocino.*

Porque el Conde de Monterey, Virrey de la nueva españa dará mas cumplido aviso del despacho y avio del descubrimiento de los puertos y bayas de la costa de la mar del sur hasta el cabo Mendocino que se hace por horden de vuestra magestad el dicho virrey me lo a encargado en dos bageles una lancha y un barco luengo pertrechandolos con gente de mar y guerra y bastimentos para once meses todo con mucho cuidado como de tan buen gobernador zeloso del servicio de Dios y aumento de la rreal corona se esperava. Oy domingo cinco de Mayo a las cinco me hago a la vela en el nombre de dios y de su vendita madre y de vuestra magestad muy deseoso de acertar en todo lo que se me a hordenado como leal criado y espero en su divina magestad de que se le a de hazer muy gran servicio, a vuestra magestad yre avisando siempre de lo que sucediere en este viaje a quien nuestro señor guarde por largos y felices años como todos los reynos de vuestra magestad avemos menester de Acapulco a cinco de Mayo de mil seiscientos dos años.

Sebastián Vizcaíno

[1] In the original the words are *"dos bageles una lancha y un bargo luengo."* The word *bajel* (which is the correct spelling) has the same signification as our English word *vessel*. As the passage is not punctuated it might be rendered by "two vessels, a *lancha* and a *barcoluengo;*" but the words "dos navios una lancha y un barcoluengo" are used in Vizcaíno's letter written at Monterey Bay and in his report to the King made after his return to Mexico. The word *navío* (which is equivalent to *nao* and *nave*) has about the meaning of our word *ship*, for the *navío* was decked and had three masts. It seems better, therefore, to render the passage by "two ships, a *lancha* and a *barcoluengo*," as undoubtedly there were four vessels. And it is thought better not to attempt a translation of the words *lancha* and *barcoluengo* because there are no fairly equivalent English words to express what they are. The *lancha* was a small vessel having no deck and but one mast, the movement of the vessel being aided by sweeps. A *barca* had no deck; a *barcoluengo*, or *barcolongo*, was a long *barca*, having one or two masts and a bluff bow and, probably, behaving very badly in going about in a head sea or in working to windward. Such vessels as these were useful as tenders and in the exploration of shoal waters and narrow passages. It will be interesting to note here that Mr. H. H. Bancroft's writers do not

Letter to His Majesty from Sebastián Vizcaíno, dated at Acapulco, 5th May, 1602, reporting that he is about to sail with his ships for the discovery and demarcation of the coast from Cape San Lucas to Cape Mendocino.*

Because the Conde de Monterrey, Viceroy of New Spain, will give a more detailed report concerning the fitting out and dispatch of the expedition undertaken by order of Your Majesty for the discovery of the harbors and bays of the coast of the South Sea as far as Cape Mendocino, I report merely that the said Viceroy has entrusted to me the accomplishment of the same, in two ships, a *lancha* and a *barcoluengo*,[1]† manned with sailors and soldiers and provisioned for eleven months, all this being done with great care—as was to be expected on the part of a governor so good and so zealous for the service of God and the increase of the royal crown. Today, being Sunday, the 5th of May, I sail at five o'clock, in the names of God and his blessed mother and of Your Majesty, I being very desirous of succeeding in all that I have been ordered to do, as beseems a loyal servant, and I trust in the Divine Majesty that I shall do very great service to his cause. As I proceed on the voyage, of what may happen I shall advise Your Majesty, whom may our Lord guard many and happy years, as is necessary for the well-being of Your Majesty's whole realm. From Acapulco, the fifth of May, one thousand six hundred and two.

Sebastián Vizcaíno

* Original in AGI, Mexico 121. Spanish versions are in Carrasco, *Documentos de las Californias*, 56, and in *Docs. para la demarcación de California*, I, 370–71.

† The two "ships" were the *San Diego* and *Santo Tomás*. The launch was probably the frigate *Tres Reyes*. There is also mention of a *barcoluengo*, or longboat, in the various accounts of the expedition under the command of Vizcaíno.

seem to be certain about the number and class of Vizcaíno's vessels. The writer of chap. VII, Vol. X, *History of the Pacific States*, says that the fleet consisted of two *navios*, a *fragata*, and a *lancha*. In no instance, it will be noted, does Vizcaíno in his own reports mention a *fragata*. This writer, by the way, gives four o'clock as the hour of sailing. The writer of chap. III, Vol. XIII of the work cited says that Vizcaíno commanded a "fleet of three vessels." Comparisons are odious; at times, nevertheless, the results obtained from comparisons are curious. Such mistakes are many in *The History of the Pacific States*; but that such is the case can not cause astonishment when it is remembered that the work was written by many hands. When a publisher adopts the plan of having the account of a series of connected events written by more than one person, ordinary caution, it might be thought, should suggest to a competent editor a comparison of the statements made in different parts of the work.

Document No. 14

Letter of Sebastián Vizcaíno, dated at Monterey Bay, 28th December, 1602, giving some account of what he has seen and done during his exploration of the coast of the Californias

Cᴀʀᴛᴀ de Sebastian Vizcaino al Consejo de Indias, fechada en puerto de Monterrey el 28 de Dice de 1602, en que dá cuenta de sus descubrimientos.*

Ya Vra. Alteza abra tenido noticia como el Conde de MonteRey, Virey de la nueba españa, en conformidad de la horden que de Su Magd tiene me encargo El descubrimiento de los Puertos y bayas de la costa de la mar del Sur desde el puerto de acapulco al cauo Mendocino dandome para ello dos nauios, una lancha y un barco luengo con gente de mar y guerra armas y municiones con bastimentos para once meses y en conformidad de la horden que para ello me dió salí de acapulco a cinco de mayo de este año y he vendio haciendo el dicho descubrimiento aUnque con mucha dificultad y trauajo por no ser sauida la nauegacion y auer sido siempre los vientos contrarios. Mas ayudados de Dios y del buen deseo que siempre hetenido de acertar a servir a su Magd he descubierto muchos Puertos, bayas y Islas hasta este puerto de MonteRey que esta en altura de treynta y siete grados demarcandolo todo y sondandolo con su derrotero como lo pide el arte de la mar sin dejar cossa sustancial que de ello y de lo que muestra Prometer la tierra y la mucha gente que en ella ay envio copia al dicho Conde Para que la envie a su Magd y a vra. Alteza. Lo que este puerto de MonteRey de más de estar en tan buena altura para lo que su Magd pretende Para amparo y siguridad de las naos que bienen de Philipinas en el pueden Redimir la necesidad que tragerén Porque tiene gran suma de pinales para arboles y entenas aUnque sea nauío de mill toneladas, ensinas, y Robles muy grandes Para fabricar nauíos y esto junto a la marina agua dulce en cantidad y el puerto es muy seguro de todos los Bientos. La tierra esta toda Poblada de yndios y es muy fertil y es del temple y terruño de Castilla y se dara en ella qualquier

---

1 *Encina* I translate *live oak*. The California tree so called is *quercus agrifolia* and not the *quercus virens* of the trans-sierran coast. *Roble* is *quercus robur*, which is not found in California; I use the word *white oak*, a tree of which there are several varieties in California. In Mexico the name *roble* is applied to all oaks other than live oaks.

LETTER of Sebastián Vizcaíno to the Council of the Indies, dated in the port of Monterey, 28th of December, 1602, in which he gives account of his discoveries.*

Your Highness will have had notice already of how the Conde de Monterrey, Viceroy of New Spain, in conformity with the orders which he has from His Majesty, charged me with the exploration of the harbors and bays of the coast of the South Sea from the port of Acapulco to Cape Mendocino, giving me for that purpose two ships, a *lancha*, and a *barcoluengo*, together with seamen and soldiers, arms and ammunition, and provisions for eleven months; that, in accordance with the orders given to me for that end, I sailed from Acapulco on the 5th day of May of this year; that I have prosecuted said exploration, although with great difficulty and labor, because the navigation was unknown and head winds were constant. But with God's help and the good desire I have ever felt for serving His Majesty, I have discovered many harbors, bays and islands, as far as the port of Monterey, a harbor which is in thirty-seven degrees of latitude, surveying all and sounding, and noting the sailing-directions, according to the art of navigation, without neglecting any substantial thing concerning the same, and noting what the land and the numerous peoples dwelling therein seemingly promise. I send a copy to the said Conde, in order that he may transmit the information to His Majesty and to Your Highness. As to what this harbor of Monterey is, in addition to being so well situated in point of latitude for that which His Majesty intends to do for the protection and security of ships coming from the Philippines: In it may be repaired the damages which they may have sustained, for there is a great extent of pine forest from which to obtain masts and yards, even though the vessel be of a thousand tons burden, very large live oaks and white oaks[1] for

---

* Original in AGI, Guadalajara 133. Spanish versions appear in Carrasco, *Documentos de las Californias*, 57–58, and in *Docs. para la demarcación de California*, I, 374–77. In Chapman, *Catalogue of AGI*, this item is listed on p. 71 as No. 13. The transcription originally printed in the 1891 edition of the Sutro Documents was difficult to follow, for the paleographer failed to distinguish breaks between various words and supplied breaks within words, both of which made the text unclear. The present text is borrowed from Carrasco's book and checked with a Bancroft Library microfilm of the original.

A translation of this document appeared as a collector's item published by the Book Club of California in 1933 entitled *The Voyage of Sebastián Vizcaíno to the Coast of California, together with a map & Sebastián Vizcaíno's letter written at Monterey, December 28, 1602*. The letter was taken without appreciable alteration from Griffin's translation of 1891.

semilla que se sembrare, ay grandes de essas y munchos generos de animales aves como en la dicha Relacion se contiene.

Yo aBiso a su Magd del grandor de este Reyno y quan poBlado esta y lo mucho que promete y lo que los yndios me han dado a entender ay en la tierra adentro de poBlaciones, y como la gente es mansa y afable que con facilidad entiendo Resibiran El Santo ebangelio y se Redusiran a la corona Real, y Pues su Magd es señor y dueño de todo prouera en ello Lo que mas conbenga que lo que fuere de mi parte Le seruire con fidelidad hasta morir.

Respecto de hauerme detenido mas tiempo del que se entendio Para hacer este descubrimiento Por las dificultades que tengo dichas se me an gastado la mayor Parte de los Bastimentos y municiones que se me dieron y con el mucho trauajo que la gente ha tendio a enfermado Alguna cantidad y muertosse algunos, de manera que Para hazer el dicho descubrimiento de Una vez ansi del cauo Mendocino como ensenada de californias que es la horden que traygo, se me ofrecio dificultad para podello hazer todo sin nuebo socorro de Bastimentos, gente y municiones, y ansí despacho paraello a la almiranta de auisso al dicho conde pidiendole lo necessario y adBirtiendole en que paraje y a que tiempo me lo aya de enuiar con la Relacion de marcacion y derroteros y todo lo que he hecho en dicho descubrimiento hastaoy para que lo enuie a Vra. Alteza si me lo enuiare espero en Dios hacer un gran seruicio a su Magd y lleuar descubierto grandes Reynos y Riquezas de todo lo que fuere haciendo en las ocaciones que sse ofrecieren auissare de ello a Vra. Alteza con berdad y fidelidad. Guarde nro. Señor a Vra. Alteza como la cristian ha menester y yo criado de SS. Deste Puerto de MonteRey a 28 de diciembre de 1602.

Sebastian Bizcayn
(hay rúbrica)

ship-building, and this close to the seaside in great number. There is fresh water in quantity and the harbor is very secure against all winds. The land is thickly peopled by Indians and is very fertile, in its climate and the quality of the soil resembling Castile, and any seed sown there will give fruit, and there are extensive lands fit for pasturage, and many kinds of animals and birds—as is set forth in the report.

I advise His Majesty concerning the great extent of this land and its numerous population, and what promise it holds forth, and what the Indians have given me to understand concerning the people of the interior, and of how gentle and affable the people are, so that they will receive readily, as I think, the holy gospel and will come into subjection to the royal crown; and, since His Majesty is lord and master of all, let him provide as may seem best to him. As to what it behooves me to do on my part, I will serve him faithfully till death.

With regard to my having delayed longer than the time which was thought necessary for this exploration: Because of the many difficulties of which I have spoken, the greater part of the provisions and ammunition which were furnished to me has been expended; while, owing to the great labors which my crews have gone through, a number of men have fallen ill and some have died—so that in making the exploration at the same time, both of the region of Cape Mendocino and of the Gulf of California, as is called for by my orders, I have met with obstacles to the completion of all the work without new succor in the way of provisions, men and ammunition, and speedy dispatch of these. So I am sending the consort vessel to notify the Count,* asking him for what is necessary, and letting him know to what place and at what time he must dispatch these things to me (sending to him also the map, report and sailing-directions concerning all I have done in said exploration to the present time) so that Your Highness may order that the same be sent to me. I trust in God that I may do a great service to His Majesty and that I shall discover great realms and riches. Of all that may be done I shall advise Your Highness, as opportunities for doing this may present themselves, with truth and faithfully. May Our Lord guard Your Highness, as christendom has need of you. I am the servant of Your Highness.

Harbor of Monterey, 28th December, 1602.

Sebastián Vizcaíno
(a rubic)

*The consort vessel was the *Santo Tomás.*

Document No. 15

Letter of Sebastián Vizcaíno to the King of Spain, announcing his return from the exploration of the coast of the Californias, as far as the forty-second degree of the north latitude—dated 23rd May, 1603

Carta a S. M. de Sebastian Vizcaino fechada en Megico a 23 de Mayo de 1603, participando su regreso del descubrimiento y demarcacion de las costas de las Californias hasta los 42 grados de latitud norte.*

El año pasado de seiscientos dos por órden de vuestro virrey Conde de Monterrey, fuí a descubrir la costa de la mar del sur con dos navios una lancha y un barco luengo, con la gente de mar y guerra pertrechada y bastecida de lo necesario para un año, sali del puerto de Acapulco como entonces di avisso a vuestra magestad a cinco de Mayo del dicho año y en conformidad con la orden é instruccion que lleve descubri muy puntualmente toda la costa sin dejar puerto, baya, ysla ni ensenada que no se sondase y demarcase conforme a buena cosmografia y arte de marcar, porque como a vuestra magestad escrivió su virrey llevé un cosmografo de confidencia y ciencia en tablas geograficas en mi compañía para que muy estensamente pusiese y apuntase en mapa y carta lo que vuestra magestad mandara ber por la que el dicho virrey enbia agora con la demarcacion y relaciones de todo. entre los puertos que hallé de mas consideracion fué uno en altura de treinta y siete grados que le nombré Monterrey. Como de alli escrivi a vuestra magestad a los veinte y ocho de Setiembre del dicho año que es todo lo que se puede desear para comodidad y escala de las naos de la carrera de Filipinas donde vienen a reconoscer esta costa, es el puerto abrigado de todos los vientos y en la marina tiene muchos pinos para arbolar las naos del tamaño que las quisieren y tambien encinas, robles, romero, xara, rosas de Alejandria, mucha caza de conejos, liebres, perdices y otros generos y especies de españa mas que en cierra morena y abes bolatiles de diferentes maneras. La

1 Making the month September must be a mistake of the copyist. Vizcaíno is made to say here that he wrote to the King from Monterey Bay on the 28th September. He did not anchor in that bay until the 16th of December. On the 28th of this latter month he wrote the letter, of which a copy precedes this.

Letter to His Majesty from Sebastián Vizcaíno, dated at Mexico, on the 23d of May, 1603, announcing his return from the exploration and demarcation of coasts of the Californias as far as latitude 42° north.*

In the past year of six hundred and two, by order of your Viceroy, the Conde de Monterrey, I set out on the discovery of the coast of the South Sea with two ships, a *lancha*, and a *barcoluengo*, with the requisite sailors and soldiers, armed and provisioned with everything necessary for a year. I sailed from the port of Acapulco, as I advised Your Majesty at the time, on the 5th of May of said year; and, in conformity with the order and instructions I had, I explored very diligently the whole coast, not leaving harbor, bay, island or gulf without sounding and delineating it in accordance with the rules of good cosmography and the art of demarcation; for, as your Viceroy wrote to Your Majesty, I was accompanied by a cosmographer† in whom confidence can be reposed and scientific in the matter of geographical computations, in order that he might put down and note in the most complete manner on map and chart the result of the examination Your Majesty should order, which the Viceroy now forwards, together with the delineation and reports concerning the whole. Among the ports of greatest consideration which I discovered was one in thirty-seven degrees of latitude, which I called Monterey. As I wrote to Your Majesty from that port on the 28th of September[1] of said year, it is all that can be desired for commodiousness and as a station for ships making the voyage to the Philippines, sailing whence they make a landfall on this coast. This port is sheltered from all winds, while on the immediate coast there are pines from which masts of any desired size can be obtained, as well as live oaks and white oaks, rosemary, rock roses, the rose of Alexandria, a great variety of game, such as rabbits, hares, partridges, and other sorts and species

---

* Original in AGI, Mexico 122. Spanish versions appear in Carrasco, *Documentos de las Californias*, 60–63, and in *Docs. para la demarcación de California*, I, 455–58.

† Shortly before assignment to the expedition, the cartographer, Gerónimo Martín Palacios, arrived in New Spain after a twenty-year career in Spain. During the expedition a beautiful color series of California maps was drawn. As a result of his activity with the Vizcaíno expedition, Martín Palacios was rewarded by the Conde de Monterrey with an appointment on the Manila galleon. Viceroy Montesclaros, successor to the Conde de Monterrey, had the cartographer tried for forgery, a crime not associated with the map maker's California service. Martín Palacios was found guilty of having forged both the King and the Viceroy's signatures and was subsequently executed.

tierra es de apacible temple y de buenas aguas y muy fertil por el vicio de la arboleda y planta porque vi algunos frutos de ella y particularmente de castañas y bellotas, mayor que las de españa y muy poblada de gente cuya condicion vi ser suave, mansa y docil y muy abta para reducirlos a el santo evangelio y corona de vuestra magestad, su comida es de muchas y barias semillas que tienen y tambien carne de caza como son ciervos que los ay mayores que vacas y ossos y ganado vacuno y cibolas y otros muchos. Son los yndios de buen cuerpo, blancos de rrostro y las mugeres algo menores y bien agestadas, su bestido es de la gente de la playa de pellejos de lobos marinos que los ay en abundancia que los curten y aderezan mejor que en Castilla, tienen tambien gran cantidad de hilo de lino de Castilla, cañamo algodon de que hacen cordeles para pescar y redes para conejos y liebres y tienen sus embarcaciones de madera de pino muy bien fabricadas en que salen a la mar con catorce remeros por banda con gran ligereza aun con grande tormenta. Tomé relacion de ellos y otros muchos que descubrí en la costa en mas de ochocientas leguas que anduve toda poblada sin numero de yndios que decian haver la tierra adentro grandes poblaciones conbidandome fuese con ellos. Con muestras de mucha amistad y querer la contratacion de nosotros aficionados a la ymagen de nuestra señora que les enseñé y muy atentos al sacrificio de la misa. Usan de barios ydolos como me rremito a la dicha relacion de vuestro virrey y conocen bien la plata y oro y decian aberlo la tierra adentro.

Y aviendose de poblar algun puerto ó parage de esta costa ninguno es mas aproposito que este de Monte-Rey por las causas dichas a donde las naos de tornaviaje de Filipinas podran benir a él y si les diese tormenta despues de enmaradas no arribar al Japon como otras veces lo an hecho y perdidose tantas con tan gruesa hacienda que si este estuviera descubierto no se ubiera deservido tanto vuestra magestad. Conocidos los tiempos de verano se podrá entrar por este paraje la tierra adentro y descubrirla porque promete muchas riquezas y por la costa se pueda tambien descubrir el resto de ella que aunque yo llegué a cuarenta y dos grados que fué el limite de mi instruccion pasa adelante la costa y esta cerca del Japon y costa de la gran china ques una corta travesia y lo mismo de la tartaria y famosa ciudad de quinsay con innumerables gentes que conforme a la relacion que tube son del propio yndibiduo y natural de los dichos que para la propagacion de

found in Spain and in greater abundance than in the Sierra Morena, and flying birds of kinds differing from those to be found there. This land has a benign climate, its waters are good, and it is very fertile— judging from the varied and luxuriant growth of trees and plants; for I saw some of the fruits, particularly chestnuts and acorns, which are larger than those of Spain. And it is thickly settled with people whom I found to be of gentle disposition, peaceable and docile, and who can be brought readily within the fold of the holy gospel and into subjection to the crown of Your Majesty. Their food consists of seeds which they have in abundance and variety and of the flesh of game, such as deer which are larger than cows, and bear, and of cattle and bison and many other animals. The Indians are of good stature and fair complexion, the women being somewhat less in size than the men and of pleasing countenance. The clothing of the people of the coast consists of the skins of the sea-wolves abounding there, which they tan and dress better than is done in Castile; they possess also, in great quantity, flax like that of Castile, hemp and cotton, from which they make fishing-lines and nets for rabbits and hares. They have vessels of pine-wood very well made, in which they go to sea with fourteen paddle-men on each side, with great dexterity—even in very stormy weather. I was informed by them, and by many others I met with in great numbers along more than eight hundred leagues of a thickly settled coast, that inland there are great communities, which they invited me to visit with them. They manifested great friendship for us and a desire for trade; were fond of the image of Our Lady which I showed to them and very attentive to the sacrifice of the mass. They worship different idols, for an account of which I refer to said report of your Viceroy, and they are well acquainted with silver and gold, and said that these were found in the interior.

And, as some port or place on this coast is to be occupied, none is so proper for the purpose as this harbor of Monterey. For the reasons given, this port can be made by ships on the return voyage from the Philippines; and if, after putting to sea, a storm be encountered, they need not, as formerly, run for Japan, where so many have been cast away and so much property lost; and, had this port been known previously, Your Majesty would not have been so badly served. The time of the occurrence of the dry seasons being known, from this place the interior can be reached and explored, such exploration promising

la fe y rreduccion de tantas almas a Dios se abrirá la puerta para que la semilla del santo evangelio se produzca a tanta gentilidad.

Once meses se gastaron en el viaje en que se padecieron notables trabajos y con el mucho que tuvo mi gente enferma toda y se murieron cuarenta y dos hasta llegar al puerto de acapulco, yo e acudido señor a continuar el servicio de vuestra magestad en este descubrimiento como lo hice en la jornada de la California, y otras muchas de que tengo avisado a vuestro Real consejo por papeles que presente en él con mucho cuidado y puntualidad como tambien me rremito a los nuevos que agora ban en que e gastado la mayor parte de mi hacienda y salud. mas la poca que me queda y mi persona está dedicada a vuestro Real servicio con la entereza, amor, fidelidad de leal vasallo y criado de vuestra magestad a quien suplico mande se bean los mios remunerandolos con las mercedes de tan poderossas y reales manos mandando tambien hacerla a los oficiales de mar y guerra que llevé conmigo rrecomendando sus personas a vuestro virrey de esta nueva España. dios guarde la Real y Catolica persona de vuestra magestad de Mexico a 23 de Mayo de 1603.

Sebastián Vizcaíno

2 Vizcaíno's letters, generally, are full of exaggerated statements and falsehoods; and in this letter he gives his fancy a slack rein. We know that Monterey Bay is not land-locked. At the time of his visit many of the beasts and plants he mentions did not exist, nor had they ever existed, in California; nor did he meet with any natives such as he describes. His object in thus exercising his talent for romancing was, of course, further employment.

rich returns; and proceeding along the coast, the remainder of it can be examined, for, although I went as far as the forty-second degree of latitude, this being the limit fixed in my instructions, the coast-line trends onward to near Japan and the coast of Great China, which are but a short run away, and the same is the case with regard to Tartary and the famous city of Quinsay; and, according to the reports I received, there are to be found very numerous peoples akin to those I have referred to—so the door will be opened for the propagation of the faith and the bringing of so many souls to a knowledge of God in order that the seed of the holy gospel may yield a harvest among all these heathen.

Eleven months were spent on the voyage, during which noteworthy hardships were suffered; and, notwithstanding the unhappy experience of my men, who were all sick and of whom forty-two died before our return to the port of Acapulco, I again offer to serve Your Majesty in continuing this exploration, as I did on the voyage to California and on many others, of which I have given account to your royal council in carefully and exactly prepared documents which I have presented there; and I refer, furthermore, to others now forwarded, in which it is shown I have spent the greater part of my fortune and of my health. Yet the little of these remaining to me, as well as my person, is devoted to your royal service with the constancy, love and fidelity of a loyal vassal and servant of Your Majesty, who, I pray, will order the necessities of my men to be considered and that they be rewarded with favors from those powerful royal hands, and that the same be ordered to be done for the naval and military officers who accompanied me, their persons being recommended to your Viceroy of this New Spain. God guard the royal and catholic person of Your Majesty. Mexico, 23d of May, 1603.

Sebastián Vizcaíno[2]

Document No. 16

Letter of Fray Junípero Serra, President of the missions of California, to Don Frey Antonio María Bucareli y Ursúa, Viceroy of New Spain, giving some account of the condition of the missions and complaining of the conduct of Captain Pérez and of the Governor—dated 9th September, 1774

Va Jhs Ma Jph

Muy vendo Señor mio Excmo acabo de escrivir a V. E. largamte*
pr un correo qe por California despachó, quatro dias ha, el Sr Capn
Dn Fernando Rivera, en contestacion dela de V. E. de 25 de Mayo, qe
en 6 de Agosto por el mismo conducto y mano de dho Sr Capitan,
recibio el P. Lectr Fr. Francisco Palou, qe en esta me acompaña, y con
los demas assumptos ocurrentes en estas Missiones, incluyendo el
Diario de uno de los dos Religiosos qe acompañaron la la expedicion
de mar embiada pr V. E. baxo el comando del official de mar Dn
Juan Perez. El motivo de haver despachado dhas cartas y papeles por
un conducto qe es regular qe sea de bastante demora, fue porqe
haviendo llegado el 27 del vencido Agosto a este puerto la dha expedicion de mar en la fragata Santiago y en ella con salud los dos religos
capellanes (a Dios las gs) nos dixo su capitan ser su animo detenerse
en este Puerto hasta mediados de Octubre y entonces (qe ya es regular
qe esten aca las familias qe Dn Fernando espera) pasar al reconocimo
del Puerto de Sn Francisco pa la fundacion de la Mission, ó Missiones
qe parescan necessarias pa qe aquel Puerto quede ocupado segun las
ordenes de V. E. é intenciones de N. Cathco Monarca. Y haviendo de
ser assí, de lo qe yo, y todos estavamos contentissimos, parecio el unico

---

[1] This is a customary invocation placed at the beginning of all documents and letters
written by Spanish friars of the order of St. Francis. Literally it means "Live Jesus,
Mary, Joseph!"

[2] Meaning Lower California.

[3] Fathers Serra and Palóu had been inmates of the same religious house at La Palma,
in the island of Mallorca where the former was born. They came to America together in
1749, and, twenty years later, to California. Father Palóu survived his companion and,
three years after Serra's death, in 1787, published a biography of him, which may be
regarded as the earliest Californian book, although it was printed at the City of Mexico.
An English translation of this life of Serra was made by a distinguished member of the
Historical Society of Southern California, the Very Rev. J. Adam, Vicar-General of the
diocese of Los Angeles, and was published in 1884, at the time of the centennial com-
memoration of Serra's death.

[4] The *Santiago* was built expressly for the service of the Californian missions and was
used as a transport.

[5] Captain Don Fernando Rivera y Moncada.

Hail Jesus, Mary and Joseph![1]

My greatly venerated, most excellent Sir:

I have just written at length to Your Excellency by a courier*
whom Captain Don Fernando Rivera,† four days since, dispatched
for California,[2] and in answer to the letter of Your Excellency bearing
date 25th May, which, on the 6th August, was received by conduct
and hand of the said captain by Father Lector Fray Francisco Palou,[3]‡
who is my companion here. In that letter I gave an account of further
events at these missions, and with it sent the diary of one of the two
religious who accompanied the naval expedition dispatched by Your
Excellency under the command of Don Juan Pérez,§ an officer of the
navy. The reason for sending these letters and documents by a means
usually rather tardy was this: The naval expedition having arrived at
this port on the 27th of August last, in the frigate *Santiago*,[4]# and
on board of her in safety the two chaplains (God be thanked!), her
captain informed us that he had a mind to remain at this port until
the middle of October, by which time it is probable that the families
expected by Don Fernando[5] will be here, and then to make the ex-

---

* Original in AGI, Estado 43. In Chapman, *Catalogue of AGI*, this item is catalogued as No. 2716, appearing on p. 360. Antonine Tibesar (ed.), *Writings of Junípero
Serra*, Vol. II, 173–79, contains both Spanish and English versions on facing pages, and
the editor cites the Sutro Collection as containing a copy.

† See Ellen K. Shaffer, "Some Incidents in the Life of Captain Don Fernando de
Rivera y Moncada," M. A. thesis, University of Southern California, 1954, for the most
detailed account of his life.

‡ Fr. Francisco Palóu, O. F. M., was author of several works on early California. See
Herbert E. Bolton (ed.), *Historical Memoirs of New California* by Francisco Palóu, 4 vols.,
and Maynard J. Geiger, *Palóu's Life of Fray Junípero Serra*.

§ Until his death at sea aboard the *San Carlos*, October 13, 1775, Pérez was the out-
standing naval figure in California. A biographical note of his career is in Hubert H.
Bancroft, *History of California*, Vol. IV, 774. Greater detail is found in James G. Caster,
"The Last Days of Don Juan Pérez, the Mallorcan Mariner," in *Journal of the West*, Vol.
II, No. 1, 15–21.

The frigate *Santiago* had been built in San Blas the previous year, 1773, and was
a vessel of 225 tons burden, being the largest up to that time employed in the California
service. Museo Naval, California y Costa N. O. de América, Tomo II (332). This vessel
was frequently called the *Nueva Galicia*.

medio pa dar a V. E. las noticias convenientes el despacharlas pr California. Ahora despues ha tomado nueva determinacion dho Dn Juan Perez, y es de salirse con la fragata de su cargo pa S. Blas y ahuqe le hemos rogado mucho el P. Palou y yo, de qe si hare dable, se estuviese en su prima determinacion, pa qe de esta vez quedase evacuado lo de Sn Francisco se negó totalme diziendo tener varios motivos pa no detenerse y pr ellos haver resuelto su prompta salida. Y considerando qe primero llegaran estas cartas qe aquellas voy a resumir con la brevedad a qe me obliga lo repentino de la noticia y brevedad del tiempo algo de lo antes escrito. Y sea lo primero qe el ganado vacuno de las dos Missiones Sn Francisco, y Santa Clara, en vista de la dha carta de V. E. me lo remitio sin nuevo pedimo el Sr Capn Dn Fernando en 16 de Agosto segun lo ordenado pr la Real Junta y pr V. E. y aqui lo tenemos señalado desde dicho dia. Di el recibo y ya nada queda qe hazer en tal assumpto, pues fue muy a gusto y satisfaccion de ambas partes.

Tambien dezia qe el otro dia de recibida dha carta de V. E. pase con ella al Rl Presidio y communique su contenido al Sr Capitan pa si resolvia qe se diesse algun passo azia el Puerto de San Francisco, pero me respondio hallarse sin gente y ahun sin armas pa empresa alguna, como qe ni el Capn Anza dexo soldo alguno, ni han llegado las familias. La lastima es de que quando las tendremos ya no habra barco, y que reconosco mucha mayor inclinacion a ocuparlos en hazer Presidio nuevo a quatro ó cinco leguas de distancia del Puerto y seys de esta Mission qe en fundar alguna nueva Mission. Assumpto es sobre que iva a representar por escrito a V. E. hallandome en essa Ciudad, quando supe qe el nuevo official proponia tal demanda, pero como me dixeron que no se le permitia desamparar el Puerto, ni tal translacion, lo dexe; ahunque ya me arrepentí despues, quando en Guadala, en Tepic, y en otras partes hallava esparcida la noticia de qe iva el nuevo Capn a mudar el Presidio, como si ello fuesse el principal objeto de su destino. Ya con una circunsta nada me pesaria, y es qe a una legua mas lexos (supuesto que es camino pa S. Franco) pusiesemos una Mission y con esto el nuevo Presidio estaria facil y exactame

---

[6] Juan Bautista Anza was a very meritorious officer of the Spanish army, as his father had been also. He, the younger Anza, commanded the expedition sent to explore the peninsula of San Francisco, and the first immigrant expedition which came to California by land from eastward of the Colorado river.

ploration of the port of San Francisco, with a view to the founding of the mission, or missions, which may seem necessary, in order that the region about that port be occupied in accordance with the orders of Your Excellency and the intention of our catholic monarch. And it having so to be—with which circumstance I and all were very content—it seemed that the only way of giving desired information to Your Excellency consisted in sending it by way of California. Since then Don Juan Pérez has come to a new determination—that is, to sail for San Blas* with the frigate under his command; and, although Father Palou and myself have besought him earnestly that, were it possible, he adhere to his prior determination, in order that the matter of the occupation of San Francisco might be attended to at this time, he has utterly refused to do so, saying that he has many reasons for not delaying and for resolving on a speedy departure. And, considering that this letter will reach you before the arrival of those already sent, I proceed to relate, with the brevity made necessary by this sudden notice and the little time remaining in which to do so, some portions of that which has been written already. And, first: As to the cattle for the two missions of San Francisco and Santa Clara, mindful of the directions contained in the said letter of Your Excellency, Captain Don Fernando turned the cattle over to me on the 16th of August, without renewed demand, in accordance with the disposition of the Royal Junta and the orders of Your Excellency; and that same day we branded them here. I gave a receipt, and now nothing remains to be done in that matter, which was arranged very much to the liking and satisfaction of both parties.

I wrote also, that, on the day after receiving the said letter of Your Excellency, taking it with me to the royal presidio, I communicated its contents to the Captain, for the purpose of learning whether he would resolve to do anything in the matter of the port of San Francisco. But he replied to my request that he found himself without men, or even arms, for any undertaking, as Captain Anza[6]† had not left him a single soldier and the families had not arrived. It is a pity that when we do have them here then there will be no longer any vessel

---

* San Blas was founded as a supply base and home port for the vessels in the California service and those engaged in Northwest Coast exploration. A study in depth of this activity is found in Michael E. Thurman, *The Naval Department of San Blas, New Spain's Bastion for Alta California and Nootka, 1767 to 1798* (Glendale, 1967).

† Herbert E. Bolton (ed.), *Anza's California Expeditions*, 5 vols.

provehido de pasto espiritual y los Gentiles, de ambos sexos, de aquellos contornos, se harian feligreses de los PP Misioneros y no de los Soldados. Estaria la tal Missn a siete leguas de distancia de esta qe no es poco respecto de occurrir con ella a quitar los inconvenientes qe concibo de lo contrario. Si no fuesse pr lo qe tiene de respectivo a Misiones no hablara en tal assumpto, po siendolo, y tanto, no me parece qe voy en la propuesta fuera de mi Ministerio y qe siempre en aquello me conformo gustoso que V. E. tenga pr mas conveniente. Es dolor pa mi (Sr Excmo) verme abunde de Religs y de viveres, y qe no se dé un paso, por un lado ú otro, a algun nuevo espiritual laborío, y me rezelara de fatigar a V. E. con esta mi repetida cantinela si no estuviere tan seguro de qe son tan conformes a los de V. E. mis anhelos.

Dava a V. E. tambien las buenas noticias de qe estos nuevos christianos con el exemplo de algunos peones qe he logrado de los Barcos se van bien aplicando al trabajo con el azadon en la mano, con la barra, en los adobes, en la pisca ó cosecha del trigo y su acarreo y demas quehaceres a qe se les aplica; y qe este año se ha levantado en esta Missn de cosecha a mas de 20 fans de cevada 125 de trigo, algo de avas y mas de frijol a mas del contínuo socorro de la huerta de qe participan todos, y se espera una razonable cosecha de maiz qe ya está muy adelantado y bueno, y de le abunda de sardina qe estuvo varando en la playa immta a esta Missn en 20 dias continous, y los adelantams espirituales qe cada dia vamos experimentando a Ds gs. En todas las Misiones se van disponiendo pa el año siguiente siembras mayores, y espero en Dios qe sean los trabajos con felizes resultas.

Respecto del Diario qe incluí a V. E. dezia qe no nos quedavamos aca con copia pa remitarla a su tiempo a nro Colegio y lo mismo escriví al R. P. Guardn de dho Colegio pr qe quando concluí y firmé las cartas hize fixo concepto qe no habria lugar pa copiarlo; pero en fin lo huvo, se copió a toda prisa. Ahora qe no dudo iran a V. E. los de los Pilotos lo remito a dho R. P. Guardn y el del otro Religo ira despues. Ya digo al R. Pe Guardn qe si vuestra excelencia no obste los otros gustare, lo ponga prompte en sus manos, qe supuesto lo hecho no lo envio ahora directame

En lo demas me remito a las dhas qe ahunque algo mas tarde

---

7 The City of Mexico.
8 Captain Fernando Rivera y Moncada.

available; and I recognize a far greater inclination to employ them in establishing a new presidio, at a distance of four or five leagues from the port and six from this mission, rather than in founding any new mission. This is a matter concerning which I was about to present to Your Excellency a written memorial, at the time I was in that city,[7] when I learned that the new official[8] proposed making such a demand; but, as I was told that any failure to protect the port would not be allowed, nor any such change of plan, I abandoned that design. Yet I afterwards repented of this, when in Guadalajara, Tepic, and other places, I found that tidings had gone abroad to the effect that the new captain was about to move the presidio—as though this were the principal object of his appointment. Still, for one reason this would not grieve me, and that is because at the distance of a league farther— on the road to San Francisco, be it understood—we might plant a new mission; and in this way the new presidio would be easily and in a perfectly fitting way provided with spiritual food, and the heathen of both sexes of those parts would become parishioners of the missionary fathers and not of the soldiers. Such mission would be at a distance of seven leagues from this one—which is not a matter of slight importance when it is considered that such an establishment would be likely to be of service in the prevention of disadvantages which I fancy might arise from a different condition of things. Were it not a matter connected with the missions I would not speak of it; but, being such, and to so great a degree, it does not seem to me that in this proposition I am advocating anything not within the scope of my clerical functions. And in this matter I conform to what Your Excellency may consider most fitting. It is a grevious thing for me, Most Excellent Sir, to find myself well provided with religious and with provisions, while no steps are taken in one way or another, towards some new spiritual labor; and I should fear to fatigue Your Excellency with this my oft-repeated importunity were I not sure that my desires are so much in accord with those of Your Excellency.

I gave to Your Excellency, also, the agreeable tidings that these new christians, following the example set by some of the workmen of the vessels whose services I managed to secure, are learning how to apply themselves to labor, hoe in hand and with the bar and in making adobes, in reaping or harvesting the wheat and in carting these crops, as well as in other work in which they take part. I reported, also, that

espero en Dios no dexaran de llegar y qe despues de su salida no hay mas novedad qe el embarcarse los volunts qe se quedaron en la salida de Dn Pedro Fages, menos los seys pa quienes pedí las licencias que los 3 son aca casados y los otros estan proximos a casarse y ahun de estos he ohido qe se va el uno. Con las dhas va tambien carta del P. Palou a V. E. qn al prte reproduce sus afectos pa con V. E. y sus preceptos Y quedo rogando qe

Dios N. Sr gde la salud, vida, y prosperidad de V. E. ms as en su

[9] The *fanega* was not always the same measure, even in Spain, where the *fanega* of one province was not that of some other province. At the respective missions of California the missionary whose duty it was to superintend the labors of the farm appears to have kept his accounts of the sowings and yield of wheat, and the like, in *fanegas* of that part of Spain where he was born and bred. The *fanega* may be taken as equivalent to from two to two and one quarter hectolitres and may be calculated as equal to about one and one quarter of our bushels. The equivalent given for a *fanega* in the books published by Mr. H. H. Bancroft is not correctly calculated.

[10] I translate *haba* (written *ava* by Father Serra) by *horse-bean*, and *frijol* by *kidney-bean*. The *haba* is the *faba* of the Romans—in many Spanish words the letter "h" replacing the Latin "f"—and was a *broad* bean. In Spanish-America the *haba* may have been either the bean known in Spain, or the variety called botanically *canvalia*, indigenous to the island of Jamacia, and, perhaps, other parts of America. What we call the "Lima bean" is probably of this variety. The word *frijol*—or *frejol*—is of American origin. Whether the bean so called was cis-Atlantic in its origin, or the *judia* of Spain (the *phaseolus* of the Romans, and *kidney-bean* among English-speaking people) can not be determined. Nor is it known in what part of Spanish-America the word *frijol* originated; now, at least, it is common from California to Cape Horn and is used to signify any kidney-shaped bean. In southern Mexico the *frijol* is a small black bean; in California it is a larger bean of a light chocolate color, and even the abundant small white bean is called by that name.

[11] It is impossible to tell exactly what fish is meant by *sardina*. In Spanish-America, as in Spain, this name is given to many different fish—to the sardine, the herring, the shad, and others. Father Serra here uses the word *varando* for *barrando*, an older form of *embarrando*, meaning *covering with mud*.

[12] This was the college of San Fernando de México, headquarters of the Franciscan friars of the vice-royalty of New Spain. The head of the house was called the *guardian*.

[13] The first soldiers sent to California were detailed for the service from the regiment called "Voluntarios de Cataluña," a corps raised in the Spanish province of that name. When the regiment came from Spain the men, as well as the officers, were of white Spanish birth; after many years' service in New Spain the rank and file had come to be composed of men of mixed race. This is true also of all the troops sent to California by the vice-royal government.

[14] In these early days no soldier, other than a commissioned officer, who came to California a bachelor was allowed to remain for a very long time in a state of single blessedness; as a rule the new comer was married out of hand to some neophyte of the missions. Very many of the men who at a later date figured in California affairs were sons and grandsons of native Indian women.

this year there have been harvested at this mission, in addition to twenty *fanegas*[9] of barley, one hundred and twenty-five of wheat, some horse-beans and a greater quantity of kidney-beans,[10] and together with continuous help from the vegetable garden—in the consumption of which all share. There is reason for expecting a fair return from the maize sown, and it is well-grown and in good condition, and there will be obtained a goodly number of fish from the abundance of sardines which, for twenty consecutive days, have been spawning along the beach near this mission,[11] and a reasonable harvest from the spiritual advancement we are experiencing each day —thanks be to God! At all the missions they are making preparation for more extensive sowings in the coming year, and I trust God that a happy outcome may attend the work.

Concerning the diary that I remitted to Your Excellency, I said that no copy remained here for transmission to our college[12] at a suitable time, and to that effect I wrote to the Reverend Father Guardian of said college, because, when I had finished and signed the letter, I came to the conclusion that time to copy it was wanting; but, as it fell out, there was time, and it was copied in great haste. Now that I doubt not those of the navigating officers will be sent to Your Excellency, I remit it to the Reverend Father Guardian; that of the other religious will go later. I have already told the Reverend Father Guardian that, despite the other diaries, if Your Excellency desires he will place them in your hands; supposing that this will be done, I am not now sending it directly to you.

For the rest I refer to my said letters, which I trust in God, will not fail to reach your hands somewhat later. Since dispatching them nothing noteworthy has happened, other than that the volunteers[13] who remained here at the time Don Pedro Fages* left have taken passage in the ship, excepting the six whose permits I asked for, and of whom three have married here while the other three are about to marry[14]—although one of them, I hear, is going away too. With this letter there goes, also, to Your Excellency one of Father Palóu, who

---

* At this time Pedro Fages was Lieutenant of the Catalonian Volunteers. His military career found him as acting governor of California and later as civil and military governor. For a shortened biography see Bancroft, *History of California*, Vol. I, 481–87. An extended treatment is found in Donald A. Nuttall, "Pedro Fages and the Advance of the Northern Frontier of New Spain, 1767–1782," Ph.D. dissertation, University of Southern California, 1964.

Sta gracia. De esta favorecida de V. E. de S. Carlos de Monte-Rey, y
Septe 9 de 1774.

Excellmo Señor

B. l. m. s. de V. E. su mas affo y rendo Svo y Capellan
que le venera y ama
Fr. Junípero Serra
(hay rúbrica)

[15] This letter, as well as that which follows, was written to the forty-sixth viceroy of
New Spain, who was—not to curtail his name and titles—His Excellency the Bailio Frey
Don Antonio María Bucareli y Ursúa Henestrosa Lasso de la Vega Villacis y Córdoba,
Knight-Commander of la Bóveda de Toro in the Military Order of St. John of Malta,
Lieutenant-General of the Royal Armies of Spain. Later he became, in addition to all
this, a gentleman of the royal bedchamber. Of these two letters I fail to find any mention
in the works published by Mr. H. H. Bancroft. I may be allowed to suggest, in this connection, that, considering the number of letters which must have been written by a
president of missions so active and zealous as President Serra, it is rather astonishing that
Mr. Bancroft's writers saw so few of them. President Serra's manuscript is very legible,
as may be judged by the facsimile of document No. 17, page 130 of this edition. The
abbreviations he makes use of are common to Spanish manuscripts of his time. His
spelling is peculiar at times, and occasionally he makes use of an archaic word or a
provincialism rather than the idiomatic *lengua Castellana* of the eighteenth century.

sends again his affectionate regards to Your Excellency and the assurance of his prayers for you. And I continue praying that God our Lord guard the health, life and prosperity of Your Excellency for many years in His holy grace. From this mission favored by Your Excellency of San Carlos de Monterey, Sept. 9, 1774.[15]

> Most Excellent Sir:—Your most affectionate and humble servant and chaplain, who venerates and loves you, kisses the hands of Your Excellency.
>
> *Fray Junípero Serra**
> (a rubric)

* Father Serra, most famous of California's Franciscans, has had many biographers. Geiger's edition of *Palóu's Life of Fray Junípero Serra* and Tibesar's edition of the *Writings of Junípero Serra* present the most recent and the best scholarly material on the subject.

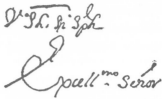

J. M. J.

Exmô Señor

Muy Venᵈᵒ Sʳ mio. Exmô. La nueva detencion de
la fragᵃ en este Puerto con ocasion d su arribada aⱼᵃ
los dias d haver salido ya pª el Sᵗ Blas, ha dado
tiempo pᵃ q se sacase en limpia el Diario del P F
Juan Crespi, el q remito en esta ocasion à VE su
poniendo le tengo ya remitido, y q duplicado d sᵘ
Antᵉ el P F Thomas dela Peña d q se servà V dios
de perdonar los defectos assegurandose d la buena vo
luntad q yo, y todos tenemos d servir à VE y à N So.
berano q Dios guarde especialmᵗᵉ en Assumptos d esta na
turaleza tan proprios d N Sagrado Instituto. Y porque
desde las vltꞵ cartas no se ofrece novedad especial q
noticiar à VE y q no me recelo no ser molesto à q tanto
venero, yᵉ estimo solo añado el

Dios Nˢ Oᵉ à VE mᵗ aˢ con salud y su Sᵗ
gracia de esta su favorecida d VE Mission de S Carla
de Monte Rey Octᵉ 7 d 1774.

Exmô Señor

B. l. m. de VE su mas atto rendᵈ
Siervo y Capellan
Fr Junipero Serra

Document No. 17

Letter of Fray Junípero Serra, President of the missions of California, to Don Frey Antonio María Bucareli y Ursúa, Viceroy of New Spain, forwarding the journal of Fray Juan Crespi—7th October, 1774

Va Jhs. Ma Jph

Excellmo Señor

Muy Vendo Sor mio Exmo. La nueva detencion de la fraga en este Puerto con ocasion de su arribada a pocos dias de haver salido ya pa el de Sn Blas, ha dado tiempo pa qe se sacasse en limpio el Diario del P. Pr Fr. Juan Crespi, el qe remito en esta ocasion a V. E. suponiendo le tengo ya remitido, y pr duplicado el de su Compo el P. Pr Fr. Thomas de la Peña. V. E. se sirva pr Dios de perdonar los defectos assegurandose de la buena voluntad qe yo y todos tenemos de servir a V. E. y a N. Soberano qe Dios guarde especialme en Assumptos de esta naturaleza tan proprios de N. Sagrado Instituto y porque desde las ults cartas no se ofrece novedad especial qe noticiar a V. E. y qe me rezelo no ser molesto, a qn tanto venero, y estimo, solo añado el.*

Dios N. Sr Gde a V. E. ms as con salud, y su Sta gracia. De esta tan favorecida de V. E. Mission de S. Carlos de Monte-Rey Octb 7 de 1774.

Excellmo Señor
B. l. mos de V. E. su mas affo y rendo
Siervo y Capellan
Fr. Junípero Serra
(hay rúbrica)

[1] In the *History of the Pacific States* published by Mr. H. H. Bancroft Spanish words especially patronymics, have been accented, or the necessary accent has been omitted from them, without authority. One of the names accented improperly by Mr. Bancroft's writers is that of Father Juan Crespi, the name being given as Crespí. That he did not so write his name is shown by his signature to his diary, No. 19 of the documents published in this collection. To the casual observer it might seem that President Serra put an accent on the final syllable of the name of his companion—the friend by whose side he requested that his own body might be laid—and it is quite possible that in this case as in many others, Mr. Bancroft's writers jumped at a conclusion. In the President's manuscript Father Crespi's name seems to be accented, but a similar mark appears over the letter "i" in the words "detencion," "limpio," "Dios," "servir," "gracia." In no one of these words should the "i" be accented.

Hail Jesus, Mary and Joseph!

Most Excellent Sir.

My Greatly Venerated, Most Excellent Sir:*
The new detention of the ship at this port, consequent on her return a few days after her departure for San Blas, has been the means of there being time for making a clean copy of the diary of Father Preacher Fray Juan Crespi,[1] which I take occasion to send to Your Excellency, it being understood that I have already sent, in duplicate, that of his companion, Father Preacher Fray Tomás de la Peña.† May Your Excellency be pleased for God's sake, to pardon its defects, resting assured of the good will I and all have in serving Your Excellency and our sovereign—whom God guard—especially in matters of this kind so fitting for our holy institute. And inasmuch as, since the date of said letters, there is no special new occurrence of which to advise Your Excellency, and because I fear lest I might molest one I so venerate and esteem, I will add only: May God our Lord guard Your Excellency many years in health and in His holy grace. From this mission, so favored by Your Excellency, of San Carlos de Monterey, October 7, 1774.

Most Excellent Sir:—Your most affectionate and humble servant and chaplain kisses the hands of Your Excellency.

Fray Junípero Serra
(a rubric)

* For facsimile, see page 130. Original in AGI, Estado 43. In Chapman, *Catalogue of AGI*, this item is catalogued on p. 363 as No. 2738.

Tibesar, *Writings of Junípero Serra*, Vol. II, 192–93, contains both Spanish and English versions. The editor indicates that a copy exists in the Sutro Collection. In Herbert E. Bolton (ed.), *Historical Memoirs of New California* by Fray Francisco Palóu, 4 vols., facing p. 176 of Vol. III, there is a photographic copy of the original document from Sevilla.

† Fr. Tomás de la Peña y Saravia, an early California Franciscan, is author of document 18 in this collection. For more biographical data, see Geiger, *Palóu's Life of Fray Junípero Serra*, 411–12, or Bancroft, *History of California*, Vol. I, 722–23.

Document No. 18

Diary of Fray Tomás de la Peña kept during the voyage of the
Santiago—dated 28th August, 1774

Dᴵᴬᴿᴵᴼ del viaje que por mandado del Padre Fray Junípero Serra, Predicador Apostólico y Presidente de estas Misiones de Monte-Rey, del cargo de nuestro santo colegio de Propaganda fide de San Fernando de la ciudad de Mexico hago desde este Puerto de San Carlos de Monte-Rey sito en la costa de la California setentrional en 36 grados y 30 minutos de Latitud al Norte, en la Fragata de Su Magestad nombrada Santiago, alias la Nueva Galicia, mandada por Don Juan Perez Alferez graduado de Fragata, primer Piloto de los del numero en el Real Departamento de San Blas, y Capitan Comandante de la expedicion que por órden del Excelentisimo Señor Don Frey Antonio Maria Bucareli y Ursua, ha de hacer en dicha Fragata a fin de reconocer la costa desde dicho Puerto de Monte-Rey hasta la altura de 60 grados de Latitud al Norte, comenzado dia 6 de Junio de 1774, en que me embarqué en compañia del Reverendo Padre Fray Juan Crespi, Predicador Apostolico de dicho Colegio y Ministro de la mision de San Carlos de Monte-Rey, vulgo del Carmelo.*

Viva Jesus Maria y Joseph: Junio de 1774. Habiendome destinado el Reverendo Padre Presidente de estas Misiones de Monte Rey Fray Junipero Serra Comisionado del Santo oficio y Predicador Apostolico de Propaganda fide del Colegio de San Fernando de la Ciudad de Mexico para acompañar al Reverendo Padre Fray Juan Crespi Pre-

---

[1] *Alferez graduado de fragata* was a rank in the Spanish navy corresponding to that of sub-lieutenant in the army.

[2] It will be noticed that, in the letter of President Serra of which a facsimile is herewith published, the final letter of Father Crespi's name is apparently accented. A careful inspection of the President's manuscript makes it evident that in many words where the letter "i" should not be accented he appears to have accented that letter. The President's manuscript shows that he was a quick, nervous writer, who did not waste time in writing out words or in placing accents properly. Father de la Peña does not accent the final letter of his companion's name. In the document which follows this, which is Father Crespi's own diary, it will be noted that he himself wrote his name without an accent. It must be admitted that these clergymen of the Roman Catholic church knew how to spell their own names and those of their companions, and, therefore, that Mr. H. H. Bancroft's writers are in error when they give the name with an accent on the final letter.

DIARY OF THE VOYAGE which, by order of Father Fray Junípero Serra, Preacher-Apostolic, President of these Missions of Monterey entrusted to the care of Our Holy College *de Propaganda Fide* of San Fernando of the City of Mexico, I make from this port of San Carlos de Monterey, situated on the coast of Northern California, in 36° 30′ north latitude, in His Majesty's Frigate called the *Santiago*, otherwise the *Nueva Galicia*, commanded by Don Juan Pérez, *Alférez Graduado de Fragata*, Navigating Officer of the first class among those serving in the royal department of San Blas and Captain-Commanding of the expedition[1] which, by order of the Most Excellent Lord Don Frey Antonio María Bucareli y Ursúa, is to be made in that frigate, for the purpose of examining the coast from said port of Monterey to 60° north latitude, begun on the 6th of June, 1774, on which day I embarked, in company with the Reverend Father Fray Juan Crespi, Preacher-Apostolic of said college and Minister of the Mission of San Carlos de Monterey, commonly called Carmelo.*

Hail Jesus, Mary and Joseph, June, 1774

The Reverend Father President of the missions of Monterey, Fray Junípero Serra, Commissioner of the Holy Office and Preacher-Apostolic *de Propaganda Fide* of the College of San Fernando of the City of Mexico, having assigned me as companion to the Reverend Father Fray Juan Crespi,[2] Preacher-Apostolic of said College, charged me with the duty of making observations for the determination of the latitude wherever a landing shall be made during the progress of the expedition:

6th June: About four in the afternoon we set forth from the Mission

---

* There are contemporary copies of this diary in both AGI, Estado 43 and Guadalajara 515. The latter is noted in Chapman, *Catalogue of AGI*, 352, as No. 2640.

In addition to the account of Fr. Juan Crespi, which is document 19 of this work, two other diaries of the 1774 expedition exist: Estevan José Martínez, Viage executado por el Piloto Estevan Josef Martinez en la Fragata Santiago alias la Nueva Galicia propia de S. M. y por orden de Exmo Sor Baylio Fr dn Antonio Maria Bucarely y Ursua Virrey Goveror y Capitan General de los Reynos de N. E. & a los Puertos de San Diego: y Monterrey, y desde este a la Altura de 55 grados Norte segun y como en el se expresa haviendo salido del Puerto de San Blas (que se halla en 21 grados 21 minutos de latitud norte) en 24 dias del Mes de Henero de 1774, MS, in Archivo General de la Nacion (Mexico), Historia 61; and in almost identical wording and found in the same archive is Pérez' journal: Diario de la Navegacion hecha por el Alferez graduado D. Juan Pérez, de orden del Sr. Bucareli a la altura de los 55 grados donde esta situada la entrada y Bahia de su nombre, en la Fragata Santiago, alias la Nueva Galicia, MS, 1774, Historia 62.

dicador Apostolico de dicho Colegio, que va con el encargo de observar la altura del Norte, cuando se verifique saltar en tierra, durante el viage de la expedicion:

Dia 6 de Junio, como a las cuatro de la tarde, salimos de la Mision de San Carlos de Monte-Rey, que dista como una legua del Presidio y Puerto de Monte-Rey, al que llegamos como a las cinco de la tarde y habiendonos despedido de los señores capitanes, vinimos a bordo acompañandonos dicho Padre Presidente hasta la playa, en donde nos dimos el último abrazo y despedida; al ponerse el sol llegamos a bordo y habiendo cenado la gente de la tripulacion embarcaron cuatro toretes y algunos cerdos, que el Sor Capitan Comandante del presidio regalo para el rancho de la camera. Esta noche se levaron las anclas.

Dia 7 por la mañana con una espia por la proa sacaron el barco del fondeadero y lo arrimaron a un yerbasal, que está junto a la Punta de Pinos, y distante de dicho fondeadero como un tiro de fusil. Esta mañana sopló el N. O., como a las 9 de la mañana se levó la última ancla, que habia servido de espia y se alargaron velas, y habiendo hecho la ceremonia de hisar vandera española con un cañonazo, dimos dos ó tres bordos para fuera y refrescando el N. O. se volvió a dar fondo; como a las doce y media de la tarde poco mas a fuera de donde habia estado anclado para el desembarque de la carga. Todo este dia sopló el N. O. algo fresco. Por la noche se enfermó el Contra-Maestre.

Dia 8 amaneció con el mismo viento del dia antecedente y se mantuvo todo él. Como a la una de la tarde se divisó el Pacabot San Antonio, alias el Principe, el cual dió fondo como a las tres.

Dia 9 nos mantuvimos fondeados por falta de viento favorable. Este dia como a las 9 de la mañana, fuimos a dar un paseo al Real el señor capitan Don Esteban y los dos Padres, y alli encontramos al Padre Presidente, al Padre Fray Francisco Palou y al Padre Fray Joseph de Murguia, volvimos a comer a bordo, y el Padre Presidente se quedó a dormir en el Principe, para cantar al otro dia una Missa que los señores Pilotos habian ofrecido.

[3] This was Esteban (not Estevan, as given by H. H. Bancroft's writers) Martínez, assistant navigating officer of the expedition.

[4] Mr. H. H. Bancroft's writer (*History of the Pacific States*, XIII, 228) says that this mass was said "under the old oak, &c." In this diary no mention is made of an oak, and Father Crespi (see Document No. 19) says that this mass was celebrated under an *enramada*—a shelter made of boughs. He adds that they all dined together, near the old oak which Vizcaíno saw.

of San Carlos de Monterey, about one league distant from the Presidio and Port of Monterey, which place we reached about five; and, having taken leave of the captains there, we came on board, the Father President accompanying us to the shore, where he gave us his last embrace and good-bye. At sunset we arrived on board. After supper, the crew put on board ship four young bulls and some pigs which the Captain-Commanding of the Presidio presented to the cabin mess. This night we weighed anchor.

On the morning of the 7th the ship was warped out from the anchoring ground and brought near to a shallow place where the seaweed [kelp] grows to the surface of the water, close to Point Pinos and about a musket-shot distant from said anchorage. This morning the wind was northwest. About nine the anchor which had served for warping the ship was weighed and the sails were loosed; and, the ceremony of hoisting the Spanish flag and firing a gun having been observed, we made two or three tacks seaward, but, the northwest wind increasing, about a half an hour after noon we went back to an anchorage a little farther out than where the ship had anchored when her cargo was discharged. All day the wind blew from the northwest rather fresh. During the night the boatswain sickened.

At dawn on the 8th the same wind was blowing, and held all day. At one in the afternoon we saw the packet *San Antonio*, otherwise *Príncipe*,* in the offing, and about three o'clock she came to anchor.

On the 9th we remained at anchor, lacking a favorable wind. About nine o'clock the Captain [Pérez], Don Esteban[3] and we two fathers made a visit to the fort, meeting there the Father President, Father Fray Francisco Palóu and Father Fray Joseph de Murguía.† We returned on board to dine, and the Father President slept on board the *Príncipe* in order to chant a mass, offered by the navigating officers, on the day following.

On the 10th a solemn mass was chanted to Most Holy Mary for a good voyage, in the same place where the mass was first celebrated in Monterey.[4] Fathers Fray Joseph de Murguía and Fray Francisco

---

* The packetboat *San Antonio* was commonly known as the *Príncipe*. It was of 193 tons burden and constructed in the shipyards at Santiago, Mexico in 1767. Museo Naval, California y Costa N. O. de América, Tomo II (332).

† For biographical information on Murguía, see Geiger, *Palóu's Life of Fray Junípero Serra*, 441–42.

Dia 10 se cantó una Missa solemne a Maria Santisima por el buen viage en el mismo parage, en que se celebró la primera en Monte-Rey; assistieron a ella los Padres Fray Joseph de Murguia y Fray Francisco Dumez, los señores capitanes Don Fernando de Rivera, Don Pedro Fages y Don Joseph Cañizares con toda la gente asi del Presidio, como de los dos barcos. Comimos todos en el mismo parage por convite del señor capitan Don Juan. Como a las 3 de la tarde confese al Contra-Maestre Manuel Lopez, y luego le administró la extrema uncion el Padre Fray Juan y como a las cuatro y media espiró. El cadaver se embió a la Yglesia del Presidio, para que le diesen sepultura los Padres Ministros de la Mision de San Carlos.

Dia 11 amaneció en calma y con una espia y el romolque de las lanchas de los dos barcos arrimaron la Fragata al yerbasal de la Punta: Como a las doce con viento Norte nos hicimos a la vela y habiendo quedado la lancha del Principe levando un anclote que habia servido de espia no pudo darnos alcance; toda esta tarde cabeceó mucho el barco a causa de la mar por proa. Por la noche hallandonos como 3 leguas de la Punta de año nuevo calmó el viento.

Dia 12 amaneció en calma; celebramos missa los dos padres. Por la tarde sopló el N. O., pero lento y al ponerse el sol se calmó. Como a las 9 de la noche venteó el E. variable, y luego se calmó. Toda la noche se pasó en ventolinas y con nieblina muy densa y humeda.

Dia 13 amaneció con la misma nieblina y ventolinas. Celebramos el Santo Sacrificio ambos padres. A causa de la mucha nieblina no pudimos ver la costa esta mañana, ni los señores Pilotos pudieron observar; toda la tarde y noche siguiente se mantuvo la nieblina densa y muy humeda.

Dia 14 amaneció en calma, con mucha nieblina. Esta mañana divisamos la Punta de año nuevo como a distancia de 2 leguas y las corrientes nos arrimaron tanto a la costa que a las nueve la teniamos como un cuarto de legua: a dicha hora se sondeó varias veces y se halló fondo en 25, 24 y 22 brazas. A las doce y media comenzó a ventolear lentamente el S. O. y con el nos apartamos de la tierra. Por la noche calmó a ratos y nos mantuvimos dando bordos entre las dos puntas.

Dia 15 amanecimos en frente de la punta de Pinos a la parte del Oeste y divisamos claramente la Punta de Cipreses, la ensenada del Carmelo y la sierra de Santa Lucia. Como a las 8 comenzó a soplar el

Dumetz,‡ Captains Don Fernando de Rivera, Don Pedro Fages and Don Joseph Cañizares,* together with all the people of the Presidio and the ships, were present. We all dined at the same place, by invitation of Captain Don Juan Pérez. About three in the afternoon I received the confession of the boatswain, Manuel López; soon afterward Father Fray Juan Crespi administered the rite of extreme unction to him, and he expired at about half past four. The corpse was sent to the church at the Presidio, that it might be given sepulture by the fathers ministers of the Mission of San Carlos.

The 11th dawned calm. By means of a warp, and the ship being towed by the longboats of the two vessels, she was taken to the shallow at the point where the seaweed grows to the surface. About noon we made sail, with the wind from the north. The longboat of the *Príncipe*, which had remained behind to get up the anchor used in warping, could not overtake us. All afternoon the vessel pitched heavily, for her head was to the sea. At night, the ship being some three leagues off Point Año Nuevo, the wind died away.

At daybreak on the 12th it was calm. We two fathers celebrated the mass. During the afternoon the wind was northwest, but light, and at sundown it died away. About nine o'clock at night the wind was east, but it shifted about and soon it was calm again. All night long there were light shifting winds, with a very dense and wet fog.

The 13th dawned foggy, with light shifting winds. We two fathers celebrated the mass. Because of the heavy fog we could not see the coast this morning; nor could the navigating officers take an observation. All afternoon, and the night following, there was a dense and very wet fog.

At dawn on the 14th it was calm, with a thick fog. This morning we saw Point Año Nuevo about two leagues distant, and the current bore us so near to the coast that at nine it was only a quarter of a league away. At that hour several casts of the lead were made, with bottom at twenty-five, twenty-four and twenty-two fathoms. At half past twelve a light breeze sprang up from southwest, and by its aid we drew away from the land. During the night the breeze died away at intervals, and the ship kept tacking between the two points.

At dawn on the 15th we were off of Point Pinos, and we saw clearly

‡ On Dumetz, *Ibid.*, 398.

* For a brief sketch of Cañizares' career, see Bancroft, *History of California*, Vol. II, 741. As an early naval figure in California history, he played a significant role in colonization and early exploration.

Noroeste algo fresco, pero se calmo antes de las 9. Este dia no hubo tanta nieblina como los antecedentes, pero estuvo nublado el cielo y se despejo algunos ratos. Al anochecer nos hallabamos como 6 leguas apartados de la tierra, la cual demarcaron los señores pilotos y la punta de año nuevo nos demoraba al Nordeste, la de Pinos al Este, y la de mas al Sur de Santa Lucia al S.E.

Dia 16 por la mañana se miraba la sierra de Santa Lucia como a distancia de 12 legaus; este dia amaneció nublado como el antecedente. A las 8 de la mañana refrescó un poco el Nornoroeste con aparato de agua y cayeron algunas gotas, pero cesó luego y el viento se mitiguó. Por la tarde aclaró algo el cielo y el viento se fué aflojando.

Dia 17 amaneció en calma y el cielo muy despejado y claro. Como a la una de la tarde se levantó viento del S. O. muy lento; divisamos al Noroeste la sierra de Santa Lucia como a distancia de 16 leguas. Por la noche se llamó el viento al N. O. y se viró de bordo con la proa al oestesudoeste.

Dia 18 amaneció con el mismo viento y nieblina muy obscura y humeda que parecia aguacero. Este dia amanecio enfermo el señor capitan con indisposicion del estomago y sin haber sosegado en toda la noche, pero al medio dia ya estaba mejorado. A las 12 observaron los señores pilotos y digeron nos hallabamos en 34 grados y 57 minutos de latitud al Norte. Por la tarde refrescó mas el viento.

Dia 19 amaneció con el mismo viento, pero muy fresco y mucha marejada. No se pudo decir misa por los muchos valances. A las 8 nos

---

* Spanish sailing was done on the following points (with modern azimuth equivalents supplied in the second column).

North	0°	South	180°
North ¼ Northeast	11¼°	South ¼ southwest	191¼°
Northnortheast	22½°	Southsouthwest	202½°
Northeast ¼ north	33¾°	Southwest ¼ south	213¾°
Northeast	45°	Southwest	225°
Northeast ¼ east	56¼°	Southwest ¼ west	236¼°
Eastnortheast	67½°	Westsouthwest	247½°
East ¼ northeast	78¾°	West ¼ southwest	258¾°
East	90°	West	270°
East ¼ southeast	101¼°	West ¼ northwest	281¼°
Eastsoutheast	112½°	Westnorthwest	292½°
Southeast ¼ east	123¾°	Northwest ¼ west	303¾°
Southeast	135°	Northwest	315°
Southeast ¼ south	146¼°	Northwest ¼ north	326¼°
Southsoutheast	157½°	Northnorthwest	337½°
South ¼ southeast	168¾°	North ¼ northwest	348¾°

Point Cipreses, the Bay of Carmelo and the Sierra of Santa Lucía. About eight o'clock it began to blow rather fresh from the northwest but before nine the wind died away. Today there was not so much fog as on other days, but the sky was overcast, though clear at intervals. At nightfall we were about six leagues from shore, its bearings being taken by the navigating officers, Point Año Nuevo bearing northeast, Point Pinos east, and the land to the southward of Santa Lucía southeast.

On the morning of the 16th we saw the Sierra of Santa Lucía, about twelve leagues away. The day dawned cloudy, as yesterday was. At eight in the morning the north-northwest wind freshened. There was an appearance of rain, and some drops fell; but it soon ceased to rain and there was less wind. During the afternoon the sky was clearer and the wind was dying away.

The 17th dawned calm and the sky was very cloudless and clear. About one in the afternoon a very light southwest breeze sprang up. To the northeastward we saw the Sierra of Santa Lucía, about sixteen leagues away. During the night the wind shifted to the northwest and the ship went about and stood to the west-southwest.

At dawn of the 18th the same wind held; the fog was very thick and so damp it was like a shower. The Captain arose this morning suffering from an indisposition of the stomach, having had no ease during the night; but at noon he felt better. At twelve the navigating officers took an observation and said that we were in 34° 57′ north latitude. During the afternoon the wind freshened.

At dawn on the 19th the same wind was blowing, but it was very strong and there was a heavy sea. It was impossible to celebrate mass, owing to the rocking of the ship. At eight o'clock the ship was under the foresail only, and so made three and four miles an hour. During the afternoon the wind was less strong and the main-tack was hauled aboard.

On the 20th the wind had become lighter and, the topsails being set, the ship made five miles and a half an hour. All day the wind blew from the northwest.

At dawn on the 21st the sky was very bright and clear. The wind shifted to the north and blew fresh all day. The course was west ¼ northwest, the ship going three miles an hour.* [see opposite] Today the navigating officers took an observation in 34° 08′.

quedamos con solo el trinquete, y asi se caminaba a 3 y 4 millas por hora; por la tarde aflojó el viento alguna cosa y se amuro la mayor.

Dia 20 habiendose mitiguado el viento se marearon las gavias y se caminaba a 5 millas y media por hora. Todo este dia sopló el Noroeste.

Dia 21 amaneció muy claro y despejado el ciclo. El viento se llamó al Norte y sopló fresco todo el dia, se navegó al Oeste cuarto al Noroeste a tres millas por hora. Observaron este dia los señores pilotos 34 grados y 8 minutos de latitud.

Dia 22 amaneció nublado el cielo y a las 7 de la mañana vino del Norte una nieblina muy humeda y el viento fué calmando. Al medio dia observaron los señores pilotos 34 grados y 7 minutos de latitud; el viento se mantuvo lento y variable.

Dia 23 por la mañana se llamó el viento al Nordeste pero luego se ladeó al Noroeste. Observaron los señores pilotos al sol en 33 grados y 46 minutos; todo el dia sopló el Noroeste y se caminaba al oeste-sudoeste a 3 millas por hora.

Dia 24 amaneció nublado el cielo y el viento se llamó al Norte Nordeste algo fresco y se caminó al O. N. O. Digimos misa los dos padres y celebramos alegres el cumpleaños del señor capitan Don Juan Perez. Este dia observaron los señores pilotos 33 grados y 43 minutos de latitud. Por la tarde se caminó al N. O. ¼ al O. a 3 y media millas.

Dia 25 amaneció claro el cielo y con el mismo viento que ayer se caminaba a 4 millas por hora al mismo rumbo. Este dia observaron el sol los señores pilotos en 34 grados y 26 minutos de latitud. A las 9 de la noche se llamó el viento al Este.

Dia 26 amaneció con el mismo viento fresco. Digimos misa los dos padres. Observaron los señores pilotos el sol en 35 grados y 37 minutos de latitud. A las 5 de la tarde se calmó el viento.

Dia 27 a las 6 de la mañana comenzo a ventolear del Nordeste lento y variable. En este dia observaron los señores pilotos 35 grados 59 minutos, y prosiguió el mismo tiempo.

Dia 28 prosiguió el mismo viento y se caminaba a 2 millas por hora. Este dia nos hallamos en 36 grados y 26 minutos casi al paralelo de Monte-Rey. Por la tarde refrescó algo el viento y prosiguió toda la noche.

Dia 29 amaneció con el mismo viento. Digimos misa ambos padres. Al medio dia observaron el sol los señores pilotos en 37 y 20 minutos. Por la tarde se llamó el viento al Este y se caminaban 4 millas.

The 22d dawned with the sky overcast and at seven o'clock there came from the north a very wet fog, the wind dying away. At noon the navigating officers got an observation in 34° 07′. The wind was light and variable.

On the morning of the 23d the wind shifted to the northeast, and presently to the northwest. The navigating officers took a sun sight in 33° 46′. All day the northwest wind blew and the ship sailed three miles an hour, the course being west-southwest.

At dawn on the 24th the sky was cloudy, and the wind rather fresh from north-northeast. The course was west-northwest. We two fathers said mass, and all celebrated joyously the birthday of Captain Don Juan Pérez. Today the navigating officers took an observation in 33° 43′. During the afternoon the ship sailed three and a half miles an hour, the course being northwest ¼ west.

On the 25th the sky was clear, and the ship sailed on the same course at the rate of four miles an hour with the wind as it was. Today the navigating officers took a sun sight in 34° 26′. At nine o'clock at night the wind hauled to the eastward.

At dawn on the 26th the same wind was blowing fresh. We two fathers said mass. The navigating officers observed the sun in latitude 35° 37′. At five in the afternoon the wind died away.

At six o'clock on the morning of the 27th the wind began to come from the northeast, light and variable. Today the navigating officers took an observation in latitude 35° 59′, and the weather was the same.

On the 28th the same wind was blowing, and we made two miles an hour. Today we were in 36° 26′ latitude, almost that of Monterey. The wind freshened during the afternoon and continued to blow during the night.

At dawn on the 29th the same wind was blowing. Both fathers said mass. At noon the navigating officers observed the sun in 37° 20′. During the afternoon the wind shifted to the eastward, and the ship sailed at the rate of four miles an hour.

On the 30th the wind continued to blow from the east, although it was light, and at seven o'clock it shifted to the east-southeast, being very light. The navigating officers took an observation in latitude 38° 35′. In the afternoon the wind was fresher.

JULY, 1774

At dawn on the 1st it was almost calm, and at ten o'clock the wind

Dia 30 prosiguió el viento del Este aunque lento y como a las 7 se llamó el Este Sudeste muy flojo. Observaron los señores pilotos 38 grados y 35 minutos de latitud. Por la tarde refrescó algo el viento.

JULIO DE 1774

Dia 1 amaneció casi calmado el veinto y a las 10 se calmó del todo. Este dia observaron los señores pilotos 39 grados 45 minutos. A las doce y media comenzó a ventear el Sur muy lento y cargó mucha nieblina. A las 5 se calmó el viento.

Dia 2 como a las 3 de la mañana cayó un aguacero con ventolinas del Sudoeste y luego quedó en calma, la que duró todo el dia y calentó bien el sol. Por la noche sopló del E. S. E. muy lento.

Dia 3 amaneció con mucha nieblina y el viento algo fresco. Digimos misa los dos padres. A las 8 se calmó el viento, y la nieblina comenzó a descargar agua. A las 10 volvió a ventolear del E. Observaron los señores pilotos 40 grados 34 minutos de latitud, como a las dos se llamó el viento al S. E. algo fresco, y duró toda la tarde y noche siguiente. Esta tarde al ponerse el sol se vieron algunos pajaros y digeron que eran de mar y que muchas veces se ven sin que haya tierra en muchos cientos de leguas.

Dia 4 amaneció el cielo nublado y con mucho rocio, el viento fresco del S. E. y se mantuvo todo el dia. No pudieron observar este dia los señores pilotos por lo mucho nublado que estuvo. Como a la una de la tarde comenzó a llover y prosiguió lo mas de la tarde. Por la noche serenó algo el cielo y cayo mucho rocio.

Dia 5 amaneció con el mismo viento aunque no tan fresco, y el cielo nublado. Observaron este dia los señores pilotos 43 grados 35 minutos de latitud, pero digeron que no era segura dicha observacion, por no haberse aclarado los orizontes. Al ponerse el sol vimos un pajaro grande como gavilan y digeron que era de tierra, pero esta no se pudo divisar desde el tope: hicimos juicio que por el O., a donde caminaba dicho pajaro, habrá alguna isla. Por la noche sintieron los marineros un bufido que les pareció de ballena, pero Don Esteban que estaba de guardia me dijo que le parecia ser de lobo marino.

Dia 6 amaneció con grande rocio y nieblina muy densa, el viento algo mas fresco que ayer; pero a las 8 ya comenzó a escasearse. No pudieron observar los señores pilotos por la mucha nieblina. Como a la una se llamó el viento al S. O.; a las 4 vimos un pato posado en la agua, como sesenta varas del barco y segun digeron es señal de que hay

has ceased. The navigating officers took an observation in 39° 45′. At half past twelve a very light wind set in from the south, and a dense fog arose. At five o'clock the wind died away.

About three o'clock on the morning of the 2d there was a shower, with light variable winds from the southwest, which soon died away. The calm lasted all day, and the sun shone with great warmth. During the night there was a light wind from the east-southeast.

There was a thick fog at dawn on the 3d and the wind was fresh. We two fathers said mass. At eight o'clock the wind died away, and the fog became rain. At ten o'clock the wind came from the east again. The navigating officers took an observation in latitude 40° 34′. About two the wind shifted to the southeast, and was quite fresh during the afternoon and the following night. At sunset this afternoon some birds were seen; it was said that they were sea-fowl, and that they were seen often although there was no land within a distance of many hundreds of leagues.

At daylight on the 4th the sky was overcast and there was a heavy dew. The wind was fresh from the southeast and blew all day. As it was so cloudy the navigating officers could not get an observation. About one o'clock in the afternoon it began to rain, and rain fell during almost all the afternoon. During the night the sky became clearer and there was a heavy dew.

At dawn on the 5th the same wind was blowing, although it was not so strong, and the sky was clouded over. The navigating officers observed a latitude of 43° 35′, but said that this position was uncertain as the horizon was not clear. As the sun went down we saw a large bird like a hawk; it was said that it was a land-bird, though from the masthead land could not be seen. We concluded that towards the west, in which direction the bird was going, there must be an island. At night the sailors heard what they thought was the blowing of a whale, but Don Esteban, who was on duty, told me he thought it was made by a seawolf.

At daybreak on the 6th there was a heavy dew and a very thick fog, the wind being rather more fresh than it was yesterday. At eight o'clock it began to die away. On account of the thick fog the navigating officers could not get an observation. About one o'clock the wind hauled to the southwest. At four o'clock we saw a duck sitting on the water, distant about sixty yards from the vessel, and this was said

tierra no muy lejos. Como a las 5 se calmó el viento, y luego aclaró el cielo y orizontes. El gaviero registró desde el tope y dijo que no divisaba tierra por parte alguna. Al anochecer vi otro pato.

Dia 7 amaneció en calma con mucha nieblina, y tanto rocio que parecia aguacero. Esta mañana vimos varios lobos marinos al rededor del barco. No pudieron observar los señores pilotos por la mucha nieblina. Como a las 7 de la tarde comenzó a ventolear del N. y toda la noche se pasó en ventolinas.

Dia 8 amaneció con nieblina como los dias antecedentes, y las ventolinas del N. muy lentas y variables que a cada rato calmaban, y cuando mas se caminaba a milla por hora. A las 9 se calmó totalmente. No pudieron observar los señores pilotos con certeza por haber aclarado muy poco el sol y estar los orizontes ofuscados con la nieblina, que ya 5 dias no nos ha faltado ni una hora. Por la tarde hubo algunas ventolinas del S. E., pero muy calmosas. Esta tarde vimos tambien varios pajaros.

Dia 9 amaneció con tanta nieblina y rocio que parecia haber llovido toda la noche, pues las velas estaban como si las hubieran mojado y de la agua que destilaban habian llenado algunos valdes los marineros que los habian puesto debajo para recogerla. La calma siguió todo el dia salvo algunos ratos que venian algunas ventolinas del S. E. Al medio dia aclaró algo el cielo, con que pudieron hacer su observacion los señores pilotos y dijeron que estabamos en 45 grados de que nos alegramos todos, pues estaban ya con cuidado los pilotos y luego que observaron volvió la nieblina muy oscura a cerrar los orizontes. Por la tarde calmaron mas las ventolinas y la nieblina descargó mucha agua.

5 The writer employed by Mr. H. H. Bancroft who alludes to the voyage of Pérez (*History of the Pacific States*, XIII, 288) says that the ship was "driven back and forward along the coast," until "the 9th July, when they were again able to make observations." This diary and that of Father Crespi show that on the 18th June, the day after that on which a final departure from the coast was made, the latitude was determined by an observation of the sun; and that, from that date until the 9th July, observations were made on no less than fourteen days. Captain Pérez knew that he had plenty of sea-room and that the general trend of the coast to the northward of Monterey, so far as it was then known, was to the northwestward. He stood out to sea, though he was driven farther south than was desirable, in order to get an offing, and then sailed to the northwestward until the 14th July, when he put the ship's head to the northward—in order to make the land in about the latitude sought. It is very evident that Captain Pérez was an officer who understood his instructions, which were that he should go to 60° north latitude, and thence return southward, making an examination of the coast as he came. The Bancroftian writer seems to intimate that Pérez did not know what he was about.

to be a sign that land was not very far away. About five o'clock the wind died away and presently the sky and horizon were clear. The lookout at the masthead said that he saw no land anywhere. At sundown I saw another duck.

At dawn on the 7th it was calm and there was a dense fog, and dew so heavy that it was like a shower. This morning we saw several seawolves about the vessel. On account of the fog the navigating officers could not get an observation. About seven o'clock at night it began to blow from the north and all night the wind was variable.

As on previous mornings, at dawn on the 8th there was a fog, and there were light and variable breezes from the north, which at intervals died away. At most the ship made a mile an hour. At nine o'clock there was a dead calm. The navigating officers could not get a sure observation because the sun was not very clearly visible and the horizon was obscured by the fog, which for five days has not been absent a single hour. During the afternoon there were light breezes from the southeast. This afternoon, also, we saw several birds.

At dawn on the 9th there was so much fog and dew that it seemed as if it had rained all night long. The sails seemed as if they had been wetted, and the water from them had filled some buckets which the sailors had placed under them for the purpose of catching it. The calm lasted during the day, except that at times there were light breezes from the southeast. At noon the sky cleared a little, so that the navigating officers were able to take an observation. They said we were in 45°. Of this result all were glad, for the navigating officers had been uneasy. After the observation had been obtained the fog became very thick again and the horizon was obscured. During the afternoon the force of the breezes was less and a great deal of rain fell.[5]

On the 10th the calm and fog continued. Both fathers celebrated mass. About ten o'clock it began to blow very gently from the south. At noon it cleared a little, and the navigating officers took an observation in 45° 35′. During the afternoon a great deal of water fell from the fog and every little while the wind ceased to blow. Today a seawolf was seen which swam around the vessel several times. At half past eight at night it began to blow rather fresh from the southeast and during the night the ship made two miles and a half an hour.

The wind and dense fog were present, as previously, at dawn on the 11th. About eight o'clock the wind shifted to the south and the

Dia 10 prosiguió con nieblina y calma. Digimos misa ambos padres. Como a las 10 comenzó a soplar muy lento el S. Al medio dia aclaró algo el cielo y observaron los señores pilotos 45 grados 35 minutos. Por la tarde cayó mucha agua de la nieblina y el viento calmaba a cada rato. Este dia se vió un lobo marino el cual dió algunas vueltas al barco. A las 8 y media de la noche comenzó a soplar el S. E. algo fresco y se caminó toda la noche a dos millas y media por hora.

Dia 11 amaneció con el mismo viento y mucha nieblina como los dias antecedentes; como a las 8 se llamó el viento al S. y se caminaba a 3 millas por hora. Esta mañana se vieron dos gaviotas y varios pajaros. Al medio dia se aclaró algo el sol y lo observaron los señores pilotos en 46 grados y 32 minutos de latitud; por la tarde se llamó el viento al S. O. y la nieblina comenzó a descargar mucha agua y parecia lluvia de temporal y esto duró todo el dia y noche siguiente. Esta tarde hizo bastante frio, y mas por la noche, que digeron caia elada la agua.

Dia 12 amaneció con nieblina y rocio como los dias pasados, pero mas frio. El viento se llamó al O. S. O. como a las 5 de la mañana y la nieblina prosiguió llovisnando hasta las 10: en dicha hora se llamó el viento al O. algo fresco. Esta mañana se vieron algunos patos. No pudieron observar los señores pilotos por estar muy nublado el cielo y oscuros los orizontes. Por la tarde se llamó el viento al O. N. O. muy fresco y hubo mucha marejada y grande frio; viendo que el viento era contra a nuestro rumbo, (que ha sido al N. O. ¼ al O. desde que comenzamos a subir siempre que lo ha permitido el viento) y que las nieblinas eran tan continuas, pusieron la proa al Norte, para recalar a tierra ganando alguna altura. Como a las 3 de la tarde aclaró un poco el cielo, y toda la noche se mantuvo algo despejado, pero muy oscuros los orizontes.

Dia 13 amaneció con el mismo viento O. N. O. aunque no tan fresco y el cielo claro como por la noche pero a las 7 se volvió a cubrir de nubes. Al medio dia aclaró muy bien el dia y observaron los señores pilotos 48 grados 55 minutos de latitud y dijeron que tenian mas satisfaccion de esta observacion que de las antecedentes por haber estado mas despejados los orizontes. Por la tarde volvió a nublarse el cielo. Como a las 7 se llamó el viento al S. O. bien fresco y se puso la proa al N. O. en dicha hora vino la nieblina tan oscura que apenas se veia la proa del barco y con tanta agua que parecia aguacero y asi continuó toda la noche.

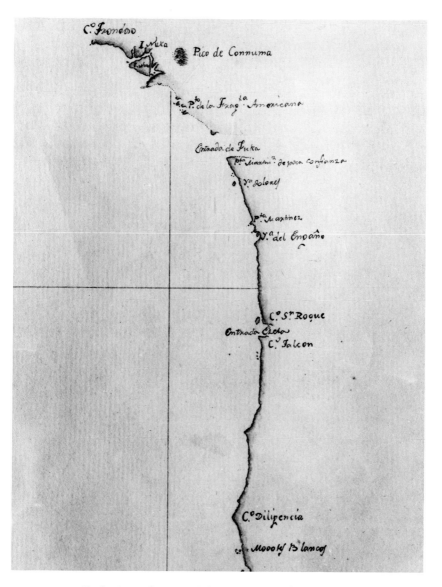

Early Spanish map of the Pacific Northwest Coast.

Early Spanish map of the Pacific Coast from just below Monterey to
58° N. latitude.

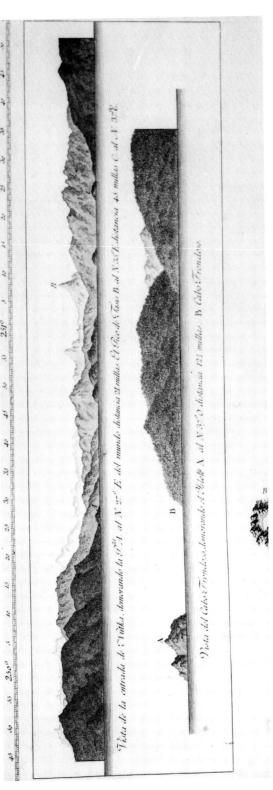

Coastal profiles of San Lorenzo de Nutka with Tasis Peak in the background and of Cabo Frondoso (Woody Point).

Native of the Entrance of the Strait of Juan de Fuca.

Native of the Pacific Northwest Coast wearing basketry hat and otter cape.

Another native of the Pacific Northwest Coast wearing typical basketry hat.

Nootka type wearing whaling hat. See Document Nos. 18 and 19.

Plebian of the Nootka tribe. See Document Nos. 18 and 19.

Native woman
and child of the
Pacific Northwest Coast
showing labial distortion.

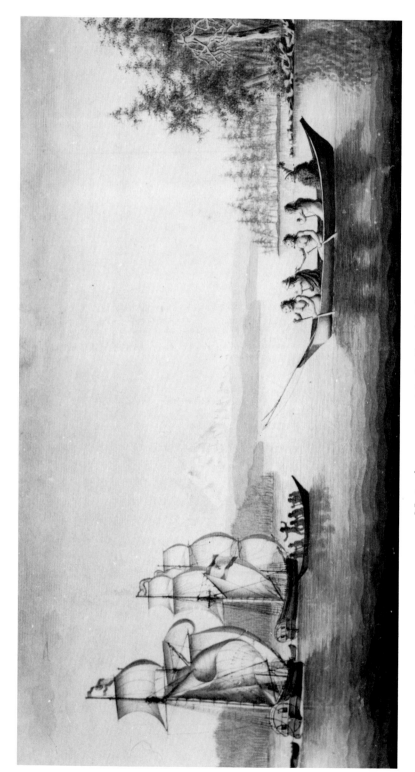

Native boats out to visit the Spanish sloops.

Indian canoes out to meet a Spanish longboat off Vancouver Island.
See Document Nos. 18 and 19.

Nootkan village.

ship made three miles an hour. This morning we saw two seagulls and several other little birds. At noon the sun was seen more clearly and the navigating officers took an observation in 46° 32'. In the afternoon the wind hauled to the southwest, and a great deal of water came from the fog so that it seemed a storm of rain. This continued all day and the night following. The afternoon was cold and the night more so, and they said that rain fell frozen.

The 12th dawned foggy and with dew, like the preceding days, but the cold was greater. The wind went to west-southwest about five in the morning, and the drizzling fog lasted until ten o'clock. At this hour the wind hauled to the west and blew somewhat stronger. This morning some ducks were seen. The navigating officers could not get an observation because the sky was very much overcast and the horizon obscure. In the afternoon the wind hauled to west-northwest and was very strong; there was a heavy sea and it was very cold. As this was a head wind, for since we began to sail northward, as we have done whenever the wind allowed, the course has been northwest ¼ west, and as fogs were continual, the ship's head was put to the north, in order to make land at a point farther to the northward. About three in the afternoon the weather cleared a little, and the sky remained rather clear all night, though the horizon was very much obscured.

At dawn on the 13th the wind continued at west-northwest, although it was not so strong, and the sky was as clear as during the night, but at seven o'clock it was overcast again. At noon it cleared, and the navigating officers got an observation in 48° 55', and said that this was more satisfactory than preceding observations because the horizon was more distinct. During the afternoon the sky became overcast again. About seven o'clock the wind hauled to the southwest, very fresh, and the course was changed to northwest. At that hour so thick a fog came on that barely the prow of the ship could be seen and it was so wet that it seemed to be raining. Thus it continued all night long.

At dawn on the 14th the same fog and dew were present, and the wind blew fresh from the west. About nine in the morning the Captain ordered the ship's head to be put to the northward, in order to get in with the land and determine whether in nearing the coast the sky would become clearer. At noon the navigating officers got an

Dia 14 amaneció con la nieblina y rocio dichos, y el viento fresco del O.; como a las 9 de la mañana mandó el señor capitan poner la proa al Norte, para recalar y ver si arrimandonos a la costa se halla despejado el cielo. Al medio dia observaron los señores pilotos (aunque no con seguridad por el mucho nublado) 50 grados y 24 minutos de latitud. Por la tarde se mantuvo fresco el viento y variable del O. al S. En este dia se reconoció la aguada y halló haber agua para dos meses y medio. Por la noche prosiguió dicho viento variable con mucha nieblina y rocio.

Dia 15 amaneció muy nublado, con mucho rocio y el viento del S. muy fresco. A las 9 de la mañana convocó el señor capitan a todos los oficiales del barco y habiendoles manifestado el estado de la aguada, les pidió su parecer sobre si convenia seguir en demanda de la altura de 60 grados que pide Su Excelencia, ó ir en busca de la tierra para reconocer si se halla proporcion de refrescar la aguada y con ella hacer la diligencia de subir a los 60 grados; todos fueron de sentir, que convenia recalar a tierra para surtirse de agua y al mismo tiempo tener parage conocido a donde recalar de arribada en caso de hacerse necesario por algun acaecimiento. Visto el parecer de los oficiales mandó el señor capitan governar al N. E.; en dicha hora se llamó el viento al S. O. bien fresco. Estos dos dias se ha caminado a cuatro y media millas por hora con mucha marejada y frio. Al medio dia observaron los señores pilotos 51 grados y 42 minutos. Por la tarde prosiguió el mismo viento aunque no tan fresco y el tiempo aclaró un poco.

Dia 16 amaneció nublado el cielo, pero no hubo nieblina ni rocio; el viento se mantuvo del S. O. y a las 9 aclaró muy bien el dia y quedó templado el tiempo. Este dia se hizo una cruz grande de madera con el fin de fijarla en tierra en señal de posesion cuando se verifique el primer desembarque. Al medio dia observaron los señores pilotos 52 grados y 41 minutos de latitud. Por la tarde se aflojo el viento y se mantuvo variable del S. al S. O. Esta tarde se vieron algunas ballenas y yerbas del mar que los marineros llaman porras, y se crian muchas en las costas de Monte-Rey ó cerca de ellas.

Dia 17 amaneció nublado el cielo, sin nieblina ni rocio y el viento casi en calma, pues no se caminaba a milla y media por hora. Digimos misa los dos padres. Como a las 7 vino la nieblina y cayó un aguacero corto, pero pasó luego, y el tiempo comenzó a levantar. Este dia no

observation in 50° 24', although not sure of it on account of a very cloudy sky. During the afternoon the wind was fresh and shifted about between west and south. Today an inspection of the water-supply was made, and it was found that there was sufficient for two months and a half. At night the same shifting wind continued, and there was a good deal of fog and dew.

The 15th dawned very cloudy: there was a heavy dew and the wind was very fresh from the south. At nine o'clock in the morning the Captain called a council of all the officers of the ship; and, having made known to them the condition of the watersupply, he asked their opinion as to whether it were better to go on to latitude sixty, as was exacted by His Excellency, or to make land for the purpose of endeavoring to renew the watersupply, afterwards going to 60°. All were of the opinion that it were better to make land, for the purpose of getting a supply of water and at the same time to gain the knowledge of some place where a refuge might be had in case some accident should make it necessary to seek one. In conformity with this opinion of the officers, the Captain ordered the ship's head to be put northeast. At that hour the wind hauled to southwest, and was very fresh. During the past two days the ship has sailed at the rate of four and a half miles an hour, with a heavy sea and great cold. At noon the navigating officers got an observation in 51° 42'. During the latter part of the day the wind held, though it was not so fresh, and the weather cleared a little.

At daylight on the 16th the sky was overcast, but there was neither fog nor dew. The wind was still in the southwest. At nine o'clock the day was clear and the weather moderate. Today a great wooden cross was made, with the intention of planting it on land in token of taking possession when the first landing shall take place. At noon the navigating officers got an observation in 52° 41'. During the afternoon the force of the wind lessened and it shifted about between south and southwest. This afternoon some whales were seen, and some seaweed, called *porras** by the sailors, which abounds along the coast at and near Monterey.

---

* *Porras*, frequently mentioned by Pacific Coast mariners, were seaweed, bulbous on one end and long and thin. A drawing is given in Ayensa, Diario, MS, 1796 in Museo Naval (201). The reference is apparently to the Spanish breakfast dish of *porras*, which is somewhat similar to American doughnuts, but is long and thin. It is eaten hot, having been cooked in oil. The Pacific Coast variety of *porras* is kelp.

hubo frio. Al medio dia ya estaba despejado el cielo y el sol calentó muy bien: observaron los señores pilotos 53 grados y 13 minutos de latitud. Por la tarde prosiguió la misma bonanza de tiempo con algunas ventolinas del S. O. y vimos algunas ballenas. La noche quedó buena y clara sin rocio.

Dia 18 a las 5 de la mañana vino un chuvasco del S. E. con alguna agua y prosiguió con ventolinas y nieblina muy humedas. Esta mañana se sangró el piloto Don Esteban por causa de una inflamacion en la cara. Como a las diez entró un poco de viento del N. O. pero muy variable y flojo. A las 11 divisamos tierra por la proa que es al N. E. Bendito sea Dios alabado de todas las criaturas. No se pudo observar este dia por no haberse descubierto el sol. A las dos reparamos que la tierra vista al N. E. estaba nevada no solo en la cumbre de la sierra sino tambien en las faldas. Mas al N. se miraban otras tierras sin nieve. Cuando divisamos la tierra que seria a distancia de veinte leguas poco mas ó menos, mandó el señor capitan poner la proa al N. N. E.; el viento se mantuvo flojo y caminabamos a milla y media por hora. Esta tarde se volvió a sangrar D. Esteban. A las 5 se llamó el viento al O. N. O. y se caminaba a dos millas, pero luego se escaseó. Al ponerse el sol demarcaron la tierra y la sierra nevada demoraba al E. N. E. y la punta de tierra mas al N. que parece cabo al N. N. E. Por la noche hubo algunas ventolinas del O. N. O., pero lo mas de ella se pasó en calma; el cielo quedó nublado pero no cayó rocio.

Dia 19 amaneció en calma, el cielo nublado, pero los orizontes claros. Como a las 7 de esta mañana se ofuscaron los orizontes con nieblina. D. Esteban se sacó una muela por no haber tenido alivio con las sangrias: a las 11 entró un poco de viento del S. E. muy lento y se puso la proa al N. ¼ al N. E. para montar el cabo de tierra que demoraba al N. E. y ver a donde corre la costa mas arriba de dicho cabo, pues al N. de ál no se vé mas tierra. Al medio dia observó el señor capitan 53 grados y 41 minutos de latitud; el viento fué refrescando muy bien y hallandonos a distancia de tres leguas de la punta de tierra mas al N. se reconoció que desde dicha punta corre al N. N. O. la costa de tierra baja. Como a las 5 de la tarde se puso la proa al N. E. para arrimarnos a la falda de la sierra que demoraba a dicho rumbo y ver si habia paraje donde fondear. Como a las 6 estando ya muy fresco el viento comenzó a llover, por lo cual, y estar muy oscuro el tiempo por la nieblina y la noche muy proxima determinó el señor

The 17th began with a cloudy sky, but there was neither fog nor dew; there was scarcely any wind, the ship not making a mile and a half an hour. We two fathers celebrated the mass. About seven o'clock the fog came on and there was a light shower; it did not last long and the weather began to lighten. It was not cold today. At noon the sky was clear and the sun made it quite warm. The navigating officers took an observation in 53° 13′. The same fair weather continued during the afternoon, with light winds from the southwest; we saw some whales. The night was fine and clear and there was no dew.

At five on the morning of the 18th there was a squall from the southeast accompanied by rain and followed by light winds and a very wet fog. This morning navigating officer Don Esteban was bled for the purpose of alleviating an inflammation of the face. About ten o'clock a little wind came from the northwest, but it was very light and variable. At eleven land was descried on the bow, in the northeast. Blessed be God and let Him be praised by all creatures. No observation was taken today as the sun did not shine out. At two o'clock it was noticed that the land seen in the northeast was snowy, not only on the summits of the sierra but on the slopes. Farther towards the north more land was seen but it was not snowy. When we made out the land, which might be a little more or less than twenty leagues distant, the Captain ordered the ship's head to be put to the north-northeast. The wind remained light and we made a mile and a half an hour. This afternoon Don Esteban was bled again. At five o'clock the wind went around to west-northwest and we made two miles an hour, but this speed soon diminished. At sunset the bearings of the land were taken. The snowy range bore east-northeast; the point of land farthest north, which seemed to be a cape, bore north-northeast. During the night there were light winds from the west-northwest, but most of the time there was a calm. The sky was overcast, but no dew fell.

The 19th dawned calm; the sky was overcast but the horizon was clear. About seven o'clock in the morning the horizon was obscured by fog. As bleeding had brought no relief to Don Esteban, he had a tooth pulled. At eleven a very light breeze from the southeast sprang up, and the ship was headed north ¼ northeast for the purpose of doubling the cape which bore northeast and determining the trend of the coast beyond it, for to the northward of that cape no land was seen. At midday the Captain took an observation in 53° 41′. The

capitan hacernos un poco afuera y ponernos a la capa como se hizo a las 7 de la tarde y asi pasamos la noche; la nieblina prosiguió con bastante agua.

Dia 20 habiendo amanecido se llamó el viento al E. S. E. y nos pusimos a camino con la proa al N. ¼ al N. E., la nieblina se mantuvo muy humeda y oscura; como a las 9 se puso la proa al E. N. E. para reconocer la tierra baja que se miraba al estremo de la punta, y a las diez desde el tope conocieron que eran tres islas chicas y proximas a la tierra. A estas islas llamó el señor capitan las islas de Santa Margarita, por ser dia de la gloriosa señora. No se pudo observar este dia por la mucha nieblina que todo el dia estuvo arrojando agua. Como a las tres de la tarde estabamos cerca de la tierra (que habia parecido islas y no se pudo asegurar lo fuesen por lo poco que la nieblina dejaba estender la vista con ser que estabamos como tres leguas de ella) y se biró de bordo para fuera con animo de mantenernos bordeando sobre la tierra para en aclarando el tiempo registrar fondeadero y hacer la aguada. En dicha hora vimos humaderas en tierra y luego se vió venir una canoa con 9 hombres dentro: esta se acercó a nuestro barco cantando los gentiles pero no quisieron arrimarse de modo que le pudiesemos hablar por señas, y habiendonos seguido un buen rato se volvieron para tierra. Como a las 5 vino en nuestro seguimiento, dicha canoa juntamente con otra en que venian 6 gentiles y habiendonos alcanzado se arrimaron las dos a nuestra popa, y el señor capitan les regaló algunas sartas de abalorios y ellos dieron pescado seco, pero no quisieron subir a bordo. Son gente bien dispuesta, blancos, con pelo largo, cubiertos de pieles y gamuzas y algunos son bordados. En sus canoas traian algunos hierros, pero no pudimos averiguar de donde los han habido porque luego se retiraron a su tierra convidandonos con ella y ofrecieron darnos agua al dia siguiente. Como a las 6 llegó otra canoa con 7 gentiles, y se arrimaron con el mismo canto que los primeros; estos nos siguieron como una hora sin querer subir a bordo y cuando se volvieron a su tierra estabamos ya apartados de ella como ocho leguas y bastante marejada. Las canoas son como las que tienen en la canal de Santa Barbara, pero de mayor cavidad. Esta tarde corrió el viento S. E. y a las diez de la noche se calmó.

Dia 21 como a las 12 de la noche comenzó a ventear el S. E. muy fresco, y se prosiguió para fuera con la proa al S. O. ¼ al S. A las 8 de la mañana se viró de bordo para tierra con la proa al E. ¼ al N. E.

wind freshened considerably; and, when we were three leagues from the point of land farthest to the northward, it was noted that beyond that point a low coast stretches to the north-northwest. About five in the afternoon the course was altered to northeast, so that we might draw near to the shore of the land lying in that direction and see whether there were any place to anchor. About six, the wind being very fresh, it began to rain, on which account and because the weather was obscure by reason of the fog and night was coming on, the Captain determined to go a little farther off the land and lie to. This was done at seven o'clock; and thus the night passed, the fog continuing with a good deal of water.

After dawn, on the 20th, the wind came from east-southeast, and the ship's head was put on a course north ¼ northeast, the fog continuing very dense and wet. About nine o'clock the course was altered to east-northeast, that we might examine the low land that showed at the end of the point. At ten o'clock it was noted from the masthead that it consisted of three small islands which were near to the mainland. These the Captain named the Islands of Santa Margarita,* this being the day of that glorious lady. It was impossible to get an observation today on account of the heavy fog and drizzle. About three in the afternoon we were near the land which had appeared to consist of islands, although this could not be verified because the fog so limited the view when we were about three leagues away, and we went about and stood off shore with the intention of continuing tacking along the land, so that when the weather cleared we might find anchorage ground and take in a supply of water. At that hour we saw bonfires on the land, and presently there came to us a canoe with nine men in it. This canoe drew near to the vessel, the pagans in it singing; but they would not come near enough for us to communicate by means of signs. Having followed us for some time, they returned to the land. About five o'clock this canoe, and another in which there were six pagans, caught up with us, both drawing up to our stern. The Captain made them a present of some strings of beads and they gave us some dried fish. But they would not come on board the ship. These persons are well-built, white, with long hair; and they were clothed in pelts and skins, some of them were bearded. They had some iron imple-

* Santa Margarita is identified by Bancroft, *History of the Northwest Coast*, Vol. I, 153–54, as Cape North of Queen Charlotte Island.

Esta mañana hubo mucha nieblina. No pudieron observar los señores pilotos por estar nublado el cielo. Como a las 12 del dia llegamos sobre la punta de tierra del N. de Santa Margarita a distancia de un cuarto de legua y la fuimos costeando hacia al E. como media legua con animo de registrar si tras de una punta al E. en donde parece hace recodo habia fondeadero, pero no se pudo montar esta punta porque las corrientes nos rechazaban al S., por lo cual se viró de bordo y habiendonos apartado como una legua al S. O. de la tierra se calmó el viento que toda la mañana habia soplado muy fuerte y habia levantado grande marejada. Como a las dos y media de la tarde comenzaron a venir canoas de gentiles, unas mayores que otras; las mayores tendran de largo doce ó trece varas, y al parecer son de una pieza, escepto un cerco de tablas por arriba, y la proa. En dichas canoas vinieron como doscientas almas; en una se contaron veinte y una personas, en otra diez y nueve, en las demas habia a cinco, a siete, a doce y a quince almas. Vino una canoa con doce ó trece mugeres sin hombre alguno; en las otras habia tambien algunas mugeres, pero el mayor numero era de hombres. Al tiempo de llegarse a nuestro barco la canoa de mugeres sucedió que esta topando con su proa en la de otra canoa de hombres se la quebró, de lo que se enfadaron mucho los hombres, y uno de ellos cojiendo en sus manos la proa de la canoa de las mugeres se la hizo pedazos, para vengarse del descuido de ellas. Toda la tarde se estuvieron las canoas que eran veinte y una entre todas, al rededor de nuestro barco, comerciando con los de abordo para lo cual traian gran prevencion de petates, pieles de diversas especies de animales y peces, sombreros de junco, gorras, de pieles, plumages con varias figuras y sobre todo muchas colchas, ó tejidos de lana muy bordados como de vara y media en cuadro con sus flecos de la misma lana al rededor y varios labores de distintos colores. De todo compraron los nuestros por ropa, cuchillos y abalorios, varias piezas. Se conoció que tienen mucha aficion al comercio y que lo que mas apetecian eran cosas de hierro, pero querian piezas grandes y de corte, como espadas, machetes, &c., pues mostrandoles velduques daban a entender que eran chicos, y ofreciendoles aros de barril, que no tenia corte. Subieron a bordo dos gentiles, y les cuadró mucho nuestro barco y las cosas de él. Las mugeres tienen taladrado el labio inferior y en él pendiente una rodeta plana que no pudimos saber que cosa era, ni de que materia. Su vestido es una esclavina con fleco al rededor y una

ments in their canoes, but we were unable to inquire where they obtained them, for presently they went back to land, inviting us thither, and offering to give us water on the following day. About six o'clock there arrived another canoe with seven pagans, who drew near, singing the same air the others had sung. These followed us for about an hour without being willing to come aboard the ship. When at length they went back to land we were about eight leagues from it, and there was a high sea on. These canoes resemble those used in Santa Barbara Channel, but are of greater burden. This afternoon the wind was in the southeast, and at ten o'clock it died away entirely.

Shortly after midnight, it being the 21st, it began to blow very fresh from the southeast, and the ship stood off shore with her head to the southwest ¼ south. At eight in the morning we went about toward the land on a course east ¼ northeast. This morning there was a dense fog. The navigating officers could not take an observation, for the sky was overcast. About noon we made the point of land to the northward of Santa Margarita, a quarter of a league away, and we coasted along it to the eastward for about half a league with intent to discover whether there were an anchorage behind a point to the eastward where there seemed to be an indentation in the coast line. But we could not double this point, for the current carried us to the southward. For this reason we went about, and, after we had sailed about a league to the southwestward, the wind, which all the morning had blown with much force and had raised a heavy sea, died away. About half past two, canoes, some larger than others, all full of pagans, began to arrive. The larger canoes were twelve or thirteen yards in length, and appeared to be of a single piece, excepting that there was planking along the sides and at the bow. In these canoes were some two hundred persons; in one there were counted twenty-one, in another nineteen, while in the others were five, seven, twelve and fifteen. One canoe contained twelve or thirteen women and no men. In others, also, there were women but the majority consisted of men. At the time the women's canoe arrived at the ship it happened that its prow struck that of another canoe whose occupants were men and broke it; at this the men became very angry, and one of them, seizing the prow of the women's canoe, broke it to pieces in order to repay their carelessness. All the afternoon these canoes, twenty-one in all, were about the ship, their occupants trading with the ship's people,

ropa talar de sus tejidos de lana, ó de pieles que las cubre todo el cuerpo; tienen pelo largo y hecho trenza a las espaldas, son blancas y rubias como cualquiera española; pero las afea la rodeta que tienen en el labio y cuelga hasta la barba. Los hombres andan tambien cubiertos ya de pieles, ya de tejidos de lana, y muchos con esclavinas como las mugeres; pero no reparan en quedarse desnudos cuando ven ocacion de vender su vestido. A las seis se fueron despidiendo las canoas para su tierra y demonstraron que deseaban el que fuesemos a ella. Algunos marineros saltaron a las canoas y los gentiles los embijaron con mucha algazara y contento. Dieron a entender estos gentiles que no pasasemos al Norte porque era mala gente que flechaban y mataban; (cuento comun entre gentiles decir que todos son malos menos ellos). Toda la tarde duró la calma y las corrientes nos apartaron mas de la tierra como dos leguas.

Dia 22 como a las dos de la madrugada comenzó a ventear el S. E. muy lento y a las 5 distariamos de la tierra como cuatro leguas, y la teniamos al E. S. E., y una isla que ayer se demarcó al N. O. ¼ O. a distancia de 8 ó diez leguas se miraba al N., y otra tierra alta demarcada ayer al N. ¼ al N. O. que no se supo si era isla demoraba al N. Caminamos sobre la tierra con la proa al E. ¼ al N. E. para ver si se podia montar la punta al E. de Santa Margarita y registrar si hay fondeadero en el recodo que hace tras de dicha punta; pero por lo mucho que las corrientes nos sotaventaban no se pudo llegar a dicha punta y asi dimos bordo para fuera con la proa at S. S. O. Al medio dia dijo el señor capitan que habia observado al sol en 55 grados de latitud; como a la una se viró de bordo para tierra y a las tres y media se llamó el viento al E. S. E. y se viro para fuera con la proa al S. pero luego se llamó otra vez el viento al S. E. y se puso la proa al S. S. O. Toda esta tarde se mantuvo dicho viento fresco con muchisima nieblina, tan espesa que parecia de noche y tan humeda que parecia aguacero de temporal y grande marejada. Con motivo de ser el viento contrario, la nieblina tan espesa y humeda, la marejada tan grande y las corrientes que nos sotaventaban sobre la tierra alta que está al Norte de la punta de Santa Margarita, caminamos toda la tarde y noche para fuera y perdimos de vista la punta de Santa Margarita.

---

[6] Of course these Indians had no woolen stuffs. It is not probable that any of the natives seen during the voyage possessed any implements or weapons of iron or copper. The men were certainly not white; nor the women as fair and rosy as Spanish women.

for which purpose they had brought a great quantity of mats, skins of various kinds of animals and fish, hats made of rushes and caps made of skins, bunches of feathers arranged in various shapes, and, above all, many coverlets, or pieces of woven woolen stuffs very elaborately embroidered and about a yard and a half square, with a fringe of the same wool about the edges and various figures embroidered in different colors. Our people bought several of all these articles, in return for clothing, knives and beads. It was apparent that what they liked most were things made of iron; but they wanted large pieces with a cutting edge, such as swords, wood-knives and the like—for, on being shown ribands they intimated that these were of trifling value, and, when offered barrel hoops, they signified that these had no edge. Two of the pagans came aboard the ship, and were much pleased with the vessel and things on board of it. The women have the lower lip pierced, and pendent therefrom a flat round disk; we were unable to learn the significance of this, nor of what material the disk was made. Their dress consists of a cape with a fringe about the edge and a cloth reaching to the feet, made of their woven woolen stuff, or of skins, and covering the whole body. Their hair is long and falls in braids to the shoulder. They are as fair and rosy as any Spanish woman, but are rendered ugly by the disk they have in the lip, which hangs to the chin. The men also are covered, with the skins or with the woven cloths of wool, and many have capes like those of the women; but they do not hesitate about remaining naked when occasion for selling their clothing offers. At six o'clock, taking leave of us, they made for the land, and they made evident their desire that we should go thither. Some sailors went down into the canoes and the pagans painted their faces with delight and shouts of joy. These pagans gave us to understand that we should not pass on to the northward because the people there were bad and shot arrows and killed.[6] How common it is for pagans to say that all are bad except themselves! The calm lasted all the afternoon and the current took us about two leagues farther from the land.

About two o'clock in the morning of the 22d a very light wind set in from the southeast, and at five we were at a distance of about four leagues from the land, which bore east-southeast, and an island which yesterday bore northwest ¼ west, distant about eight or ten leagues, now bore north, and high land which yesterday bore north ¼ north-

Advierto que toda la tierra de Santa Margarita y la demas al Este, está tan poblada de arboleda que no se mira parte alguna que no sea bosque muy tupido de maderage alto y nos pareció ser cipreses. En las canoas de los gentiles vieron los nuestros palos de pino, de cipres, de fresno y aya, aunque yo no vi mas que de cipres y de pino.

Dia 23 amaneció con el mismo viento, nieblina, agua y marejada que ayer y se prosiguió para fuera con la misma proa caminando solamente a milla por hora, (estando con demasiada fuerza el viento) por la mucha marejada que nos venia por proa. Antes de medio dia se llamó el viento al E. S. E. y se caminó todo el dia al S. a tres millas y a dos y media por hora. No se pudo observar por no haberse visto el sol en todo el dia. Por la tarde prosiguió llovisnando con bastante frio; viendo el tiempo tan malo y los vientos contrarios para vajar, determinamos hacer una novena al Señor San Juan Nepomuceno, que se comenzó este dia y otra a la Señora Santa Clara que se comenzará dia 4 del proximo Agosto (dandonos Dios vida) para alcanzar de Su Magestad Santisima por la intercesion de dichos santos la mejoria de tiempo que necesitamos. Advierto que el señor capitan nos dijo este dia que la isla demarcada al N. O. ¼ al O. dia veinte y uno estando sobre la punta de Santa Margarita se llama isla de Santa Cristina, y la otra tierra alta demarcada al N. ¼ l N. O. se llama el cabo de Santa Maria Magdalena. Este cabo está al N. O. de la punta de Santa Margarita y entre él y dicha punta hace a la parte del E. una como ensenada muy grande que no pudimos conocer, (porque las corrientes nos rechazaban como tengo dicho) si es golfo, estrecho ó bahia con desemboque de algun caudaloso rio como imagina el señor capitan. El dicho cabo de Santa Maria Magdalena dista 10 leguas de la punta de Santa Margarita y esto es lo que tiene de ancho la boca ó entrada de dicha ensenada ó golfo. El cabo de Santa Maria Magdalena sale para fuera del E. al O. y junto a la punta que hace al O. está la isla de Santa Cristina, la cual nos pareció ser chica y apartada de tierra como dos leguas; esta noche a las once comenzó a ventear el S. O.

Dia 24 amaneció algo claro y el viento fresco del S. O. Desde las 11 de la noche antecedente hasta las 5 de esta mañana caminamos al S. E. A las 5 se puso la proa al E. S. E. para recalar a tierra. Este dije yo misa y el padre Fray Juan no la dijo porque antes de comenzarla se vió venir un chuvasco y cayeron algunas gotas de agua y refrescó mas el viento. Este dia observaron los señores pilotos 53 grados y 48 minutos

west, and which we thought might be an island, bore north. We stood for the land on an east ¼ northeast course, for the purpose of trying to double the point lying to the eastward of Santa Margarita, in order to discover whether there were anchorage ground in the indentation of the coast behind that point, but the current took us so far to leeward that we were unable to reach the point; so we stood off shore on a south-southwest course. At noon the Captain said that he had taken an observation of the sun in 55°. About one we went about and stood toward the land. At half-past three the wind hauled to east-southeast and we went seaward on a course due south, but presently the wind shifted back to the southeast and the course was altered to south-southwest. All this afternoon this wind blew fresh and there was a heavy fog, so thick that it seemed night and so wet that it was like a rainstorm, and there was a great deal of sea on. As there was a head wind, together with a dense and wet fog and a heavy sea, and as the current was carrying us to leeward upon the high land to the north-ward of Point Santa Margarita, all the afternoon and during the night we stood out to sea and lost sight of Point Santa Margarita. I note that all the land of Santa Margarita, as well as that to the eastward of it, is so thickly covered with forest that no part of it can be seen which is not clothed with a very thick growth of tall timber, the trees appearing to be cypresses. In the canoes of the pagans our people saw pine, cypress, ash and beech wood although I noticed only some cypress and some pine.

The same wind held at daybreak on the 23d; also yesterday's fog and the heavy sea. We continued to stand out to sea on the same course, making only a mile an hour, the wind being too fresh on account of the heavy head sea. Before noon the wind hauled to east-southeast and all day we stood due south, at the rate of two and a half or three miles an hour. No observation for latitude could be taken as the sun was not seen during the whole day. During the afternoon the drizzling rain continued to fall and it was quite cold. Seeing that the weather was so bad and the wind so contrary for running down the coast, we determined on a novena to San Juan Nepomuceno, to commence today, and another to Santa Clara, to commence on the 4th of August (God giving us life), in order to obtain from the Most Holy Majesty, through the intercession of these saints, that bettering of the weather which we need. I note that today

de latitud. Por la tarde aflojó el viento y por la noche se calmó. Al ponerse el sol se divisó tierra y nos pareció ser la primera que vimos en la recalada dia 18 del presente. A las 11 de la noche se vieron en el cielo a la parte del Norte y N. E. unos resplandores muy luminosos.

Dia 25 amaneció en calma y el cielo muy claro y despejado. A las 6 comenzó a ventolear muy lento del E. Digimos misa ambos padres y le administré por viatico el Santisimo a un marinero enfermo. Como el viento era de tierra la cual se miraba al E. no pudimos ir en demanda de ella, que distaria de nosotros como doce leguas y se puso la proa al S. ¼ al S. E. Al medio dia observaron los señores pilotos 53 grados y 21 minutos de latitud. Como a la una de la tarde se llamó el viento al N. E. muy lento y con la proa al S. E. ¼ al E. caminabamos a milla por hora: esta tarde se vió bien clara la costa y la sierra nevada; al pie de esta se vé una tierra alta que hace cuchilla en la cumbre tendida del E. al O. y a la parte del O. hace la tierra un mogote redondo como un horno y parece ser islote; aunque no se pudo conocer, si lo es, como tampoco si la dicha tierra alta es continente con la falda de la sierra nevada, ó isla apartada de ella. Al N. O. de esta tierra alta, y mogote con figura de horno parece que hace ensenada. Esta tarde como a las 7 murió un grumete llamado Salvador Antonio, natural y casado en el pueblo de Gaynamota. Como a las 6 comenzó a cargar la nieblina, y a llovisnar. A las 9 se llamó el viento al N. E. ¼ al E. y comenzó a llover con mucha fuerza especialmente hasta las 11, y toda la noche prosiguió lloviendo con el mismo viento.

Dia 26 amaneció llovisnando con mucha nieblina; a las 4 de la mañana comenzó a ventear al S. S. E. y caminamos con la proa al O. S. O. hasta las 6 y media que se viró para tierra con la proa al E. Dige misa y enterré al grumete que murió ayer: el padre Fray Juan no dijo misa por el mal tiempo que sobrevino de aguaceros con tanto viento y marejada que no podiamos mantenernos en pié; a las diez se viró para fuera con la proa al O. S. O. por estar el tiempo tan malo para arrimarnos a tierra asi por el mucho viento como por la marejada y oscuridad del dia que todo él estuvo lloviendo con mucha fuerza; no se pudo observar; por la tarde se arreció mas el viento y se mantuvo

---

[7] Mr. Bancroft's writer says, (*History of the Pacific States*, XXVII, 154) that Father Crespi says Pérez named this island Santa *Catalina*. A reference to the diary of Father Crespi, which is Document No. 19, will show that, among his notes of the 21st July, he also says that the island was named Santa *Cristina*.

the Captain told us the island which bore northwest ¼ west on the twenty-first instant, lying off Point Santa Margarita, is called the Island of Santa Cristina,[7]* and the other high land bearing north ¼ northwest is called Cape Santa María Magdalena.† This cape is to the northwestward of Point Santa Margarita; and, between it and said point, to the eastward is what appeared to be a large gulf. The current drifting us away, as I have noted, we were unable to know whether this were gulf, strait, or bay into which some great river discharges, as the Captain fancies. This Cape Santa María Magdalena is distant ten leagues from Point Santa Margarita, and this also is the width of the mouth of, or entrance to, said bay or gulf. Cape Santa María Magdalena stretches out from east to west, and close to its western extremity is the Island of Santa Cristina, which seemed to us to be small and to lie about two leagues from the mainland. Tonight, at eleven o'clock, the wind began to blow from the southwest.

The dawn of the 24th was rather clear and the wind was fresh from the southwest. From eleven o'clock last night until five this morning our course had been to the southeast. At five it was altered to east-southeast, that we might draw in with the land. Today I celebrated the mass; Father Fray Juan did not because just before it began a squall came upon us, some drops of rain fell and the wind freshened. Today the navigating officers obtained an observation in 53° 48′. During the afternoon the wind died away; to a dead calm during the night. At sundown land was seen, and it seemed to us to be that which we saw first as we approached the coast on the eighteenth instant. At eleven at night there was an appearance in the sky, in the north and the northeast, of some very brilliant northern lights.

The 25th dawned calm, the sky being very clear and cloudless. At six o'clock a light breeze sprang up from the east. Both fathers celebrated mass, and I administered the most holy sacrament to a sick sailor. As the wind blew off shore, the land being in sight to the eastward, about twelve leagues away, we could not sail toward it, and our course was south ¼ southeast. At noon the navigating officers obtained an observation in 53° 21′. About one in the afternoon the wind shifted to northeast and was very light; we sailed at the rate of

* The Island of Santa Cristina was Forrester Island, *Ibid.*, Vol. I, 154.

† Cape Santa María Magdelena was Point Muzon, Prince of Wales Island, *Ibid.*, Vol. I, 154.

variable del S. E. al S. S. O., pero siempre lloviendo; por la noche se llamó el viento al S. O. y se puso la proa al S. S. E.

Dia 27 amaneció oscuro el cielo y lloviendo como el dia antecedente con grande marejada; el viento del S. O., pero no tan fresco; a las 8 de la mañana cesó la lluvia, y desde las 10 comenzó a aclarar el tiempo y mitigarse el viento. Al medio dia observaron los señores pilotos 52 grados y 59 minutos de latitud; por la tarde hizo buen sol y el viento se mantuvo flojo hasta la noche que se quedó en calma.

Dia 28 amaneció en calma y el tiempo claro, se miraba bien la tierra a distancia como de 8 leguas; es la tierra alta con muchos cerros tajados a la mar: como a las 7 comenzó a ventolear del S. y nublarse el cielo, pero el viento se calmó luego y el cielo se despejó algo al medio dia con lo cual pudieron observar los señores pilotos y segun dijeron nos hallamos en 52 grados y 41 minutos: tambien demarcaron la costa y lo mas al N. de ella demoraba al N. N. O. y lo mas al S. demoraba al E. S. E. Esta costa desde los 54 grados hasta aqui corre del N. O. al S. E. y toda es tierra muy alta. A esta tierra llamó el señor capitan la sierra de San Cristoval, y está nevada no solo en el cerro que está en los 53 grados de latitud, sino tambien en otros varios mas al S. Por la tarde como a las 3 comenzó a soplar muy lento el S. S. O., luego se fué llamando al S. O. y se puso la proa al S. S. E. pero fué tan lento el viento que se navegaba a milla por hora y varios ratos se calmaba totalmente asi por la tarde como por la noche siguiente que se mantuvo dicho viento; el tiempo se mantuvo esta tarde y noche sin llover con mucho nublado y algun frio.

Dia 29 amaneció nublado el cielo pero sin nieblina y asi se veia bien la costa que tambien distaría como 8 leguas y es tierra muy alta y quebrada, en la cumbre tiene muchos picachos que hacen diversas figuras, como lo demas de la sierra de San Cristobal. En toda la costa desde Santa Margarita en los 55 hasta aqui no se ha podido reconocer si hay puertos, ensenadas, bahias, rios, &c., asi por lo apartado que hemos navegado como por los muchos nublados de los mas dias que han ofuscado los orizontes y playage; esta mañana continuó el S. O. con la misma lentitud é intervalos que ayer; como a las 11 se llamó el viento al S. S. E. y se viró de bordo para fuera con la proa al S. O. ¼ al O. No se pudo observar este dia por lo mucho nublado que estuvo el cielo; por la tarde se quedó causi calmado el viento y a anochecer se calmó totalmente y duró la calma toda la noche.

a mile an hour on a course southeast ¼ east. This afternoon the coast and the snowy range were very clearly visible. At the foot of this range appears a high land with a knife-like summit and stretching from east to west. At its western extremity there is an insular round rock with a flat top, resembling an oven, which seems to be an island, although we could not discover whether it is or not. Nor could we make out whether the high land referred to joins the slope of the snowy range or whether it is an island separated from it. To the northwestward of this high land and the insular, oven-like rock there appears to be a bay. About seven o'clock this evening a ship's boy named Salvador Antonio, a native of Gaynamota* and married there, died. About six o'clock the fog began to thicken and it began to drizzle. At nine the wind hauled to northeast ¼ east, and it began to rain very heavily, especially so until eleven, and all night it continued raining with the same wind.

At dawn on the 26th it was drizzling, and there was a heavy fog. At four in the morning it began to blow from the south-southeast, and the course was west-southwest until half past six, when we went about for the land with the ship's head due east. I celebrated the mass and the funeral service over the ship's boy who died yesterday. Father Fray Juan did not celebrate the mass on account of the bad weather, for there were showers of rain accompanied by a high wind and a sea so heavy that we could not keep our feet. At ten we went about and stood off shore with the ship's head to west-southwest, the weather being too bad for us to draw near to the land, for the wind was very high, a heavy sea was running and the day very dark, as it rained heavily all the time. It was impossible to get an observation. During the afternoon the wind went on increasing and shifted about from southeast to south-southwest; and it rained continuously. During the night the wind hauled to the southwest, and the course was south-southeast.

At dawn on the 27th the sky was overcast, it was raining as it had rained the day before and a high sea was running. The wind was from the southwest, but not so fresh. At eight in the morning it stopped raining, and after ten o'clock the weather began to clear and the

---

* Gaynamota, Guainamota in Crespi, or Guayamota on contemporary maps, is today Huaynamota on the river of the same name in Nayarit, Mexico. It was a settlement that dated from the early conquest.

Dia 30 por la mañana hubo algunas ventolinas del E. S. E. y con ellas nos apartamos mas de la tierra con la proa al S.; como a las 8 se llamó el viento al S. S. E. muy lento y variable y se puso la proa al S. O. ¼ al S., luego se fué llamando al S. y cada vez mas fresco; a las 12 se viró de bordo con la proa al E. S. E., y a la una habiendose vuelto el viento al S. E. se viró con la proa para fuera al S. O. ¼ al S. y se caminaba tres millas por hora. Este dia no pudieron observar los señores pilotos por estar nublado el cielo; por la tarde se arreció mucho el viento con grande marejada y antes de anochecer fué preciso aferrar el velacho para que no se viniese abajo el mastelero, se quebrase el trinquete con las grandes cabezadas que daba el barco; luego que anocheció comenzó a llover y duró la agua toda la noche: a las 12 aferraron la gavia, porque el viento iba tomando fuerza y nos quedamos con las dos mayores: todos pasamos mala noche por lo mucho que se valanceaba el barco: el viento a prima noche se llamó al E. S. E. y de la media noche abajo se volvió al S. E. y S. S. E.

Dia 31 amaneció lloviendo y el tiempo muy cerrado aunque el viento no estaba ya tan fuerte. No pudimos decir misa por estar malo el tiempo y haber mucha marejada y valances. Como a las 8 y media marearon las gavias habiendose mejorado algo el tiempo y cesado la agua; el viento se mantuvo del toda la noche y mañana y se caminó con la proa al S. O. ¼ al O.: como a las 10 volvió a tomar mayor fuerza el viento y a cerrarse mas el tiempo con amenazas de agua, pero no llovió. A las 12 se aclaró un poco y observaron los señores pilotos 51 grados, y 58 minutos de latitud. Por la tarde prosiguió el mismo viento muy fuerte y el cielo muy cerrado y oscuro; como a las 7 cayeron algunas gotas de agua muy gruesas y frias pero luego cesaron.

AGOSTO DE 1774

Dia 1 a la una de la madrugada habiendose llamado el viento al S. O. viraron de bordo para tierra y con la proa al S. S. E., se caminaba a cuatro millas por hora; como a las 7 de la mañana se llamó el viento al S. S. O. siempre muy fresco y se puso la proa al S. E. A las 8 aclaró el cielo y se dejó ver el sol; como a las 10 se llamó el viento al O. S. O. no tan fuerte como por la mañana ni tan frio; al medio dia observaron los señores pilotos el sol en 51 grados y 35 minutos de latitud al N. Por la tarde prosiguió dicho viento algo mas fresco y lento, y se caminó al mismo rumbo a tres millas por hora; como a las 7 se llamó el viento

wind to go down. At noon the navigating officers got an observation in 52° 59'. In the afternoon the sun shone clear, and the wind was light until nightfall, when it was calm.

The 28th dawned calm, with fair weather. The land was plainly visible at a distance of about eight leagues; it is high land, with many hills all running downward towards the sea. About seven o'clock the wind began to blow from the south and the sky to become overcast; but the wind soon died away and the sky cleared—so that at midday the navigating officers could get an observation. According to what they said, we were in 52° 41'. They took the bearings of the land also. The more northerly part bore north-northwest; the more southerly, east-southeast. The coast, from the fifty-fourth degree to this point, trends northwest and southeast, and the land is all very high. The Captain named this land Sierra of San Cristóbal;* and it is snowy, not only the hill in 53° but several others more to the southward. About three in the afternoon the wind began to blow very gently from the south-southwest, presently hauling to the southwest, and the course was made south-southeast. But the wind was so light that we made only a mile an hour, and it died away entirely at times during the afternoon and the following night. During this time there was no rain, but it was cloudy and rather cold.

At daybreak on the 29th the sky was overcast; but there was no fog, and the coast was seen plainly. It was about eight leagues distant, and the land is very high and broken. Along the summit are many peaks of different figures, as is the case in the rest of the Sierra of San Cristóbal. On the whole coast, from Santa Margarita in 55° to this place, we have not been able to discover whether there are any harbors, gulfs, bays, rivers, and the like, as well on account of the distance from it which we have kept, as because most of the time it has been cloudy and the horizon and the shore line have been obscured. This morning the wind came from the southwest, with the same gentleness and intervals of calm as yesterday. About eleven o'clock the wind hauled to south-southeast, and we went about and stood out to sea on a southwest ¼ west course. No observation was possible because of the very cloudy sky. During the afternoon it was almost calm, and by nightfall the wind died away entirely. The calm lasted all night.

* Sierra de San Cristóbal is identified as Queen Charlotte Island by Bancroft, *History of the Northwest Coast*, Vol. I, 154–55.

al O. el cual duró toda la noche y se prosiguió navegando al S. S. E. a tres millas por hora; la noche estuvo muy clara y despejado el cielo. Dia 2 como a las cuatro y media de la mañana se llamó el viento al O. N. O. y se puso la proa al S. E. para recalar a tierra; esta mañana aunque no era muy fuerte el viento por ser cuasi en popa y la marejada favorable, caminabamos a tres millas por hora. Al medio dia observaron los señores pilotos y dijeron que nos hallabamos en 50 grados y 20 minutos de latitud: en dicha hora mandó el señor capitan governar al E. ¼ al S. E. para caer a tierra sin perder tanta altura; por la tarde prosiguió el mismo viento hasta las 6 que se llamó al O.; por la noche cargó mucha nieblina y rocio, esta noche se governó al mismo rumbo hasta las 12.

Dia 3 desde las 12 a las 4 se governó al S. E. ¼ al E. por medio de la costa que por estar tan oscura la nieblina no se podia ver si estaba cerca; a las 4 se puso otra vez la proa al E. ¼ al S. E., el viento se mantuvo fresco del O. hasta las 8 que se llamó al N. O. (viento que ya mucho tiempo se deseaba y no se habia logrado ni una hora). La nieblina duró toda la mañana, por lo cual no pudimos divisar la costa. Al medio dia observaron los señores pilotos el sol en 49 grados y 24 minutos de latitud; desde las 12 de este dia por mandado del señor capitan se governó al E. para recalar a tierra y reconocer la costa, en caso de levantarse la nieblina; pues segun sus cuentas debemos estar muy cerca de ella; a las 3 de la tarde viendo que la nieblina no aclaraba y que el viento iba refrescando mandó dicho señor capitan tomar rizos a las gavias y poner la proa al S. E. ¼ al S. hasta que Dios quiera darnos tiempo claro como se necesita para ir por la costa; a las 5 comenzó a levantarse la nieblina, y habiendo aclarado y no viendose la costa alargaron rizos a las gavias y marearon todo el velamen y pusieron la proa al E. para ver si antes de anochecer se descubria la tierra; el viento fué tomando cada vez mas fuerza y se caminaba a 5 millas por hora y lo demas del dia se habia caminado a 4 y a 4 y media. No pudimos divisar la costa por lo cual a las 9 se aferraron las velas y nos quedamos con solo el trinquete y asi andaban a dos millas y media por hora; a las 12 volvió a cerrarse la nieblina espesa.

Dia 4 a las 12 de la noche se puso el barco a la capa con la mayor y a las 4 habiendo amanecido con la nieblina muy densa se marearon las gavias y trinquete y nos pusimos a camino con la proa al E.; el viento se llamó al N. muy fresco y luego levantó mucha marejada; a las 8

During the morning of the 30th there were light winds from the east-southeast, and these took us farther away from the land, our course being south. About eight o'clock the wind went to south-southeast; it was light and variable and the ship's head was put to the southwest ¼ south. Presently the wind hauled to the southward and was fresher. At noon we went about and stood east-southeast. At one, the wind having gone back to southeast, we went about and stood out to sea on a southwest ¼ south course, making three miles an hour. The navigating officers could not get an observation as the sky was overcast. During the afternoon the force of the wind increased and there was a very high sea. Before night it was necessary to furl the fore-topsail, so that the topmast might not be carried away, or the foremast itself, by the heavy pitching of the ship. As the night came on it began to rain and it rained all night. At midnight the main-topsail was furled, for the wind increased in force, only the fore and main courses remaining set. The ship rolled so much that all passed a bad night. During the first quarter of the night the wind was east-southeast; after midnight it went back to southeast and south-southeast.

At dawn on the 31st it was raining and the weather was very thick, although the wind was not so strong. We could not celebrate the mass because the weather was so bad, and there was a heavy sea causing great rolling of the ship. About half past eight the topsails were set, as the weather was better and the rain had ceased. The wind held all night and continued this morning, and the course was southwest ¼ west. About ten o'clock the wind freshened again and the weather became worse; there was a threat of rain, but none fell. At noon it cleared a little, so that the navigating officers could get an observation in 51° 58′. During the afternoon the same wind blew very fresh, and the sky was very much overcast and dark. About seven some drops of rain fell; they were heavy and cold but soon ceased.

August, 1774

At one o'clock on the morning of the 1st, the wind having gone to southwest, we went about and stood in for the land, on a south-southwest course, the ship going four miles an hour. About seven in the morning the wind, which was still very strong, hauled to south-southwest, and the course was altered to southeast. At eight the sky

viendo que la nieblina no aclaraba y que el viento y mar iban en aumento se volvieron a aferrar las gavias y quedandonos con el trinquete se puso la proa al E. S. E. por no verse la costa, que se imagina muy cerca segun las cuentas de los señores pilotos. A las 11 comenzó a aclarar un poco el tiempo y no se divisó la tierra. A las 12 observaron los señores pilotos el sol en 48 grados y 52 minutos de latitud; a la una de la tarde habiendose aclarado bien el tiempo se marearon la mayor y gavias y con la proa al E. N. E. fuimos en demanda de la costa caminando a 4 millas por hora: esta tarde se llamó el viento al N. N. E. y sopló con tanta fuerza como al N. por la mañana. Este dia es el unico que durante toda la navegacion se ha visto claro ponerse el sol. Por la noche prosiguió dicho viento con la misma fuerza y por ser tanta la marejada hubo mucho valanceo y poco sosiego. Esta tarde dimos principio a la novena de la Señora Santa Clara, como lo habiamos prometido para implorar el auxilio divino por intersecion de la gloriosa santa a fin de que el Señor nos conceda vientos favorables y tiempos claros para poder costear la tierra y dar cumplimiento a los encargos y ordenes del superior goviero, si conviene al servicio de Dios y del Rey Nuestro Señor.

Dia 5 amaneció claro y despejado el cielo sin nieblina y no se pudo divisar la costa que segun cuentas debiamos estar ya dos dias sobre ella, y sin duda ha estado el yerro en la variacion de la hauja, que segun se ha podido demarcar estas noches el Norte, no destea dicha hauja dos cuartas. Esta mañana se volvió el viento al N. pero ya no tan fuerte y se puso la proa al N. E. ¼ al E., a las 5 de la mañana; como a las 7 se alargaron los rizos a las gavias y se mareó todo el velamen; el viento se fué escaseando poco a poco. Al medio dia observaron los señores pilotos 48 grados de latitud; por la tarde se escaseó tanto el viento que no se caminaba mas que dos millas por hora, el sol calentó muy bien y fué el mejor dia que hemos tenido en toda la navegacion asi de calor como de claridad. Este dia vimos varias yervas de mar que los marineros llaman porras y son buena señal de no estar muy lejos la tierra; el viento se mantuvo muy flojo toda esta tarde y noche siguiente con tiempo muy claro.

Dia 6 a las 12 de la noche se llamó el viento al N. O. muy lento y se puso la proa al N. E.; a las 4 de la mañana habiendo amanecido bien claro el dia y no divisandose la tierra se puso la proa at N. E. ¼ al N.; el viento desde dicha hora comenzó a refrescar y se caminaba a 3

cleared and the sun was seen. About ten the wind went to west-southwest, but it was not so strong, nor was it so cold as it had been. At noon the navigating officers observed the sun in 51° 35′. During the afternoon the wind was in the same quarter and rather fresher, the ship being on the same course and going at the rate of three miles an hour. About seven o'clock the wind hauled to west and so remained all night, during which we stood south-southeast at the rate of three miles an hour. The night was very clear and the sky cloudless.

About half past four on the morning of the 2d the wind went to west-northwest and the ship's head was put to southeastward, in order to draw in to the land. This morning the wind was not very strong, but it was almost a stern wind, and the send of the sea was favorable, so we made three miles an hour. At noon the navigating officers took an observation and said that we were in 50° 20′. At that hour the Captain ordered the ship's head to be put east ¼ southeast, so as to make a landfall without losing too much latitude. The same wind continued until six o'clock in the evening, when it hauled to west. During the night the fog and dew were heavy. We sailed on the same course until midnight.

On the 3d, until four o'clock in the morning, the course was southeast ¼ east, for fear of the coast, and as the fog was so thick we could not see if it were near. At four o'clock we again stood east ¼ southeast. The wind blew fresh from the west until eight o'clock, when it hauled to the northwest. This was the long desired wind which we had not had for one single hour. The fog lasted all morning, for which reason we could not make out the land. At noon the navigating officers took an observation of the sun in 49° 24′. After midday, by order of the Captain, the course was east, so that we might draw in to land and examine the coast in case the fog should lift, for, according to his reckoning, we should be very near it. At three in the afternoon, seeing that the fog did not lighten and that the wind freshened, the Captain ordered the topsails to be reefed and the ship's head to be put southeast ¼ south, until such time as it may please God to give us the fair weather necessary for us to go to the coast. At five the fog began to lift; and, it being clear and the coast not visible, the reefs in the topsails were shaken out, all sail was set and the ship's head was put to the eastward, so as to see whether before night fell we might make the land. The wind freshened continually and we made five

millas; a las 11 se divisó la tierra muy a lo lejos y pareció ser tierra alta, pues se miraba por proa un cerro nevado y al parecer muy elevado. A las 12 observaron los señores pilotos y Don Juan nos dijo que estabamos en los 48 grados como ayer; pero Don Esteban nos dijo que habia observado 48 grados y 52 minutos; no se por que motivo hayan discordado, siendo asi que este dia como los demas se han comunicado el punto de observacion. Por la tarde prosiguió el mismo viento pero cada vez mas lento, a las 8 de la noche se calmó totalmente el viento y comenzó a caer mucho rocio con alguna nieblina aunque no muy densa; a las 11 se espesó mucho la nieblina.

Dia 7 amaneció en calma y con la nieblina tan espesa que no se podia ver de popa a proa con muchisimo rocio. Este dia celebramos el santo sacrificio los dos padres. No pudieron observar el sol los señores pilotos porque la nieblina se mantuvo todo el dia y no se vió el sol en todo el dia. Por la tarde vimos algunos peces grandes que parecian taurones, pero dijeron que no lo eran; estos son los primeros peces que se han visto en todo el viaje. Todo este dia y noche siguiente se mantuvo en calma.

Dia 8 a las 4 de la mañana comenzó a ventear al E. lento y variable y se puso la proa al N., este dia amaneció muy oscuro el cielo, pero sin nieblina baja ni rocio; como a las 8 se llamó el viento al S. E. lento y con la proa al N. E., caminamos para la tierra que no se divisaba ya fuese porque las corrientes nos hayan apartado de ella durante la calma, ó ya por lo nublado del tiempo; como a las 11 se vió la tierra y no se divisaba el cerro nevado porque la costa estaba cubierta de niebla; la tierra que se miraba al N. E. como a distancia de 6 leguas es tierra medianamente alta poblada de arboleda, y a la parte del S. E. hace una punta tajada a la mar. Toda esta mañana se caminó a 3 millas por hora. Al medio dia aclaró muy poco el sol y observaron los señores pilotos; segun me dijo Don Esteban nos hallamos en 49 grados y 5 minutos de latitud; el señor capitan no dijo que latitud habia observado; como a las dos de la tarde hallandonos 3 leguas de la tierra comenzó a calmarse el viento, pero con algunas ventolinas nos acercamos como a distancia de 2 leguas; aqui se sondeó varias veces y se encontró fondo en 24 y 22 brazas. Como a las 4 vinieron 3 canoas de gentiles, en una venian 4 hombres, en otra 3 y en la otra 2; estas se estuvieron algo apartadas de nuestro barco dando gritos con ademanes de que nos fueramos de alli, pero a largo rato habiendoles hecho señas

miles an hour; the rest of the day we had made four and four and a half. But we could not see the coast, for which reason, at nine o'clock, sail was reduced to the foresail only, and thus we made two miles and a half an hour. At twelve the fog shut in again, very thick.

It was now the 4th, and the ship was hove to under her mainsail. It was daybreak at four o'clock, and, the fog being very thick, the foresail and the topsails were set and we went to the eastward. The wind hauled to the northward, very fresh, and soon there was a heavy sea on. At eight o'clock, as the fog did not lift, while both wind and sea were increasing, the topsails were furled again, and, under the foresail, the ship stood east-southeast, for we could not see the coast, which, according to the reckoning of the navigating officers, is thought to be very near. At eleven the weather began to clear a little, but no land was seen. At noon the sun was observed in 48° 52'. At one o'clock, the weather being clear, the mainsail and the topsails were set, and we went towards the coast, our course being east-northeast, the ship making four miles an hour. This afternoon the wind went to north-northeast and blew as strong as it had blown from the north in the morning. Today is the only one during the voyage on which we have seen the sun set clear. During the night the wind held the same strength; and, as the sea was very high, there was much pitching and tossing and little rest. This afternoon we commenced the novena to Santa Clara, as we had promised, for the purpose of imploring divine aid through the intercession of this glorious saint, to the end that the Lord may concede to us favorable winds and fair weather, so that we may sail along the coast and comply with the charge and orders of the superior government, if it be acceptable to the service of God and the King Our Lord.

The 5th dawned clear, the sky was cloudless and there was no fog. Yet we could not see the coast; though, according to the reckoning, we should have made land two days ago. Undoubtedly the error consists in miscalculating the variation of the needle; but, from observations of the North Star we have made, the needle does not vary more than two points. This morning the wind went back to the northward, though now not so strong; and, at five o'clock, the course was made northeast 1/4 east. About seven the reefs were shaken out of the topsails and all sail was made. The wind died away, little by little. At noon the navigating officers observed our latitude as 48°. During the

de que se arrimasen sin miedo, se acercaron y les dimos a entender que ibamos en busca de agua; pero ellos no debian estar muy satisfechos de nuestras señas y asi se volvieron a sus tierras. Al retirarse estas encontraron otras dos canoas que venian para nuestro barco, pero habiendo comunicado con los que iban de retirada se volvieron a tierra juntamente con ellos. A las 6 habiendonos acercado a la tierra como una legua y encontrado buen fondo en 25 brazas, se dejó caer una ancla, para poder al dia siguiente saltar en tierra y tomar posesion de ella en nombre del Rey nuestro señor; cuando se dió fondo ya se habia calmado totalmente el viento. Como a las 8 de la noche vinieron otras 3 canoas con 15 gentiles los que se estuvieron apartados del barco dando gritos en tono de lloros; los llamamos y se acercaron y a breve rato se despidieron, pero se estuvieron como un tiro de fusil de nuestro barco hasta mas de las 11 de la noche, hablando entre si mismos dando algunos gritos. Las canoas de estos gentiles no son tan grandes como las que vimos en la punta de Santa Margarita en las 55 grados, ni de la misma figura, las mas grandes tendran como 8 varas en largo, tienen la proa larga en canal y son mas chatas de popa; los remos son muy hermosos y pintados, que forman una paleta con una punta como de una cuarta al extremo. Dichas canoas parecen ser de una pieza aunque no todas, pues vimos algunas cosidas, pero todas estan muy bien trabajadas.

Dia 9 amaneció en calma y claro a la parte del N. O., pero por los demas vientos cubiertos de nieblas; habiendo amanecido comenzó la gente a hechar la lancha a la agua para ir a tierra; cuando se estaba en esta maniobra llegaron 15 canoas en que venian como cien hombres y algunas mujeres; dandoles a entender que se arrimasen sin miedo, se acercaron luego y comenzaron a comerciar con los nuestros cuanto traian en sus canoas, que se reducia a cueros de nutria y otros animales, sombreros de junco pintados con una pera en lo alto de ellos, y tegidos de una especie de cañamo con sus flecos de lo mismo con que se cubren y los mas tienen una esclavina de este tegido; los nuestros les compraron varias piezas por trajes viejos, conchas de lapas que habian traido de Monterey, algunos cuchillos; a estos y a las conchas manifestaron mas aficion. No vimos entre estos gentiles tegidos de lana como en Santa Margarita, ni andan tan cubiertos como aquellos; las mugeres no tienen rodeta en el labio. Tambien a estos se les vieron algunos hierros y cobre. Como a las 6 de la mañana estando ya la

afternoon so light was the wind that we made but two miles an hour. The sun gave out a great deal of heat, and it was the most pleasant day of the voyage as to warmth and clearness. Today we saw much seaweed of the kind called *porras* by the sailors, and this is a good sign that we are not far from land. The wind was light during the afternoon and night, and the weather was very fine.

At midnight the wind was very light, from the northwest; and the course was changed to northeast. At four o'clock on the morning of the 6th, the day breaking very clear and no land being seen, the ship's head was put northeast ¼ north. From this time the wind began to freshen, and we made three miles an hour. At eleven o'clock land was seen, but very far away. It appeared to be high land, for over the bow we saw a snowy hill which seemed to be very lofty.* At noon the navigating officers took an observation, and Don Juan said we were in 48°, the same as yesterday, but Don Esteban said that he obtained an observation in 48° 52'. I do not know why the results of these observations were not alike; today, as on all other days, we were informed of the ship's position. During the afternoon the wind held from the same quarter, but it died away gradually until, at eight o'clock at night, it was a dead calm, and the dew began to fall and a fog to arise, though this was not very thick. At eleven o'clock the fog was thicker.

At dawn on the 7th it was calm, and the fog was so thick we could not see the length of the ship; there was a heavy dew. Today both fathers celebrated the mass. The navigating officers could not obtain an observation of the sun, for the fog lasted all day and we did not see the sun. During the afternoon we saw some great fishes which seemed to be *taurones*, but it was said that they were not. These are the first fish we have seen during the voyage. The calm continued all day and during the following night.

On the 8th, at four o'clock in the morning, the wind came from the east, light and variable, and the course was north. The day dawned with the sky very much overcast, but there was no low-lying fog nor dew. At eight o'clock the wind hauled to the southeast, although it was light, and we stood in towards land on a northeast course. Whether it was that the current had carried us away from it during the calm, or because of the cloudy weather, we saw no land. At about

---

* Pico de Conuma or Conuma Peak, elevation 4845' and located at the head of Tlupana Arm, Nootka Sound. Also known as Tasis Mountain.

lancha en la agua se levantó el viento del O., y se reparó que nos
echaba sobre la tierra arrastrando la ancla, luego se empezó a levar
dicha ancla, para ponernos a la vela y salir del peligro pero el mucho
viento y marejada nos llevaban por instantes sobre la costa, por lo
cual fué preciso cortar el cable y perder la ancla. Cortado el cable nos
hicimos a la vela con la proa al S. O. ¼ al S. y con mucho trabajo
pudimos rebasar una punta de piedras que sale de la tierra como una
legua. Al dicho fondeadero llamó el señor capitan la Rada de San
Lorenzo, a unos cerros que estan al N. O. de la Rada llamó los cerros
de Santa Clara, y a la punta que está al S. E. le puso el nombre de
San Estevan. Dicha Rada segun nos dijo el señor capitan está en 49
grados y 30 minutos de latitud al N. Habiendo rebasado la punta de
piedras y apartadonos de la tierra como 3 leguas era tanta la marejada
y viento que fué menester aferrar todas las velas menos la trinquetilla
para poder subir a bordo la lancha que costó mucho trabajo y faltó
poco a perderla con algunos marineros; subida la lancha se alargaron
las velas y se puso la proa al S. S. O., el viento era cada vez mas recio y
mayor la marejada. Al medio dia observaron los señores pilotos y
segun nos dijo el señor capitan nos hallamos en 49 grados y 12
minutos; por la tarde se llamó el viento al N. O. y se fué mitigando
cada vez mas de modo que al anochecer era ya muy poco y a la noche
se calmó.

Dia 10 amaneció en calma y el cielo nublado pero sin nieblina baja
y se miraba la costa aunque confusa a distancia de 15 leguas. Este dia
digimos misa los dos padres. Al medio dia no aclaró el sol, por lo que
no pudieron los señores pilotos observar su elevacion. Todo este dia
estuvo nublado el cielo y en calma aunque por la tarde hubo tal qual
ventolina del N. O. pero tan lenta que apenas se percibia el movimiento del barco; por la noche se despejó algo el cielo, y prosiguió
la calma.

Dia 11 amaneció en calma y nublado el cielo como el dia antecedente; la costa se miraba bien clara al N. E. como a distancia de 10
leguas y a la parte del E. y del N. mas retirada. El mar venia del N. O.
con algunas ventolinas interpoladas y se conocia que nos iba llevando
al E. N. E. a donde se governaba el barco desde que calmó el viento

---

[8] Mr. Bancroft's writer gives this date as the 7th, and the date of cutting the cable
as the 8th. (*History of the Pacific States*, XXVII, 155). Reference to the account of
Father Crespi shows that he also gives these dates as they are given by Father de la Peña.

eleven o'clock we caught sight of land, but did not see the snowy hill, for the coast was covered with a fog. The land which we saw bore northeast, about six leagues away; it was rather high and covered with forest. In the southeast there was a point stretching out to the sea. All morning the ship made three miles an hour. At midday the sun was a little clearer and the navigating officers took an observation. Don Esteban told me that our position was 49° 05′; the Captain did not say what latitude he had observed. About two o'clock in the afternoon, when we were about three leagues from the land, the wind began to die away; but, aided by puffs, we reached to within about two leagues of it. Here several casts of the lead were had, with bottom in twenty-two and twenty-four fathoms. About four o'clock three canoes came out to us; in one were four men, three in another, and two in the third. They remained at some distance from the ship, crying out and making gestures that we should go away. After some time, we having made signs to them that they should draw near without fear, they did so, and we gave them to understand that we were in search of water; but they could not have been very satisfied with our signs, and went back to land. In going back they met with two other canoes which were coming out to the ship; but, after communication had between them, they turned back towards the land. At six, having arrived within about a league of land, and good holding-ground being found in twenty-five fathoms, the ship came to anchor,[8] so that on the following day we might go ashore and take possession of the land in the name of the King Our Lord. At the time of anchoring the wind had died away completely. About eight o'clock at night three canoes, with fifteen pagans in them, came to us; but they remained at a distance from the ship, their occupants crying out in a mournful tone of voice. We called to them, and they drew near. Shortly afterward they said goodbye, but, until after eleven o'clock, they remained at a distance of about a musket-shot from the ship, talking among themselves and sometimes crying out. The canoes of these pagans are not so large as those we saw at Point Santa Margarita in latitude 55°, nor of the same shape. The largest are about eight yards in length, with a long prow, hollowed out, and their sterns are blunter. The paddles are very handsome and are painted and are shaped like a shovel with a point about a quarter of a yard long at the end. These canoes appear

fresco. Al E. se divisaba un cerro muy alto cubierto de nieve que parecia una barranca blanca a primera vista; lo demas de la tierra tambien es alta y muy quebrada pero sin nieve toda ella a escepcion de dicho cerro. Como a las 10 aclaró algo el sol, y al medio dia observaron los señores pilotos 48 grados y 9 minutos de latitud segun dijo el señor capitan. Por la tarde prosiguieron las ventolinas del N. O. algo mas fuertes pero no continuas. A las 3 se puso la proa al E. y desde las 4 comenzó a refrescar el N. O. y se caminaba a dicho rumbo a 3 millas por hora; a las 5 estando a distancia de 7 leguas del cerro nevado (al que llamó el señor capitan el cerro de Santa Rosalía) se conoció que no era barranca blanca como aseguraban algunos, y mas al N. se divisaban otros picachos nevados; el dicho cerro nevado de Santa Rosalía parece desde lejos que está tajado a la mar pero en acercandose se conoce que está tierra adentro algo apartado de la costa como el cerro nevado que está al N. de la rada de S. Lorenzo. A las 6 se cerró todo de una nieblina tan espesa y humeda que no se veia de popa a proa pero se desvaneció en menos de una hora quedando el tiempo claro y oscuros los orizontes. Desde las 7 se gobernó al S. E. con animo de mantenernos sobre la costa para ver si el dia siguiente se podia hallar surgidero; el viento prosiguió lento del N. O. y a las 10 de la noche volvió la nieblina.

Dia 12 a las 12 de la madrugada se cambió el viento al S. S. E. y se puso la proa al E., la nieblina arrojaba tanto rocio que parecia aguacero; a las 4 se viró de bordo para fuera con la proa al O. ¼ al S. O. por estar tan oscuro el tiempo a causa de la nieblina que no se podia ver la tierra estando tan cerca; esta mañana llovió bastante con algunos chuvascos; el viento no fué muy fresco pero se sentia el frio por la mucha humedad; a las 9 se llamó el viento al S. O. y se viró de bordo para tierra con la proa al S. E. Este dia no pudieron observar por estar tan nieblinosa que no se vió el sol en todo él; a las 4 de la tarde volvió a llamarse el viento al S. y se volvió a virar para fuera con la proa al O. ¼ al S. O., por la noche cargó mucho la nieblina y estuvo llovisnando hasta el amanecer; el viento se mantuvo variable del S. al S. O. y muy lento toda la noche que pasamos dando bordos sobre la tierra.

Dia 13 al amanecer aclaró el cielo y tuvimos como dos horas de buen sol; como a las 7 se volvió a nublar el cielo. Esta mañana amanecimos cerca de la costa como a distancia de 5 leguas y se divisaba bastante tramo de tierra no muy alta poblada de arboleda que hace varias

to be of a single piece; though not all of them, for we saw some of pieces bound together. All are very well made.

The 9th dawned calm and clear towards the northwest, but in other quarters there was fog. Having been aroused, the crew began to get the longboat over the side, in order to go ashore. While this was going on there arrived fifteen canoes with about a hundred men and women. We gave them to understand that they might draw near without fear, and presently they came to us and began to trade with our people what they brought in their canoes, which consisted only of skins of otters and other animals, hats of rushes, painted and with the crown pointed, and cloths woven of a kind of hemp, having fringes of the same, with which they clothe themselves, most of them wearing a cape of this material. Our people bought several of these articles, in exchange for old clothes, shells which they had brought from Monterey and some knives; for these and the shells they manifested greater liking.* We did not see cloths woven of wool among them, as at Santa Margarita, nor are they so fully clothed as were those natives. These women do not have a disk pendent from the lip. In the possession of this people were seen some implements of iron and copper. About six o'clock in the morning, the longboat being now in the water, the wind was set in from the west, and it was noticed that it was forcing us towards the land, the anchor not holding. Immediately preparations for weighing anchor were made, so that sail might be made and peril avoided. But the high wind and the sea carried us steadily towards the shore, so that it was necessary to cut the cable and lose the anchor. The cable being cut, sail was made with the ship's head to the southwest ¼ south, and with great difficulty we managed to weather a rocky point that stretched out about a league into the sea. The Captain named the anchorage the Roadstead of San Lorenzo, some hills which were to the northwestward of this roadstead he

---

* Though there is no mention of it in any of the journals of the 1774 expedition, at a later time when Martínez was in command of the Spanish garrison at Nootka Sound, the story was circulated that the local Indians had stolen some silver spoons from the *Santiago*. This story explains the account of Captain Cook and his men to the effect that they found such items among the Nootkans. The Martínez version was of some importance in strengthening the Spanish claim to sovereignty in the Pacific Northwest, allegedly proving the primacy of their visit. Estevan Josef Martínez to Manuel Antonio Flores, Fragata Princesa in the Port of San Lorenzo de Nuca, July 13, 1789, in Archivo Histórico Nacional, Madrid, Estado, 4258. Also found in Archivo General de la Nación, Mexico, Historia 65. See also Andrew Kippis, *Captain Cook's Voyages*, 308f.

† The Roadstead of San Lorenzo was the outer harbor at Nootka, while Friendly

habras como ensenadas, pero como el viento era poco y de travesia no se podia arrimar a ella: como a las 9 refrescó muy bien el S. O. con mucha marejada. Toda esta mañana caminamos al S. E. y al S. ¼ al S. E. No pudieron observar por estar nublado el cielo; por la tarde aclaró algunos ratos el sol y el viento se llamó al O. no muy fresco pero con mucha marejada; por la noche sopló variable del O. al N. O. y balanceó mucho el barco; toda esta tarde y noche se gobernó al S. ¼ al S. E. y se caminaba a dos millas y media por hora, el cielo quedó nublado con nubes muy gruesas y negras que arrojaron algunas gotas de agua.

Dia 14 amaneció con el cielo nublado aunque no como el dia y noche antecedente; el viento se llamó al N. bastante flojo y como la marejada era del O. daba tan fuertes valances el barco que no podiamos tenernos en pie, por lo cual no fué posible decir misa este dia. Aunque la costa estaba muy oscura por la niebla que en ella habia divisamos la tierra al E. a las 7 de la mañana a distancia como de 8 leguas ó algo mas; tambien hubo algunos chuvascos esta mañana con alguna agua aunque poca; a las 8 se llamó el viento al N. E. muy lento y variable, el cielo se despejó varias veces pero cada rato se volvia a nublar con chuvascos. Al medio dia observaron los señores pilotos el sol en 46 grados y 8 minutos de latitud segun nos dijo el señor capitan, pero no quedaron satisfechos de esta observacion porque estando haciendola vino un chuvasco y oscureció el sol: por la tarde prosiguió ventoleando del N. E. y la marejada del O. cuasi tan fuerte como por la mañana; a la noche se volvió el viento al N. fresco y se caminó toda la noche a 3 millas y media por hora con la proa al S. S. E.; el cielo quedó claro y despejado.

Dia 15 amaneció muy claro y limpio el cielo, el viento fresco como por la noche; este dia aunque habia bastante valanceo por venir la mar del O. dije misa con algun trabajo; el Padre Fray Juan no la dijo por miedo de los valances. Al amanecer estabamos sobre la costa como a distancia de 4 leguas y se divisaba mucho tramo de tierra medianamente alta poblada de arboleda segun me dijeron, pero yo no la distinguia; este tramo de tierra corre de N. N. O. a S. S. E. segun dijo el señor capitan. Desde las 3 de la mañana que se divisó la tierra hasta las 8 se governó al S. ¼ al S. E. y desde las 8 se puso la proa al S. S. E. Al medio dia observaron los señores pilotos y segun dijo el señor capitan nos hallamos en 44 grados y 35 minutos. Toda esta mañana

called Hills of Santa Clara, and the point to the southeastward he named San Esteban.† According to what the Captain told us, this roadstead is in latitude 49° 30′. Having weathered the point of rocks, and being about three leagues off the land, so great was the force of the wind and the sea that it was necessary to take in all sail except the fore-staysail, so that the longboat might be got on board. This was effected with great difficulty, and the boat was well-nigh lost, together with some men who were in it. The longboat being got on board, sail was made and the ship's head was put to the south-southwest. The wind kept freshening and the sea rising. At noon the navigating officers took an observation and, as the Captain told us, the position of the ship was 49° 12′. During the afternoon the wind hauled to northwest; the wind died away gradually; at nightfall its force was very slight and during the night it was calm.

At daybreak on the 10th the calm continued. The sky was overcast but the fog was not low, and the coast was made out confusedly, at a distance of fifteen leagues. Today we two fathers celebrated the mass. At noon the sun did not shine, for which reason the navigating officers could not observe its elevation. All day the sky was overcast and the calm continued, although during the afternoon there were occasional breezes from the northwest, so light that one could scarcely note the movement of the ship. During the night the sky cleared a little and the calm continued.

The 11th dawned calm and the sky was cloudy—as it was yesterday. The coast was seen very distinctly to the northeast and about ten leagues away; to the eastward and northward it was farther off. The send of the sea was from the northwest; there were light puffs of wind, and the ship was drifting to east-northeast, as had been the case since the wind had become less. To the eastward we saw a very high hill covered with snow, which, at first sight, appeared to be a white cliff. The rest of the land is high also, and all is very broken, but without snow except on the hill mentioned. About ten o'clock the sun shone out a little and at noon the navigating officers took an ob-

Cove, scene of the later Spanish post on Vancouver Island, was the inner harbor. The Spaniards also used the designation of Santa Cruz de Nutka. The Hills of Santa Clara are identified as Point Macuina, named for the principal chief of the Nootkans, Maquinna. Point San Esteban, named in honor of the second officer, Martínez, is still called Estevan Point, and a small settlement at that place is still thus named.

caminamos costeando la tierra apartados de ella como 3 leguas; por la tarde se prosiguió al mismo rumbo y se miraba muy clara la costa porque no estaba tan humeda la tierra como por la mañana. Tiene esta tierra mucha arboleda que a la vista parece Pineria, no solo en la cumbre sino en las faldas de los cerros. En la playa se miran algunas mesas sin arboleda con mucho zacate y varias barrancas blancas tajadas a la mar: tambien se ven algunas cañadas ó abras que corren N. E. S. O. y en toda la tierra que este dia vimos no divisamos nieve, y cuanto mas al S. es tierra mas baja. A las 6 se reparó que la tierra salia por la proa al S. por lo cual desde dicha hora se governó al S. O. hasta las 8 que se puso la proa al S. y asi se caminó toda la noche. Todo este dia hizo buen sol, pero el viento muy frio y tan fuerte que al anochecer caminabamos a cinco millas y media por hora solo con las dos mayores y las gavias tomados sus rizos.

Dia 16 amaneció claro y limpio el cielo, como ayer, pero los orizontes muy ofuscados con nieblina a modo de humo, el viento fresco aunque no tanto como por la noche; no se divisó la tierra por estar tan humeda, pero se hizo juicio que no estaria muy lejos porque el sol estaba ya muy alto cuando lo vimos. A las 5 de la mañana se puso la proa al S. S. E., a las 8 comenzó a calmarse el viento y la niebla cada vez mas espesa de suerte que apenas se podia ver el sol: a las 12 ya estaba del todo calmado el viento; observaron los señores pilotos y segun dijo el señor capitan estabamos en 42 grados y 38 minutos. Por la tarde cargó mucha nieblina humeda y fria con algunas ventolinas del S. E. y del E. N. E. variables; al ponerse el sol aclaró algo el cielo quedando los orizontes muy claros salvo por el O.; como a las 9 de la noche estaban despejados los orizontes por todos rumbos pero luego se volvieron a ofuscar y cayó mucho rocio. En todo este dia no se pudo divisar la costa por causa de la nieblina y porque sin duda estabamos bien apartados de ella, pues no la pudimos ver a las 9 de la noche estando muy clara la luna y los orizontes como he dicho. En esta latitud conjeturo que estará el cabo blanco de San Sebastian y aquel famoso rio hondable llamado de Martin de Aguilar descubierto por la fragata de su mando en la espedicion del general Sebastian Vizcaino, pues aunque dice la historia que dicho cabo y rio está en los 43 grados segun la obser-vacion que hizo el piloto de dicha fragata Antonio Flores, se debe pensar sea menor latitud como se ha hallado menor en los parages que se ha observado con los nuevos octantes que la que en aquellos tiempos

servation in 48° 09', according to what the Captain told us. During the afternoon light breezes still came from the northwest; they were somewhat stronger than in the morning, but not so constant. At three o'clock the ship's head was put to the eastward, and after four o'clock, the wind came stronger from the northwest. We made three miles an hour on the course mentioned. At five o'clock, being at a distance of some seven leagues from the snowy hill, which the Captain named the Hill of Santa Rosalía,* it was apparent that it was not a white cliff, as it had been thought to be by some; and, farther to the northward, other snowy peaks were seen. From a distance the snowy hill of Santa Rosalía seemed to be close to the sea; but, on drawing nearer to it, it appeared that it was inland, at some distance from the shore, like the snowy hill to the northward of the Roadstead of San Lorenzo. At six o'clock everything was hidden by a fog so thick and wet that the bow of the ship could not be seen from the stern; but, in less than an hour it had disappeared, the weather being fair although the horizon was obscured. After seven o'clock the course was southeast, the intention being to remain near the coast, in order to find out whether on the day following an anchorage might not be found. The wind continued light from the northwest, and at ten o'clock at night the fog came on again.

As the 12th began the wind went to south-southwest, and the ship's head was put to the eastward. So much moisture came from the fog that it seemed a shower. At four o'clock we went about and stood seaward on a west ¼ southwest course, for the weather was so thick by reason of the fog that the land could not be seen, although so near. This morning there was a good deal of rain and some squalls. The wind was not very strong but, because of the dampness, it was cold. At nine o'clock the wind went to the southwest, and we tacked and stood for the land, on a southeast course. Today no observation could be had on account of the fog, the sun not being seen at any time during the day. At four o'clock in the afternoon the wind went back to the southward, and the ship went about and stood off shore on a west ¼ southwest course. During the night the fog became much denser and there was a drizzling rain until dawn. The wind remained

---

* The snow-covered peak is identified as Mount Olympus; see Bancroft, *History of the Northwest Coast*, Vol. I, 156.

observaron con sus instrumentos. A las once y media de la noche comenzó a ventear lentamente del N. O. y a poco rato se llamó al N. y duró toda la noche cada vez mas recio: la proa toda la noche estuvo al S. ¼ al S. O.

Dia 17 amaneció con bastante nieblina y el viento tan fuerte que fué menester aferrar las belas y quedarnos con solo el trinquete: desde las 5 en que se hizo dicha maniobra se governo al S.; no sé lo que caminaba el barco porque ya no se hechaba la corredera; a las 6 comenzó a despejarse el cielo y aclarar algo los orizontes. A las 12 observaron los señores pilotos 41 grados y 27 minutos de latitud segun dijo el señor capitan; a la una habiendose mitigado el viento alguna cosa se mareó el velacho y la mayor; a dicha hora se puso la proa al S. S. E. y a este rumbo se caminó toda la tarde. No se vió la tierra este dia con haber estado bien claro, aunque los orizontes siempre estuvieron humados. Por la noche aflojó algo el viento y se governó al S. E. y al S. E. ¼ al S.: esta noche hizo mas frio que en todo el tiempo del viaje, pero estuvo clara hasta cerca de amanecer.

Dia 18 como a las 4 de la mañana se cubrió de niebla muy espesa y humeda, el viento se quedó cuasi calmado pero no del todo y se prosiguió con la proa al S. E. que con el poco viento y la marejada del N. algo se caminaba; esta mañana se sintió mucho mas el frio; a las 10 comenzó a aclararse el sol aunque poco. No pudieron observar este dia por la nieblina, pero me hago juicio que estariamos en 40 grados con diferencia de pocos minutos: a la una se aclaró muy bien el cielo quedando siempre oscuros los orizontes escepto por la parte del N. O.: toda esta tarde hizo buen sol con algunas ventolinas del N.: al anochecer refrescaron un poco las ventolinas y quedó la noche muy clara hasta las once y media que se calmó totalmente el viento y se cubrió todo de nieblina muy espesa y cayó tanto rocio que parecia haber llovido.

Dia 19 amaneció en calma con la nieblina y rocio, como por la noche; esta mañana apuntaron algunas ventolinas del S. E. y se tuvo la proa al S. O., pero era muy poco el movimiento del barco: no se vió el sol en toda la mañana por causa de la nieblina, ni al medio dia se pudo observar. Por la tarde prosiguió en calma y hubo algunas ventolinas del N. y N. E. variables y se mantuvo la proa al S. E. y S. S. E., como a las 7 comenzó a ventolear lentamente del N. O. y se puso la proa al S. E. ¼ al E. pero calmó antes de las 8 y toda la noche se pasó

variable, from south to southwest and was very light all night, which we passed in standing off and on.

At daybreak on the 13th the sky cleared and the sun shone out well for about two hours; about seven o'clock the sky became overcast again. At dawn we were near the coast, about five leagues away, and a considerable stretch of land was discerned, not very high and covered with forest. There were several breaks like bays; but, as the wind was light and on the beam, we could not get near it. About nine o'clock the southwest wind freshened considerably and there was a heavy sea on. All the morning our course was southeast and south ¼ southeast. No observation could be taken as the sky was overcast. During the afternoon the sun shone out at intervals and the wind went to the westward; it was not very strong, but there was a very heavy sea. During the night the wind was shifting from west to northwest, and the ship rolled a great deal. All the afternoon and night the course was south ¼ southeast, and we made two miles and a half an hour. The sky remained overcast with very dense and black clouds from which some drops of rain fell.

The 14th dawned with a cloudy sky, although it was not so overcast as it had been yesterday and during the night. The wind came from the north, very light, and, as the send of the sea was from the west, the ship rolled so that we could not keep our footing, for which reason it was not possible to celebrate the mass. Although the coast was very much obscured by the fog, about seven o'clock in the morning we saw land to the eastward, about eight leagues or more away. During the morning there were some squalls; also rain, though not much. At eight o'clock the wind went to the northeast, very light and shifting. The sky cleared several times, but every little while it was overcast again and squalls came up. At noon the navigating officers took an observation of the sun in 46° 08′, as the Captain informed us, but they were not satisfied with this observation, for, while they were taking it, a squall came up and hid the sun. During the afternoon there were light winds from the northeast, and the sea was from the west, almost as heavy as in the morning. At nightfall the wind went back to the north and blew fresh; all night long we made three miles and a half an hour on a south-southeast course. The sky was clear and cloudless.

The 15th dawned very fair and the sky was clear; the wind fresh,

en calma. En todo este dia no se quitó la nieblina ni se pudo ver el sol; hizo bastante frio y cayó mucho rocio. Estas humedades pienso son la causa de mal de Loanda, ó escorbuto; pues aunque en todo el viaje ha habido algunos tocados de este accidente, no se han visto tan agravados como ahora, pues pasan de 20 los que se hallan sin poder servir a mas de otros muchos que estan aunque en pié llagados de boca y piernas, y creo que si Dios no nos envia luego otros tiempos ha de perecer de dicho mal la mayor parte de la tripulacion segun van en enfermando estos dias de nieblina humeda y fria.

Dia 20 amaneció en calma y la nieblina tan espesa, fria y humeda como los dias antecedentes y duró todo el dia sin dejar ver el sol, salvo un poco que aclaró al medio dia, en cuanto se conocia en donde estaba; a este tiempo observó el señor capitan el sol en 39 grados y 48 minutos de latitud, pero dijo que no era segura dicha observacion por razon de la poca claridad del sol y estar oscuros los orizontes. Por la tarde se aferraron las velas porque se hacian pedazos con las golpes que daban contra la jarcia a causa de la calma y valanceo. Todo este dia y noche cayó mucho rocio y la nieblina fué en estremo espesa y fria lo cual tiene a todos en mucho desconsuelo por ver que la gente se va enfermando y que no se sabe de fijo en donde nos hallamos, por hacer ya tres dias que los señores pilotos no han podido observar con seguridad. Dios sea servido darnos lo que convenga.

Dia 21 a la una de la madrugada comenzó a ventolear lenta y variablemente del E., del E. S. E. y del S. E.: al amanecer era tanta la humedad de la nieblina que parecia aguacero. Las ventolinas se calmaron luego y solo servian para romper las velas. Este dia dije misa, y el padre Fray Juan no la dijo por hallarse algo indispuesto del estomago. A las 9 de la mañana volvió otra vez a ventear del S. E. muy lento y se caminaba aunque poco at S. S. O.; a las once y media se viró de bordo y se puso la proa al E. N. E.; al medio dia alcaró un poco el sol y el señor capitan observó aunque sin certeza 39 grados y 30 minutos de latitud; por la tarde se espesó mucho la nieblina y arrojaba mucho rocio frio como un hielo con ventolinas del S. E.; a las 6 de la tarde se levantó la nieblina y aclaró algo el tiempo aunque el cielo quedó nublado y prosiguió ventoleando algo mas fresco del S. E. y del S. S. E. variable: por la noche se aclaró algo mas el cielo y se vió la luna: toda la noche hubo algunas ventolinas y se caminó con la proa al E. N. E. y al E. ¼ al N. E.

as during the night. Today, although there was a good deal of tossing about as the sea came from the west, with some difficulty I celebrated the mass. Father Fray Juan did not celebrate as he feared the movement of the ship. At dawn we were about four leagues off the coast and saw a considerable stretch of land of medium altitude and covered with a growth of trees—as they told me, for I was unable to distinguish this. According to what the Captain said, this stretch of land trends north-northwest and south-southeast. From three o'clock in the morning, when land was seen, until eight, the course was south ¼ southeast; and, after eight, south-southeast. At noon the navigating officers took an observation, and, as the Captain told us, we were in 44° 35′. All morning we ran along the land, about three leagues from it; during the afternoon our course was the same, and the coast was very clearly visible because the land was not so obscured by vapor as it had been in the morning. This land is thickly covered with timber, apparently pine, not only on the summit but along the flanks of the hills. Immediately on the coast we saw some level land where there was no timber but a heavy growth of grass, and there were several white cliffs close by the sea, and some ravines, or openings, running northeast and southwest. In all the land seen today we could not discern any snow. More to the southward the land is low-lying. At six o'clock land stretching out ahead of us and to the southward was seen, and from that time until eight o'clock the course was southwest; at this hour the ship's head was put to the southward, and this course was held all night. All day the sun was out, but the wind was very cold and so strong that at nightfall the ship was going at the rate of five miles and a half an hour, under courses and reefed topsails.

The 16th dawned fair and the sky was clear, as it was yesterday, but the horizon was very much obscured by a smoke-like fog. The wind was fresh, although not so much so as during the night. The land could not be seen, on account of this dampness, but it was thought that it could not be very far away because the sun was already high in the heavens when we saw it. At five o'clock in the morning the ship's head was put to south-southeast. At eight o'clock the wind began to die away and the fog to thicken so that we could hardly see the sun. At noon it was dead calm. The navigating officers took an observation, and the Captain said that our position was in 42° 38′. During the afternoon a very wet, cold fog arose, accompanied by shifting puffs of

Dia 22 amaneció nublado el cielo pero sin nieblina, ni rocio y algo despejados los orizontes; como a las 5 se vió la costa a distancia de 6 leguas; a la parte del N. se miraba una punta de tierra tajada a la mar que demoraba al N. N. O. como a distancia de 9 leguas y la tierra que sigue desde dicha punta al S. E. es muy alta y quebrada por mas de 5 leguas y la que se sigue al S. E. que es la que tenemos mas cerca al E. es tierra mediana poblada de arboleda a lo menos en la cumbre que se vió bien clara al salir el sol; por el S. E. se miraba mucho tramo de tierra mas baja como lomeria. La dicha punta que nos demoraba al N. N. O. hicimos juicio que será el cabo Mendocino y siendo así estará dicho cabo en 40 grados con diferencia de pocos minutos segun la observacion que ayer hizo el señor capitan y el rumbo a que hemos caminado; a las cinco y media se viró para afuera con la proa al S. O. y al S. S. O. con ventolinas variables del S. E. y S. S. E.: esta mañana aclaró algunos el sol y a cada instante se cubria de nublados, pero estuvo mas templado el tiempo que los dias antecedentes; al medio dia aclaró muy bien el sol y los orizontes por todos vientos, observaron los señores pilotos muy a su satisfaccion y dijo el señor capitan que nos hallabamos en 39 grados y 46 minutos de latitud: como a las 3 de la tarde se cubrió otra vez el cielo de nubes; a las cuatro se viró de bordo para tierra con la proa al E. N. E. manteniendose muy lento el S. E., a las 5 se volvió a virar de bordo y luego se calmó el poco viento que habia: toda la noche se pasó en calma con tal qual ventolina del S. E. y el cielo quedó nublado no muy oscuro y con nieblina por los orizontes, pero no cayo mucho rocio.

Dia 23 al amanecer se divisó la costa aunque retirada y confusa por la nieblina que en ella habia; esta mañana comenzó a soplar muy lento del S. S. E. y navegamos al S. O. y luego se perdió de vista la costa porque se cerro de nieblina espesa por todas partes; desde las 9 aclaró algunos ratos el sol pero duraban muy poco: este dia no se sintió frio sino tiempo muy templado, a las diez comenzó a refrescar algo el viento y el cielo se oscureció mucho de modo que no pudieron observar el sol; por la tarde alfojó el viento y a las 6 se calmó totalmente; desde las 8 comenzó a llovisnar y prosiguió hasta las 12 a intervalos; como a las diez de la noche comenzó a ventear del E. muy lento y luego se llamó al N. E. algo mas recio y se caminó toda la noche al S. E. ¼ al E.

Dia 24 antes de amanecer se llamó el viento al N. medianamente

wind from the southeast and east-northeast. At sunset the sky was somewhat clearer, leaving the horizon very clear, except in the west. About nine at night, the horizon was clear in all quarters, but it soon became obscured again and a heavy dew fell. All day long the coast was not visible, on account of the fog, and because, undoubtedly, we were so far away from it; as at nine we could not see it, although the moon was very bright, for the horizon was as I have said. I conjecture that in this latitude are situated the Cape Blanco of San Sebastián and that large navigable river called the River of Martín de Aguilar,* which was discovered by the ship under his command during the voyage of General Sebastián Vizcaíno; for although it is recorded in history, in accordance with an observation made by Antonio Flores,† navigating officer of said ship, that the cape and river are in 43°, the latitude should be taken to be less than this, because observations with the modern octant have made the latitude less at other places where it had been determined by means of the instruments of that time. At half past eleven at night a gentle breeze came from the northwest; in a little while the wind went to the north and remained in that quarter during the night, constantly increasing in force. All night the course was south ¼ southwest.

Dawn on the 17th was quite foggy, and the wind so strong that it was necessary to reduce sail to the foresail only. After five o'clock, at which hour this was effected, the course was south. I do not know what the rate of sailing was for the log is no longer hove. At six o'clock the sky and the horizon began to clear partially. At midday the navigating officers got an observation in 41° 27′, as the Captain told us. At one o'clock the wind had lessened a little and the mainsail and the fore-topsail were set. At that hour the ship's head was put south-southeast and this was the course during the afternoon. Although the weather was clear all day the land was not seen, the horizon being

---

* Cape Blanco generally appears in connection with the River of Martín Aguilar, both resulting from the Vizcaíno expedition explorations. Sometimes one finds either Cape Blanco of San Sebastián, or Cape Blanco of Martín Aguilar, or it appears as "Cape Blanco or Cape Diligencia." Martín Aguilar Galeote, a native of Malaga, was Ensign on the *Tres Reyes*. He died during the course of the expedition headed by Vizcaíno. It is still called Cape Blanco.

† Antonio Flores, sometimes written Antón Flórez, was pilot aboard the *Tres Reyes* and suffered the fate of Martín Aguilar. Flores' name was temporarily affixed to the California coastline in "Cabo de Antón Flores or San Sebastián," located north of Cape Mendocino. Flores was a native of Avilés.

fresco y sopló hasta las 8 de la mañana que se quedó en calma cuasi del todo. Esta mañana celebramos misa los dos padres. El cielo se mantuvo nublado de modo que solo a las 6 se vió un poco el sol; como a las 10 volvió a ventear el N. bastante fresco pero a cada rato se escaseaba; a las 11 se oscureció mucho el cielo con amagos de agua, cayeron algunas gotas, aunque pocas, luego se cerró de nieblina humeda pero no muy espesa. No pudieron observar los señores pilotos por causa de estar tan nublado y oscuro el tiempo. A las 4 de la tarde mandó el señor capitan governar al S. E. porque aunque este dia no se vió la tierra se hizo juicio que no estariamos muy apartados de ella y que sin duda se hubiera visto a no estar tan oscuro el dia; desde las 8 de la noche valanceó mucho el barco a causa de venir la marejada muy gruesa del N.: desde dicha hora sopló el N. O. lento y se puso la proa al S. E. ¼ al E., el cielo estuvo muy oscuro y cerrados de nieblina los orizontes.

Dia 25 a las tres y media de la mañana se quedó en calma el viento, pero siempre con grande marejada del N. que sin duda ha soplado muy fuerte mas arriba; el cielo se mantuvo muy oscuro toda la mañana con bastante nieblina por los orizontes y de cuando en cuando algunas ventolinas del E. y del S. E. variables; a las 11 comenzó a soplar algo fresco el S. E. y se puso la proa al N. E.; en dicha hora se aclaró algo el cielo y se vió el sol, pero por los orizontes se quedó oscuro como antes; a las 12 ya se habia calmado otra vez el viento; este dia observaron los señores pilotos y nos dijo el señor capitan que estabamos en 38 grados y 38 minutos de latitud; por la tarde se cubrió el cielo de nubes y hubo algunas ventolinas ya del N. ya del S.; como a las 6 de la tarde se fijó el viento del N. N. O. lento y por la noche refrescó algo mas, pero variable del N. O. y del O. N. O.; desde las 6 hasta las 8 se governó al E. S. E. y lo demas de la noche al S. E. ¼ al E., toda la noche estuvo muy oscuro y con bastante nieblina humeda.

Dia 26 amaneció con mucha nieblina y rocio, el viento muy escaso: luego que amaneció se puso la proa al E. S. E.; no se pudo divisar la costa por la mucha nieblina y oscuridad del tiempo, pero vimos muchos pajaros de tierra grandes y chicos y varios patos que decian ser de agua dulce; a las 8 ya el viento se quedó en calma y la nieblina despedia tanto rocio que parecia lluvia; a las 9 volvió a ventolear del N. O. y luego refrescó muy bien y se aclaró algo el tiempo: a las 10 se

hazy. By night the wind had fallen still more, and our course was southeast and southeast ¼ south. This was the coldest night of the whole voyage, but it was clear until nearly daybreak.

About four o'clock in the morning, on the 18th, the fog was very dense and wet, the wind had almost died away, but not completely, and, the course being southeast, with the little wind that was stirring and the sea being from the northward, the rate of sailing was good. This morning the cold was felt much more. At ten o'clock the sun began to shine forth, though feebly. On account of the fog no observation was taken today, but I think that we were in 40°, although there might be a difference of a few minutes. At one o'clock the sky was very clear, but the horizon was much obscured, except in the northwest. All afternoon the sun shone and there were light puffs of wind from the north. At nightfall these were stronger and the night was very clear until half past eleven o'clock, when it was a dead calm and the sky was covered with a very thick fog, while there fell a dew so heavy that it seemed as if it had rained.

On the 19th it was still calm, with the fog and the dew as during the night. This morning light winds came from the southeast and the course was southwest, but the movement of the ship was very little. By reason of the fog the sun was not seen during the morning, nor could an observation be taken at noon. In the afternoon it was still calm, and there were shifting, light winds from the north and northeast, the ship's head being kept southeast and south-southeast. About seven it began to blow gently from the northwest, and the ship's head was put southeast ¼ east; but before eight o'clock the wind died away, and all night long there was a calm. During the whole day the fog did not lift, nor could the sun be seen. It was quite cold and a heavy dew fell. I think that this dampness is the cause of *mal de Loanda*,* or scurvy; for, although during the whole voyage there have been some persons affected with this sickness, these cases have not been as aggravated as they are now, when there are more than twenty men unfit for duty, in addition to which many others, though able to go about, have sores in the mouth and on the legs; and I believe that if God does not send better weather soon the greater part of the crew must perish

---

* Mal de Loanda, or Loanda sickness, was the name applied to scurvy, doubtlessly through association with the African trade where Loanda was then capital of Portuguese holdings in Angola.

divisaron al S. E. a distancia de legua y media los Farallones de San Francisco que estan al S. O. de la Punta de Reyes y Puerto de San Francisco como a distancia de 5 leguas segun dijo el señor capitan; en cuanto se vieron dichos Farallones mandó el señor capitan poner la proa al S. O. para dejarlos a sotavento, por no saber si hay paso bueno entre ellos y la costa; como el viento era fresco a las 11 ya estabamos sobre ellos y divisamos mas al S. E. otro monton de Farallones apartados de los primeros como dos leguas al S. E. Los primeros son siete piachos altos unos mayores que otros con algunas piedras anegadas cerca de ellos, y ocupan entre todos como el circuito de una legua: pasamos muy cerca de ellos. Los de la parte del S. E. parecen mayores; no pude conocer con certidumbre cuantos son porque pasamos algo retirados de ellos, pero me pareció que eran seis picachos y uno de los del medio es mayor que los otros; cuando estuvimos poco adelante de los primeros Farallones se puso la proa al S. ¼ al S. O. y a las 12 se puso al S. ¼ al S. E.: no se pudo divisar la costa ni observar por estar muy cargado de nieblina por todas partes. Toda la tarde sopló el viento dicho muy bonancible y navegamos al S. E., al ponerse el sol aclaró muy bien el cielo y los orizontes por el O. y N., pero por el E. y S. quedaron oscuros, por lo cual no pudimos ver la tierra: por la noche refrescó un poco el viento y se puso la proa al S. E. ¼ al E. para recalar a la costa y reconocerla el dia siguiente en amaneciendo.

Dia 27 amaneció el dia claro aunque algo nublado el cielo y oscuros los orizontes con nieblina; luego que aclaró el dia se vió la costa por el E. a distancia de tres leguas y dijeron que era la punta de Año Nuevo; caminamos al S. E. hasta las 10 que se divisó la punta de Pinos y luego se governó al E. S. E. hasta que se dió fondo. A las 9 de la mañana se aclaró muy bien el cielo y tuvimos buen sol; al medio dia observaron los señores pilotos como 4 leguas al N. O. de la punta de Pinos y dijo el señor capitan que habia observado 36 grados y 35 minutos de latitud al N. Por la tarde prosiguió fresco el viento pero se fué llamando al O. y a las tres estando sobre la dicha punta de Pinos se llamó al S. O.: a las 4 de la tarde poco menos se dió fondo en este puerto de San Carlos de Monterrey. Bendito sea Dios y alabado para siempre y su Santisima Madre Maria Señora Nuestra, Amen.

Advierto que en todo este viaje no ha habido desgracia alguna en el barco: bendito sea Dios pues no ha faltado palo, ni mastelero, ni cabo de su jarcia, en medio de haber tenido vientos y mares fuertes; pero

with this disease, from the rate they are falling sick of it during these days of wet and cold fog.

The dawn of the 20th was calm, and the fog was as dense, cold and wet as it had been during previous days. It lasted all day, without letting the sun be seen, except that it was clear for a short time at noon, sufficient for us to learn whereabouts we were. At this hour the Captain got an observation of the sun in 39° 48', but said that this observation was not reliable because of the little brilliancy of the sun and as the horizon was obscured. During the afternoon the sails were taken in because they were being threshed to pieces against the rigging owing to the calm and the rolling of the ship. All day long and during the night a great deal of moisture fell from the fog, which was extremely dense and cold. This makes all of us very disconsolate, for it is seen that the men continue sickening, and we do not know definitely where we are, there having passed three days without the navigating officers being able to observe the sun with accuracy. May it please God to give us that which may seem good to Him.

At one o'clock on the morning of the 21st it began to blow gently, and by fits and starts, from the east, east-southeast and southeast. At dawn such was the humidity of the fog that it seemed a shower. The puffs of wind soon died away, so that they only served to tear the sails. Today I celebrated the mass; Father Fray Juan did not, because he was sick of an indisposition of the stomach. At nine in the morning it began to blow from the southeast again, although very gently, and the ship moved, though slowly, to the south-southwest. At half past eleven we went about with her head to east-northeast. At midday the sun brightened a little and the Captain got an observation, though not a very reliable one, in 39° 30'. During the afternoon the fog became much thicker, and a great deal of water, as cold as ice, came from it, and there were light winds from the southeast. At six in the evening the fog lifted, and the weather was somewhat clearer, though the sky remained cloudy, and the wind, which was variable, blew rather fresher from the southeast and south-southeast. At nightfall the sky was clearer and the moon was seen. All night there were puffs of wind, and the course was east-northeast and east ¼ northeast.

The 22d dawned with a cloudy sky, but there was neither fog nor dew, while the horizon was fairly clear. At five o'clock the coast was made out, about six leagues away. To the northward was a point of

es cosa notable en esta mar que en cuanto se apacigua el viento se baja y sosiega la mar, y pienso que por esta causa le llamarian los antiguos el mar pacifico.

Tambien advierto que desde los 55 grados de latitud, termino a que llegamos hasta el puerto de Monterrey no hemos podido saber si hay puertos, ensenadas ú otros surgideros, por causa de lo retirado que hemos bajado de la tierra y por la oscuridad de los tiempos que hemos tenido los mas de los dias de toda la navegacion, de todo lo cual daran mejor razon los señores pilotos como inteligentes y practicos.

Ultimamente advierto que este diario lo he escrito dia por dia en el viaje por habermelo encargado el Reverendo Padre Presidente para lo cual el señor capitan me ha hecho el favor de comunicarme los mas dias el punto de latitud que observaba, y para saber el rumbo a que se navegaba he tenido el cuidado de mirar a menudo la haguja en la vitacora. Y para que conste ser verdad lo que en este diario tengo escrito lo firmo en esta Mision de San Carlos de Monte-Rey dia 28 de Agosto de 1774.

Fray Tomás de la Peña
(hay una rúbrica)

land close to the sea. It bore north-northwest, about nine leagues distant, and the land beyond that point to the south-eastward is very high and broken for a distance of more than five leagues. That adjoining this on the southeast is the land which is nearest to us to the eastward, and is of medium altitude and clothed with timber, at least on the summits, which were plainly seen when the sun shone out. On the southeast there was a long stretch of lower land, like a range of hills. The point referred to, which remained in sight on the north-northwest, we took to be Cape Mendocino; if this be the case, this cape must be in 40°, a few minutes more or less, according to an observation the Captain obtained yesterday and the course we have held. At half past five we went about and stood off shore, to the southwest and the south-southwest, with variable light winds from the southeast and south-southeast. This morning the sun shone out at intervals but was soon hidden by clouds, and the weather was milder than it has been. At noon the sun shone out, and all around the horizon was very clear. The navigating officers obtained a very satisfactory observation, and the Captain said that the ship was in latitude 39° 46'. About three in the afternoon the sky was overcast again. At four we tacked and stood for the land, the course being east-northeast and the wind very light from the southeast. At five we went about again, and the wind was a little less. All night long it was calm, except for an occasional puff of wind from the southeast; the sky was overcast, though not very dark, and there was fog on the horizon, although no dew fell.

At daybreak on the 23d we discovered the coast, although it was a long way off and rendered indistinct by the fog. This morning it began to blow very light from the south-southeast. Our course was southwest, and we soon lost sight of the land, for a thick fog shut down all around us. After nine o'clock the sun was seen at intervals, but these were very brief. Today no cold was felt, the weather being very mild. At ten the wind began to freshen and the sky became so overcast that no observation of the sun could be obtained. During the afternoon the force of the wind decreased, and by six o'clock it had died away entirely. After eight o'clock there was a drizzling rain, which continued at intervals until twelve. At ten o'clock at night it began to blow very gently from the east, but soon the wind hauled to the northeast and was rather stronger. All night the course was southeast ¼ east.

Before dawn on the 24th the wind went to the northward and

blew rather strong until eight o'clock in the morning, when it was almost a dead calm. This morning we two Fathers celebrated the mass. The sky remained so clouded over that only at six o'clock was the sun visible for a short time. About ten it began to blow rather gently from the north, but the wind died away gradually. At eleven the sky became very dark, and rain threatened; some drops of water fell, though they were few, and presently the fog returned, wet but not very thick. The navigating officers were not able to get an observation because the day was so cloudy and dark. At four in the afternoon the Captain ordered the course to be made southeast, because, although during the day land was not seen, it was considered that we could not be very far away from it and that undoubtedly we should have seen it had not the day been so dark. After eight in the evening the vessel rolled a great deal, for there was a very heavy sea from the north. After that hour the wind was from the northwest, very light, and the ship's head was put to southeast ¼ east. The sky was much obscured and the horizon concealed by fog.

At half past three on the morning of the 25th there was a dead calm, but all the time there was a very heavy sea from the north; farther up the coast, undoubtedly, it has been blowing strong from that direction. During the morning the sky remained very much obscured, and there was considerable fog on the horizon, and, from time to time, light, variable winds from the east and southeast. At eleven o'clock it began to blow rather fresh from the southeast, and the course was made northeast. At that hour the sky cleared a little,

9 Mr. Bancroft's writer, (*History of the Pacific States*, XIII, 228), says "beyond a mere glimpse of Mendocino and the Farallones." The "glimpse" of the *farallones* seems to have been a very decided glimpse. The writer adds: "It is to be noticed that in speaking of the latter islands as a landmark for San Francisco the diarists clearly locate that port under Point Reyes, and speak of the other bay discovered five years before as the *grande estero*, not yet named." In this diary Father de la Peña says nothing about any "*grande estero*." That Father Crespi says nothing about the "*grande estero*" will be learned from his own statement in the document printed hereinafter. Mr. Bancroft's writer, in a footnote to the page last referred to, accuses Father Crespi of making "a long and confusing argument" about whether or not these *farallones* were those seen by the expedition of 1769, an expedition of which Father Crespi was a member. As the writer makes Father Crespi say that the *farallones* seen on this 26th August, 1774, were "50 leagues from Pt. Reyes," it is not to be wondered at that, in that writer's opinion, the friar's "argument" is rather "confusing." In writing of the port of San Francisco both Fathers wrote of the "puerto de San Francisco," now known as "Francis Drake's Bay," or "Drake's Bay." The *farallones* were called "*Farallones* de San Francisco" long before the present San Francisco Bay was known or dreamed of.

and the sun was visible, although the horizon remained obscured as before. By twelve o'clock the wind had died away again. Today the navigating officers obtained an observation, and the Captain told us we were in latitude 38° 38′. During the afternoon the sky was covered with clouds, and there were light puffs of wind, at times from the north and then from the south. About six o'clock in the evening the wind went to north-northwest and was steady but light. By nightfall it was stronger, but shifted about between northwest and west-northwest. From six o'clock to eight the course was east-southeast; during the rest of the night it was southeast ¼ east. The entire night was very dark, and there was a good deal of wet fog.

At daybreak on the 26th there was a great deal of fog and dew, and a very light wind. Just after dawn the ship's head was put east-southeast. The coast could not be seen on account of the heavy fog and the thickness of the weather, but we saw many land birds, great and small, and some ducks of a kind said to frequent fresh water. At eight o'clock the wind had died away entirely, and so much moisture came from the fog that it seemed to be raining. At nine light puffs of wind from the northwest began to blow again; the wind soon freshened and the weather cleared a little. At ten o'clock, at the distance of a league and a half to the southeast, the Farallones of San Francisco* were visible; these lie southwest of Point Reyes and the Port of San Francisco,[9] about five leagues away the Captain said. As soon as these *farallones* were seen the Captain ordered the course to be made southwest, so as to have them to leeward, as it is not known whether the passage between them and the mainland is good or not. As the wind was fresh, at eleven o'clock we were already up to them; and we saw, farther to the southeast, another group of *farallones*, about two leagues to the southeastward of the first. The first group consists of seven high, sharp crags, some larger than others, and near them some rocks under water. They occupy, all together, an area of about a league in circumference. We passed very close to them. Those to the southeastward appear to be somewhat larger. I could not make out with certainty how many in number they are, for we passed them at a distance; but it seemed to me that there were six craggy peaks, one of those in the middle being greater than the others. When we had gone to a short distance beyond the first *farallones* the head of

---

* The Farallones de San Francisco were early referred to as *Los Frailes*, the friars.

the ship was put south ¼ southwest, and, at twelve o'clock, south ¼ southeast. We could not see the coast, nor get an observation, because, in all directions, the fog was very thick. All afternoon the same very favorable wind held and our course was to the southeastward. At sunset the sky cleared, and the horizon to the northward and westward; to the southward and eastward it remained obscured, for which reason we could not see the land. During the night the wind freshened a little, and the ship's head was put southeast ¼ east, in order that we might get in toward the land to make an examination of it at daybreak on the day following.

The 27th dawned clear, although the sky was rather cloudy and the horizon obscured by fog. As the day broke land was made out to the eastward, about three leagues away, and it was said to be Point Año Nuevo. We held on to the southeastward until ten o'clock, when Point Pinos was seen, and then our course was east-southeast until we cast anchor. At nine in the morning the sky became very clear and the sun shone out well. At noon the navigating officers got an observation, and our position was found to be about four leagues to the northwestward of Point Pinos. The Captain said that the latitude was 36° 35′. During the afternoon the wind remained fresh, but it was hauling to the westward; and, about three, when we were abreast of Point Pinos, it went to the southwest. It lacked a little of four o'clock in the afternoon when we came to an anchor in this port of San Carlos de Monterey. Blessed be God and forever praised, and His most holy mother, Our Lady Mary! Amen.

I note that, during the whole voyage, there has been no misfortune on board of the vessel—blessed be God! There has been lacking neither mast nor yard, nor a strand from the rigging—although strong winds and heavy seas have been met with.[10] But in this ocean it is a circumstance to be noted that, as soon as the wind is calmed, the sea falls and is at rest; I think that for this reason it was named by those of old the pacific sea.

I note, also, that, from fifty-five degrees of latitude, the altitude

[10] Father de la Peña appears to forget the death of the ship's-boy and the loss of the anchor and cable.

[11] It should be remembered that Mr. Bancroft's writer acknowledges (in a footnote to page 156, Vol. XXVII, *History of the Pacific States*) that his fragment of this diary of Father de la Peña begins with *August 9th*! He does not explain why the document could not have been obtained entire—as it is given here.

reached by us, to the port of Monterey, we have not been able to learn whether or not there are harbors, bays or other anchoring grounds, because of the distance we have kept from the coast during the homeward passage and on account of the thick weather we have had almost every day during the voyage. Of all this the navigating officers, who are intelligent and skilled in such matters, will give a better account.

Finally: I note that I have written this diary day by day during the voyage, being charged to do so by the Reverend Father President; and, that I might accomplish this, the Captain has done me the favor to communicate to me, almost every day, the latitude in which we were, while, in order to know the courses sailed, I took care to observe closely the needle in the binnacle. And, for the purpose of attesting that what I have written in this diary is the truth, I sign it at this Mission of San Carlos de Monterey, this 28th day of August 1774.[11]

Fray Tomás de la Peña
(a rubric)

Document No. 19

Journal of Fray Juan Crespi kept during the same voyage—dated
5th October, 1774

DIARIO que yo Fray Juan Crespi Misionero del Apostolico Colegio de Propaganda fide de San Fernando de Mexico formo del viaje de la fragata de su Magestad nombrada Santiago, alias la Nueva Galicia mandada por su capitan y alferez de fragata Don Juan Perez, que por orden del Exmo Sor Baylio Frey D. Antonio Maria Bucareli y Ursua Virrey da la Nueva España va a hacer de las costas del Norte de Monte-Rey, que se halla en la altura de 36 grados y medio del Norte, hasta los 60 grados a lo menos.*

Hallandome ocupado de Ministro de esta Mision de San Carlos de Monte-Rey y habiendo llegado a ella en 11 de Mayo del corriente año de buelta de su viaje de nuestro colegio y ciudad de Mexico el Padre Presidente de estas nuevas misiones Fray Junipero Serra, nos hizo saber que dicho Señor Excmo de acuerdo con el Reverendo Padre Guardian de dicho nuestro colegio el Padre Lector Fray Rafael Verger habia determinado que un religioso sacerdote de los nuestros fuese de capellan de la dicha expedicion de mar con el encargo de observar en las nuevas tierras que se pasasen las alturas del polo, de demarcar las costas, notar los genios de los gentiles que se descubriesen y demas circunstancias conducentes a un pleno conocimiento de aquellos ignorados paises y formar de todo un exacto diario. Tambien nos declaró como el religioso que venia destinado al tal encargo quedaba enfermo en la mision y puerto de San Diego y que consiguientemente se le hacia preciso asignar otro y este fuí yo; y no obstante de hallarme bien fatigado con tantos viajes por tierra, me sacrifiqué a ir a esta empresa conformandome con la obediencia esperando en Dios toda felicidad en el viaje, llevando el consuelo, que obtuvo a fuerza de suplica para con su Exca el dicho Padre Presidente, de ir en mi compañia el Padre Predicador Fray Tomas de la Peña y Saravia.

¹ *Frey* should not be confounded with *Fray*. The brother of one of the military orders was *Frey*; a friar was *Fray*.

² The religious appointed to this chaplaincy, and brought from the Franciscan college at Mexico for the purpose, was Fray Pablo Mugártegui.

DIARY which I, Fray Juan Crespi, Missionary of the Apostolic College *de Propaganda Fide* of San Fernando de Mexico, keep of the voyage of His Majesty's frigate called the *Santiago*, otherwise the *Nueva Galicia*, commanded by Captain and *Alférez de Fragata* Don Juan Pérez, which, by order of the Most Excellent Lord, Baylio Frey[1] Don Antonio María Bucareli y Ursúa, Viceroy of New Spain, is about to be made to the coast to the northward of Monterey, which is in latitude 36° 30' north, at least as high as 60°.*

While I was employed in the discharge of my duties as Minister of this Mission of San Carlos de Monterey, the Father President of these New Missions, Fray Junípero Serra, having returned on the 11th of May of the present year from his journey to our college and the City of Mexico, informed us that the said Most Excellent Lord, in accord with the Reverend Father Guardian of our said College, Father Lector Fray Rafael Verger,† had determined that a religious, a priest of our number, should go as chaplain of the said expedition, charged with the duty of observing the new lands that we might explore in the polar latitudes, of making the demarcation of the coast, and of taking note of the character of such pagans as might be met with and of other matters leading to a full knowledge of those unknown lands, of all keeping an exact diary. He said to us, also, that, as the religious who was on his way for the purpose of filling this position had remained at the Mission and Port of San Diego, being sick,[2] it had become necessary to appoint someone in his stead and that I was the man. Notwithstanding my great fatigue after so many expeditions by land, I sacrificed self in order to take part in this enterprise, in conformity with my vows of obedience, trusting in God for all happiness during the voyage and bearing with me the consolation that, by dint of entreaty, the said Father President obtained from His Excellency

* Original in AGI, Estado 43. In Chapman, *Catalogue to AGI*, 352, the diary is noted as No. 2641. A Spanish version with some variation is found in Fr. Francisco Palóu. *Noticias de la Nueva California* (4 vols.), Vol. III, 147–206.

A translation of a version of this diary appears in Herbert E. Bolton (ed.), *Historical Memoirs of New California*, by Fray Francisco Palóu, Vol. III, 147–207. Bolton's notes indicate the existence of a Mexican copy of the manuscript as well as the Sevilla (AGI) copy. An exact duplicate of the Palóu Memoirs as edited by Bolton appears in Herbert E. Bolton, *Fray Juan Crespi, Missionary Explorer on the Pacific Coast, 1769–1774,* 307–66. There are substantial differences between these versions.

† For biographical data on Rafael José Verger, see Geiger, *Palóu's Life of Fray Junípero Serra*, 327.

Y aunque el encargo de mi Prelado es solo de observar saltando a tierra, las alturas, reconocer la tierra y formar una relacion de lo que en ella viese; me he determinado a formar diario del viaje de mar, si me lo permite el tiempo y mareo, que me es indispensable en la navegacion, notando por dias lo que ocurriere.

Dia lunes 6 de Junio de 1774, como a las 4 de la tarde salimos de la mision de San Carlos de Monte Rey acompañados del Reverendo Padre Presidente y habiendo llegado al Real Presidio y despedidos de los señores capitanes y de los Padres Murguia y Palou que alli se hallaban confesando la tripulacion para el viaje, pasamos a la playa en donde nos despedimos del Reverendo Padre Presidente y tomando su bendicion nos embarcamos a bordo de la dicha fragata en donde fuimos recibidos con alegria de todos porque esperaban de nosotros su espiritual consuelo. Esta noche estuvieron en la maniobra de levar las anclas.

Martes 7 prosiguió la maniobra de levar las anclas y con una espia por delante se sacó la fragata del fondeadero y la arrimaron al yervasal que está cerca de la Punta de Pinos de este puerto como un tiro de fusil del fondeadero. Entró el viento N. O. y a las 11 ya estavamos a la vela. Bendito sea Dios a quien pido nos dé toda felicidad. Dieron dos ó tres bordos y volvieron a fondear en el mismo puerto por haber refrescado mucho el Norueste; estando anclados como a las tres de la tarde. Esta noche cayó gravemente enfermo el contramaestre con recia calentura.

Miercoles 8 amaneció con el mismo viento que se mantuvo todo el dia por cuyo motivo no pudimos salir; poco mas de la una de la tarde se divisó vela y fué el Paquebot San Antonio, alias el Principe, y entró y dió fondo en este Puerto como a las tres de la tarde, por cuyo motivo ya nos detuvimos a mas que el viento contrario no nos daba lugar a salir.

Jueves 9, viendo no saliamos al viaje por las dichas causas desembarcamos los dos Padres y fuimos al Real en donde hallamos al Reverendo Padre Presidente con los Padres Murguia y Palou y despues de haber estado un rato nos volvimos a comer a bordo: esta tarde pidió el Señor Capitan Juan Perez que el dia siguiente se cantase una misa en tierra a Nuestra Señora para la felicidad del viaje.

Viernes 10 formado el altar bajo de una enramada en el mismo sitio en donde se celebró día 27 de Diciembre de 1602 cuando la

the favor that Father Predicador Fray Tomás de la Peña y Saravia should go with me as a companion.

And, although I be charged by my prelate only with taking observations for determining the latitude, making a survey of the land and noting what I may see only at those times when we are on shore, yet I have determined to keep a diary of the sea voyage, if time and seasickness, to which I am subject whenever I go to sea, permit me, noting daily what may occur.

Monday, 6th June, 1774. Abount four o'clock in the afternoon we set forth from the Mission of San Carlos de Monterey, being accompanied by the Reverend Father President. We arrived at the royal presidio; and, after taking leave of the captains there and Fathers Murguía and Palóu who were there receiving the confessions of the crew which was to make the voyage, we went to the beach; and, after taking leave of the Reverend Father President and receiving his blessing, we went on board the frigate, where we were welcomed with joy by all, for to us they looked for spiritual consolation. This night the ship's people were engaged in preparations for weighing anchor.

On Tuesday, the 7th, the same work was going on, and by means of a warp the ship was taken from the anchorage and brought near to a place where the seaweed grows to the surface of the sea, close to Point Pinos and about a musket-shot from the anchoring ground. The wind came from the northwest and by eleven o'clock we were under sail. Blessed be God, whom I beseech to give us all happiness. After two or three tacks we came back to port, for the northwest wind had freshened greatly, and anchored at about three o'clock in the afternoon. Tonight the boatswain became seriously ill of a high fever.

Wednesday, the 8th, dawned with the wind in the same quarter; it held all day, so that we could not sail. Shortly after one o'clock in the afternoon a sail was seen, which proved to be the packetboat *San Antonio*, otherwise the *Príncipe*. She came in and anchored about three o'clock. On account of her arrival, and as the headwind did not allow us to sail, we remained in port.

Thursday, the 9th: Seeing that, owing to the reasons mentioned, we could not sail, we two fathers went ashore and to the fort, where we found the Reverend Father President and Fathers Murguía and Palóu. After having been with them a while we came back to the

espedicion del general Don Sebastian Vizcaino; y el dia 3 de Junio de 1770 cuando se vino a poblar este puerto que cantó la primera misa el dicho Reverendo Padre Presidente la cantó tambien este dia, haciendo coro los Padres Fray Joseph Murguia y Fray Francisco Dumetz y nosotros dos que ibamos a este nuevo descubrimiento. Comimos todos juntos cerca la antigua encina que vió Sebastian Vizcaino y despues de haber comido fuimos a bordo y hallamos que habia empeorado el contramaestre a quien confesó mi compañero y yo le administré los santos oleos y como a las cinco poco antes murió; cuyo cadaver embió el señor capitan al Real Presidio para que se le diese sepultura eclesiastica.

Sabado 11 amanció en calma y a remolque con las dos lanchas de la fragata y el Principe nos arrimamos al yerbasal de la punta y como a las doce nos hicimos a la vela con viento O. N. O. no muy fuerte el que nos calmó por la tarde y asi en calma pasamos toda la noche.

Domingo doce amanecimos con calma y ambos Padres celebramos el santo sacrificio de la misa y empezamos una novena al Señor San Antonio de Padua pidiendo su patrocinio para la felicidad del viaje. A las nueve de la mañana nos entró el O. el que duró hasta las doce que varió al Nornorueste y despues al Norueste bonancible que duró lo mas de la tarde aunque despues calmó. Al meterse el sol, el Señor Capitan demarcó la punta de Año Nuevo que nos demoraba al O. N. O. como unas cuatro ó cinco leguas de donde estabamos. A esta hora empezaron algunas ventolinas suaves y se levantó neblina.

Lunes trece amanció con mucha neblina; digimos ambos misa: calmaron los vientos y asi nos estuvimos este dia y su noche no muy retirados de tierra, aunque por la neblina no se divisaba muy clara.

Martes catorce amanció muy cerrado de neblina aunque en breve abrió y nos hallamos a una vista de la Punta de Año Nuevo, tuvimos algunas ventolinas suaves y calmosas y estuvieron bordeando entre las dos puntas de Pinos y Año Nuevo.

Miercoles quince amanecio cerrado de neblina aunque abrió antes de las siete y nos hallamos en frente de la Punta de Pinos, divisando la de Cipreses, la sierra de Santa Lucia y la ensenada del rio Carmelo. Como a las seis da la tarde nos hallamos como cinco ó seis leguas apartados de la sierra de Santa Lucia y lo mismo de la punta de año nuevo.

Jueves diez y seis amaneció con bastante neblina aunque en breve

ship for dinner. This afternoon Captain Don Juan Pérez requested that on the next day a mass should be sung on shore to Our Lady, for the happiness of the voyage.

Friday, the 10th: The altar was raised under a shelter of boughs on the same site where the mass was celebrated on the 27th of December, 1602, during the expedition of General Don Sebastián Vizcaíno, and on the 3d of June, 1770, when a settlement was made at this port and the first mass was sung by the Reverend Father President, who sang the mass today also, Fathers Fray José Murguía and Fray Francisco Dumetz and we two who were going on this new expedition being choristers. We all dined together near the old oak which Sebastián Vizcaíno saw. After dinner we went on board the ship, and found that the boatswain's condition was worse. He confessed to my companion and I administered the holy oil to him. Shortly before five o'clock he died, and the Captain sent the corpse to the royal Presidio that it might be given ecclesiastical burial.

Saturday, the 11th, dawned calm, and in tow of the two *lanchas* of the ship and the *Príncipe*, we were taken out to the seaweed patch near the point. About twelve o'clock we made sail with a west-northwest wind, though not very strong. It died away during the afternoon, and so in a calm we passed the night.

Sunday, the 12th, dawned calm, and both fathers celebrated the holy sacrifice of the mass, and we began a novena to San Antonio de Padua, asking his patronage for the happiness of the voyage. At nine in the morning the wind sprang up from the west and blew thence till twelve, when it went to the north-northwest, and afterwards the northwest. This was favorable and lasted almost all the afternoon, though at length it died away. At sunset the Captain took the bearings of Point Año Nuevo; it bore west-northwest, some four or five leagues from where we were. At this hour the wind began to blow gently in puffs and a fog arose.

Monday, the 13th, dawned very foggy. We both said mass. The wind died away, and thus we were all day and night not very far from land, although it could not be seen very clearly on account of the fog.

Tuesday, the 14th, dawned with a very thick fog, although it soon lifted and we caught sight of Point Año Nuevo. We caught some light puffs of wind and kept tacking between Points Pinos and Año Nuevo.

abrió y vimos la sierra de Santa Lucia ya como diez ó doce leguas apartadas. Como a las diez nos entró el N. N. O. algo fresco, que llegamos a andar dos y media millas por hora, despues varió al N. O. y este continuó todo el dia, y por la tarde apenas se divisaba la tierra.

Viernes diez y siete amaneció muy claro y despejado y la mar en calma hasta la una de la tarde que se movió el S. O. aunque muy suave: por la tarde divisaron la sierra de Santa Lucia que dijeron distariamos de ella como diez y seis leguas al N. E.: por la noche viraron de bordo con el Norueste.

Sabado diez y ocho amaneció muy cerrado de neblina muy oscura y humeda que parecia estar lloviendo, soplado el N. O. fresco, que andavamos como cuatro millas. Esta noche se vió el Señor Capitan bien malo del estomago y pasó mala noche sin poder sosegar, pero no fué cosa de cuidado, pues a las doce ya estaba bueno y pudo observar y dijo nos hallabamos en 34 grados y cincuenta y siete minutos: al medio dia nos hallabamos como siete leguas de la costa de la sierra de Santa Lucia; por la tarde refrescó mucho el N. O., embraveció mucho la mar que duró este dia y el siguiente.

Domingo diez y nueve amanecimos con el mismo viento y muy embravecida la mar, de manera que no pudimos celebrar; apretó tanto el viento que a los ocho quedamos con solo el trinquete, por la tarde aflojó algo y mas a la entrada de la noche.

Lunes veinte amanecimos con el mismo viento y aunque no tan fuerte, pero caminabamos cinco millas y media por hora.

Martes veinte y uno amaneció este dia muy claro y despejado el cielo; como a las seis de la mañana varió el viento al N. N. E. suave y a las siete de la mañana dijeron andavamos tres millas por hora. Al medio dia observó el señor capitan y nos dijo nos hallavamos en la altura de 34 grados y 8 minutos: varió despues el viento al N. y fué refrescando por la tarde, y dijeron andamos cuatro millas y a veces mas, y este mismo viento continuó la noche siguiente.

Miercoles veinte y dos amaneció este dia con viento N. aunque muy suave y el dia claro; como a las siete se levantó una neblina muy humeda y calmó algo el viento, aunque no fué tanto que no anduviesimos tres millas por hora. Este medio dia me dijo el señor capitan habia observado la latitud del N. de 34 grados y 7 minutos.

Jueves veinte y tres amaneció muy cerrado de neblina se mudó el viento al N. E. aunque despues varió al N. suave y dijeron andavamos

Wednesday, the 15th, dawned with a very thick fog which lifted before seven o'clock, when we found that we were off Point Pinos, with Point Cipreses, the Sierra of Santa Lucía and the bay into which the river Carmelo empties in sight. About six o'clock in the evening we were five or six leagues away from the Sierra of Santa Lucía and the same distance from Point Año Nuevo.

Thursday, the 16th, dawned with much fog, although it lifted soon and we saw the Sierra of Santa Lucía, now some ten or twelve leagues distant. About seven o'clock the wind came from the north-northwest rather fresh, so that we made two miles and a half an hour. Afterwards the wind went to northwest and blew thence all day. By evening we could barely make out the land.

Friday, the 17th, dawned very clear and bright. The sea was calm until one in the afternoon, when the wind came from the southwest, though very light. In the afternoon we saw the Sierra of Santa Lucía, said to be some sixteen leagues distant to the northeastward. During the night we tacked, the wind going to the northwest.

Saturday, the 18th, dawned with a thick fog, so dark and wet that it seemed to be raining. The wind was blowing fresh from the northwest, so that we made some four miles an hour. During the night the Captain was very sick at the stomach and passed a bad night, being unable to get any ease from pain. But it was not a serious matter, for at twelve o'clock he was well and able to take an observation; he told us that we were in 34° 57′. At noon we were about seven leagues off the coast of the Sierra of Santa Lucía. In the afternoon the northwest wind increased a great deal in force; the sea became very rough and so continued, this day and the next.

Sunday, the 19th, dawned with the same wind and the sea very rough—so that we could not celebrate the mass. The wind freshened so that at eight o'clock we were under the foresail only; during the afternoon its strength decreased and, after night came on, it decreased more.

At dawn on Monday, the 20th, the same wind continued to blow, although not so strong; we made five miles and a half an hour.

Tuesday, the 21st, dawned with a very bright and clear sky. About six in the morning the wind hauled to the north-northeast; it was light, and at seven o'clock it was said that we were making three miles an hour. At noon the Captain took an observation and said we

211

tres millas por hora, al medio dia observaron los señores, y me dijo el señor capitan que nos hallavamos en 33 grados y 46 minutos.

Viernes veinte y cuatro, celebramos ambos misa y en la primera comulgaron el Señor Capitan, el contra-maestre y otros dos Juanes de los marineros: amaneció el dia nublado, y con el viento N. N. E. fresco caminabamos tres millas con al proa al N. O. ¼ al N. Al medio dia observaron y dijo el señor capitan que nos hallabamos en 33 grados y 46 minutos.

Sabado veinte y cinco amaneció claro el dia y con el viento N. E. que tuvimos la noche pasada y continua bastante fresco, caminando con la proa al N. O. lo que en todo viaje no se habia logrado. Al medio dia me dijo el señor capitan que segun la observacion que habia hecho nos hallabamos en 34 grados y 26 minutos; gracias a Dios que ya vamos cobrando la altura perdida: por la tarde refrescó mas el viento y andavamos como cinco millas.

Domingo veinte y seis amaneció el dia claro con el viento E. fresco que nos habia entrado la noche pasada cuando salió la luna, con la proa al N. O. como ayer: pudimos ambos celebrar, y hacerles una platica el Padre compañero en su misa. Al medio dia observaron los señores y me dijo el señor capitan nos hallavamos en 35 grados y 37 minutos. Como a las cinco de la tarde empezó a calmar el viento de modo que al anochecer estavamos en calma y asi pasamos la noche.

Lunes veinte y siete amaneció el dia algo nublado y con la misma calma de la noche antecedente: como a las seis entraron ventolinas aunque suaves que andavamos poco mas de milla. Al medio dia nos dijo el señor capitan que habia observado 35 grados y 59 minutos; siguió la calma hasta la noche que al salir la luna nos entró el N. E.

Martes veinte y ocho amaneció el dia claro siguiendo el mismo viento N. E. que fué poco a poco refrescando y a las nueve de la mañana andavamos como cuatro millas. Al medio dia observó el señor capitan 36 grados y 26 minutos y asi nos hallamos enfrente de la sierra de Santa Lucia y muy al paralelo de Monte-Rey con la diferencia de cuatro minutos menos, aunque enmarados segun dicen los señores como doscientas leguas.

Miercoles veinte y nueve amaneció el dia claro con el mismo viento fresco N. E. celebramos ambos Padres y en una de las misas comulgó

[3] This was the day of St. John the Baptist, and the birthday—saint's day—of these persons named John.

were in 34° 08′. Later the wind went to the north and freshened during the afternoon; it was said we made four miles an hour, at times more. The wind held during the night.

Wednesday, the 22d, began with the wind in the north, though light, and the day was clear. About seven a very damp fog arose, and the wind fell, although not enough to prevent our making three miles an hour. At noon the Captain told me that he had taken an observation for latitude, which was 34° 07′.

Thursday, the 23rd dawned very foggy. The wind shifted to northeast, but afterwards went to the north; it was gentle, and they said we made three miles an hour. At midday the gentlemen took an observation and the Captain told me we were in 33° 46′.

On Friday, the 24th, we both celebrated the mass. At the first mass the Captain, the boatswain and two of the sailors, also named Juan, communed.[3] The day dawned cloudy, and with the wind fresh from the north-northeast we made three miles an hour with the ship's head to northwest ¼ north. At midday an observation was taken and the Captain said our latitude was 33° 46′.

On Saturday, the 25th, the day dawned clear; with the northeast wind we had during the night, which continued fresh, we sailed on a northwest course—what so far during the voyage we had not been able to do. The Captain told me that, according to the observation he made at midday, we were in 34° 26′. Thanks be to God; we are now regaining lost latitude! During the afternoon the wind freshened and we made about five miles an hour.

On Sunday, the 26th, the day dawned clear, with the wind fresh from the east, whence it began to blow when the moon rose last night; the course was northwest, as it was yesterday. We were both able to celebrate the mass; at his mass my father companion preached a sermon. At midday the gentlemen took an observation, and the Captain told me we were in 35° 37′.* About five o'clock in the afternoon the wind began to die away, and at nightfall there was a dead calm. Thus we passed the night.

On Monday, the 27th, the day dawned rather cloudy, with the calm that had lasted all night. About six o'clock gentle puffs of wind sprang up and we made a little more than a mile an hour. At midday the Captain told us he had obtained an observation in 35° 59′. The calm

* Bolton has 34° 37′ and Palóu's *Noticias* has 31° 37′.

el cirujano celebrando el dia de su santo. Al medio dia observó el señor capitan y nos dijo nos hallavamos en 37 grados y 20 minutos.

Jueves treinta amaneció el dia claro aunque en breve se nubló con viento fresco E. S. que anadavamos como tres millas. Al medio dia observó el señor capitan y nos dijo nos hallavamos en 38 grados y 35 minutos.

Julio: Viernes primero de Julio amaneció el dia algo nublado y siguiendo el mismo viento que toda la noche E. S. y a ratos iba refrescando mas. Al medio dia nos dijo el señor capitan que segun su observacion nos hallavamos en 39 grados y 43 minutos; como a las cinco de la tarde calmó el viento y duró la calma toda la noche.

Sabado dos amaneció el dia cerrado y en calma que duró todo el dia. Al medio dia observaron los señores pilotos y nos dijeron no llegavamos a los 40 grados.

Domingo tres de Julio amaneció el dia muy cerrado de neblina con el viento E. S. E. tan flojo que apenas se andaba. Digimos ambos misa y en una comulgaron el 2° piloto D. Esteban Martinez y dos marineros: como a las diez refrescó algo el dicho viento y como a las once se andaban dos millas y media. Al medio dia observó el señor capitan la altura del N. en 40 grados y 34 minutos. Esta tarde varió el viento al S. E. bien y en popa.

Lunes cuatro amaneció el dia muy cerrado con el mismo viento S. E. bastante fresco con el que andavamos tres millas y algunas veces cuatro por hora: se cerró bastante el dia y tuvimos algunos chuvascos con algunas rociaditas de agua aunque continuó el viento, y por estar el dia cerrado no se pudo observar.

Martes cinco amaneció el dia muy claro y con el mismo viento de ayer que se ha conservado toda la noche. Al medio dia observó el señor capitan la altura del Norte segun nos dijo de 43 grados y 35 minutos. Al medio dia varió el viento al S. O. pero en breve volvió a soplar al S. E. el que duró toda la tarde y noche.

Miercoles seis amaneció con bastante neblina y con el mismo viento S. E. con el que andavamos tres millas. Al medio dia no pudieron

---

[4] This is the day of St. Peter and St. Paul. It would appear that, when Mr. Bancroft's writer says (*History of the Pacific States*, vol. XIII, p. 228) that Dávila, whose name is given on p. 226 of the same volume, went on the expedition as surgeon, instead of the ship's regular surgeon, Costan [Castán], he must be mistaken. Dávila's name was José, and St. Joseph's day is 19th March.

[5] This was the day of St. Mark. Father Crespi does not say that it was the saint's day of the communicants. The saint's day of Martínez, that of St. Stephen, is 26th December.

lasted until night; when the moon rose the wind began to blow from the northeast.

Tuesday, the 28th, dawned clear. The northeast wind continued to blow, and freshened little by little, so that at nine o'clock we were making about four miles an hour. At midday the Captain took an observation in 36° 26'—so that we are off the Sierra of Santa Lucía and very nearly in the latitude of Monterey, the difference being four minutes less; but, as the officers say, we are some two hundred leagues off the coast.

On Wednesday, the 29th, the day dawned clear, and with the same fresh wind from the northeast. Both fathers celebrated the mass; in one of the masses the surgeon communed, celebrating the day of his saint.[4]* At mid-day the Captain took an observation and told us that we were in 37° 20'.

On Thursday, the 30th, the day dawned clear, although it was soon cloudy. The wind was fresh from the east-southeast, so that we made about three miles an hour. At midday the Captain took an observation and said that we were in 38° 35'.

July: On Friday, the 1st of July, the day dawned cloudy, with the same wind that had blown from the east-southeast all night and which now kept freshening. At midday the Captain told us that, according to his observation, we were in 39° 43'. About five o'clock in the afternoon the wind died away and the calm lasted all night.

Saturday, the 2d, dawned cloudy and calm, and these conditions continued all this day. At noon the navigating officers got an observation of the sun, and told us we had not yet reached the fortieth degree of latitude.

At dawn on Sunday, the 3d, there was a thick fog, with the wind from the east-southeast, so light that we scarcely moved. We both said mass; at one of the masses the second navigating officer, Don Esteban Martínez, and two sailors communed.[5] About ten o'clock the wind freshened, and at eleven we were making two miles and a half an hour. At midday the Captain took an observation in 40° 34'. This afternoon the wind shifted to the southeast; it was fresh and a stern wind.

Monday, the 4th, began with thick weather and with the wind still

---

* Griffin's note is in error. José Dávila had been surgeon aboard the *Santiago*, but upon arrival in San Diego he had been replaced by Pedro Castán because Dávila had an intense fear of the sea.

observar por la mucha neblina que no dejó descubrirse el sol: como a la una de la tarde varió el viento al S. O. algo fresco que andavamos tres millas, pero calmó como a las cinco de la tarde y quedamos casi en calma y de la misma manera pasamos la noche.

Jueves siete amanecimos en calma con el viento O. S. O. y con bastante neblina que tuvo tapados los orizontes, hasta pasado medio dia, por cuyo motivo no se pudo hoy observar: por la tarde nos entró ventolina calmosa, tambien del N. que nos duró lo restante del dia y noche.

Viernes ocho amaneció con la misma ventolina calmosa del Norte y neblina que duró todo el dia y noche siguiente. Al medio dia abrió lo suficiente para observar y nos dijo el señor capitan que nos hallabamos en 44 grados y 5 minutos.

Sabado nueve nos hallamos con igual neblina y calma, con ventolina llovisnosa del S. E.: antes de medio dia se descubrió bien el sol y orizontes y logró el señor capitan una observacion a su satisfaccion, lo que no en los cinco dias antecedentes no habia podido, y nos dijo nos hallavamos en 45 grados cabales.

Domingo diez amaneció con mucha neblina y llovisna con ventolina calmosa del S. E. Celebramos los dos Padres el santo sacrificio de la misa, como tambien les pudo hacer una platica el Padre compañero en su misa: como a las nueve abrió el tiempo y se descubrió el sol y empezó a refrescar el viento S. E. que era en popa, a las once andavamos como dos millas. Al medio dia observó el señor capitan y nos dijo nos hallavamos en 45 grados y 35 minutos; duró el S. E. todo el dia y por la noche varió al Sur tambien fresco. Se administró esta noche los santos sacramentos de la penitencia y extremauncion a un marinero que se halla muy malo de calentura maligna.

Lunes once amaneció con el mismo viento sur y cerrado de espesa neblina; abrió algo antes de medio dia y pudo el señor capitan observar y nos dijo nos hallavamos en la altura de 46 grados y 23 minutos, refrescó mas el viento y a las tres de la tarde andavamos tres millas y a otras horas mas; esta tarde se ha sentido bien el frio y por la noche apuró mas por la llovisna que despedia la neblina que parecia nieve.

Martes doce amanecimos con la misma neblina y mucho frio, cerca de las cinco de la mañana se mudó el viento al O. S. O. fresco, que andavamos tres millas y a las diez se mudó al O. bastante fuerte y frio; todo el dia estuvo muy cerrado por lo que no se pudo observar;

from the southeast; it was quite fresh and we made three and, at times, four miles an hour. The weather thickened, and there were squalls and showers, the wind continuing to blow from the same quarter. As the weather was so thick it was impossible to get an observation.

Tuesday, the 5th, dawned very fair, and with the wind in the quarter where it had been all night. At midday the Captain took an observation and said that we were in 43° 35′. At noon the wind hauled to the southwest, but it soon went back to southeast, remaining in that quarter all the afternoon and night.

Wednesday, the 6th, dawned very foggy; the wind still came from the southeast and we made three miles an hour. At noon no observation was possible, on account of the heavy fog which obscured the sun. About one o'clock in the afternoon the wind went to the southwest; it was quite fresh, and we made three miles an hour. About five it died away almost to a calm; and in like manner the night passed.

Thursday, the 7th, dawned calm. The wind was still west-southwest and there was so much fog that the horizon was obscured till after midday, so that no observation was possible. In the afternoon there were light puffs of wind from the north and calms; these lasted all day and during the night.

At daybreak on Friday, the 8th, the same light winds from the north and calms continued, with a fog which lasted all day and through the following night. At midday it cleared away so that an observation could be obtained and the Captain told us we were in 44° 05′.

Saturday, the 9th, was also foggy and calm with light winds accompanied by rain from the southeast. Before noon the sun shone out and the horizon was clear, and the Captain managed to get an observation which was satisfactory, a thing he has not been able to do for five days past, and he said that we were in just 45°.

Sunday, the 10th, dawned with much fog and rain and light southeasterly breezes. We two fathers celebrated the mass; during the mass my companion was able to preach also. About nine o'clock the day was clearer and the sun shone out. The wind was from the southeast, a stern wind, and at eleven o'clock we were making two miles an hour. At midday the Captain took an observation and said we were in 45° 35′. The southeast wind blew all day; during the night

como a las tres de la tarde aclaró algo y por la noche no estuvo el tiempo tan cerrado.

Miercoles trece amanecimos con el dia bien claro y con el viento N. O. ¼ al O. bastante fuerte con el que andavamos tres millas. A las siete de la mañana se cerró de mucho nublado y a las diez volvió abrir y se despejaron los orizontes y pudo el señor capitan observar a toda su satisfaccion y nos dijo que nos hallavamos en la altura de 48 grados y 55 minutos: por la tarde aflojó algo el viento aunque andavamos dos millas y media.

Jueves catorce amaneció con mucha neblina y llovisnando que de la misma manera se habia pasado la noche; a las cinco soplaba bien fuerte el O. que andavamos cuatro millas y media. A las siete y media de la mañana vimos el arco iris al O. y nos entró un chubasco bastante fuerte que causó mucha marejada y obligó a tomar rizos del belacho de gabia y pasado el chubasco se deshizo el arco iris y continuó el mismo viento O. bastante fresco: poco antes de las doce se despejó el cielo y quedaron claros los orizontes con que se pudo observar y nos dijo el señor capitan nos hallavamos en la altura de 50 grados y 24 minutos: a las nueve de la mañana mandó el señor capitan poner la proa al N. y nos dijo que habia virado para ir a caer a la costa y nos dijo el señor capitan que lo hizo porque habiendo registrado la aguada reconoció no habia mas agua que para dos meses y medio lo mas, y que por lo que podia suceder queria hacer la diligencia de registrar la costa y ver si podria hacer aguada por no saber cuanto podria tardar para la buelta a Monte-Rey: a las tres de la tarde se alargo mas el viento hasta el S. O. bien fresco que adavamos cuatro millas y media con la proa al Norte.

Viernes quince amaneció con la misma neblina espesa y humeda, con una llovisna fria como los dias antecedentes, con viento sur bien fresco y con mucha marejada que nos balanceaba bastante: toda esta mañana andavamos cuatro millas y a veces mas por hora con la proa al N.; se esplica demasiadamente el frio: a las ocho cambió el viento al S. O. bastante fresco, y con él viraron poniendo la proa al N. E. para ir a caer a la costa. Fué aclarando el dia y despejandose los orizontes con que se logró la observacion y nos dijo el señor capitan que nos hallavamos en la altura de 51 grados y 42 minutos.

Este dia el señor capitan juntó los oficiales de la fragata y les propuso el estado de la aguada y el peligro a que se esponian de pasar mas

it hauled to the south, still blowing fresh. This night the holy sacraments of penance and extreme unction were administered to a sailor who was very ill of a malignant fever.

At dawn on Monday, the 11th, the same south wind was blowing and there was a thick fog. But, a short time before noon, the weather cleared a little and the Captain was able to take an observation. He told us we were in latitude 46° 23'. The wind continued to freshen; and, at three in the afternoon, we were making three miles an hour, and at times more. This afternoon we felt the cold very keenly; during the night this was greater, because of the moisture from the fog, which resembled snow.

On Tuesday, the 12th, the same fog was present and it was very cold. About five o'clock in the morning the wind shifted to westsouthwest; it blew fresh, and we made about three miles an hour. At ten o'clock the wind went to west; it blew strong and cold. The weather was thick all day and no observation could be obtained. About three in the afternoon the weather cleared a little, and during the night it was not so thick.

At daylight on Wednesday, the 13th, the weather was very clear. The wind was northwest ¼ west, so strong that we made three miles an hour. At seven o'clock in the morning a heavy fog came on. At ten it lifted and the horizon was clear, so that the Captain obtained an observation to his entire satisfaction, and he informed us that we were in latitude 48° 55'. During the afternoon the force of the wind decreased, although we made two miles and a half an hour.

At daybreak on Thursday, the 14th, there was a heavy fog and a drizzling rain, as there had been during the night. At five the wind was blowing strong from the west, so that we made four miles and a half an hour. At half past seven we saw a rainbow in the west, and were struck by a heavy squall which caused a high sea, and it was necessary to reef the topsails. When the squall passed the rainbow had disappeared and the same rather fresh west wind continued to blow. At a short time before noon the sky and the horizon became clear, so that an observation could be obtained; the Captain said our position was 50° 24'. At nine in the morning the Captain ordered the course to be made north, and said that he had gone about in order to make a landfall. He did this, he said, because he had examined into the condition of the water-supply and found that there was water for, at

arriba sin hacer aguada, que si les parecia arrimarse a la costa para registrar fondeadero y hacer aguada, ó si les parecia que siguiesen hasta la altura de los 60 grados como encargaba su Excelencia y que en dicha altura se haria la diligencia de agua. Oida la propuesta del señor capitan fueron todos de parecer que convenia recalar a tierra para prevenirse de agua y reconocer fondeadero ó parage para arribar en caso necesario. Visto el parecer de los oficiales siguió en busca de la costa.

Sabado diez y seis de Julio amaneció el dia nublado aunque sin neblina y con el viento en popa S. O. que hemos tenido toda esta noche pasada y ha durado hasta las nueve del dia que se cambió al S., con que andavamos tres millas a la bolina: a dicha hora empezó a aclarar y tuvimos un buen sol con que pudieron los señores observar y nos dijo el señor capitan que nos hallavamos en 52 grados y 41 minutos: a las cuatro de la tarde volvió a cambiarse el viento fresco al S. O. y caminavamos con viento en popa lo mismo que por la mañana. Los carpinteros hicieron hoy una cruz de como cinco varas de alto con el rotulo de arriba I.N.R.I. y en el cuerpo de la cruz desde los pies para los brazos, *Carolus tertius: Rex Hispaniarum:* y en los brazos de ella, año 1774, con el fin de en cuanto saltar a tierra que todavia no hemos descubierto fijarla.

Domingo 17 de Julio amaneció nublado con alguna neblina y casi en calma con el viento S. O. que por la noche aflojó: digimos ambos misa, y en la suya hizo la platica el Padre compañero, como todos los domingos que ha dado lugar el tiempo se ha hecho: aunque tuvimos esta mañana alguna neblina y un aguacerito corto pero despues aclaró y se logró el poder observar y nos dijo el señor capitan que nos hallavamos en 53 grados y 13 minutos. En estas alturas se nos pone el sol en estos dias a las ocho de la noche y sale como a las cuatro de la mañana, de tal manera que a las nueve de la noche todavia hay

[6] The instructions given to Pérez were that he should proceed northward to latitude 60° and thence come back to Monterey along the coast, examining it and taking possession. Mr. Bancroft's writers do not agree on this point: The person who wrote the account of Pérez's voyage to be found at p. 227 of vol. XIII of the *History of the Pacific States* says Pérez was "to explore the northern coast up to 60°." The person who wrote the account of that voyage contained in vol. XXVII of that work says, on p. 151, that "he was to make the land wherever he might deem best, but at least as high as 60°." It is very evident that Pérez understood his instructions, if the former of the two Bancroftian writers did not, and that he intended to go to 60° before making a landfall. This intention he was forced to modify because of the necessity for obtaining a supply of water.

[7] A *vara* may be taken to be 2.75 English feet.

most, two months and a half, and that, in view of what might happen, he desired to search the coast for a place where he could take in water, as he could not know how long the return to Monterey might be delayed. At three in the afternoon the wind increased in force, until with a very fresh wind from the southwest we were making four miles and a half an hour with the ship's head to the northward.

On Friday, the 15th, the same heavy, damp fog was present at dawn, together with the cold, drizzling rain of previous days. The wind blew very strong from the south, and there was a very high sea, which tossed us about a good deal. All the morning we made four miles an hour, and at times more, heading northward. The cold increased exceedingly. At eight the wind hauled to the southwest, and the ship tacked and stood to the northeast, so as to make the coast. The day became clearer and the horizon more distinct, so that an observation could be made. The Captain told us our latitude was 51° 42'.

Today the Captain called the officers of the frigate together and made known to them the condition of the water-supply and the dangers to which we would be exposed should we go on to higher latitudes without renewing that supply, and he asked whether, in their opinion, it were better to draw in to the coast in order to find an anchoring ground and take on board water, or to go on to latitude sixty as His Excellency had ordered[6] and there attend to this matter of getting water. The Captain's proposition being heard, all were of the opinion that it were better to make the land for the purpose of obtaining water and in order to find an anchorage or a place whither the ship might go in case of need. The opinion of the officers being thus obtained, we went on in search of the coast.

Saturday, the 16th, dawned cloudy, although there was no fog. There was a stern wind from the southwest, as there had been all the past night. The wind was in this quarter until nine o'clock, when it went to the south and we made three miles an hour with a side wind. At that hour the weather began to clear and the sun shone out well; so that an observation was obtained, the Captain informing us that we were in 52° 41'. At four in the afternoon the wind changed again becoming strong from the southwest, and we sailed with a stern wind again, as in the morning. Today the carpenters made a cross of about five *varas*[7] in height, with the inscription I. N. R. I.* on the upper

---

* I. N. R. I., *Jesus Nazarenus Rex Judaeorum*; Jesus of Nazareth, King of the Jews.

claridad, y por la mañana como a las tres ya empieza a aclarar; y si hubieramos llegado un mes antes segun dicen habriamos visto ponerse el sol a las nueve.

Lunes diez y ocho de Julio amaneció el dia muy cerrado de neblina y llovisna y a las cinco de la mañana vino un chubasco con ventolinas del S. y S. E. que poco se andaba: como a las once y media dijeron se descubria tierra y asi fué que empezamos a ver la costa y la mas cerca la teniamos a la proa hacia el N. E. como a diez y seis leguas de distancia y al N. O. ¼ al N. parecia que remataba, pero por lo muy ahumado y muy retirado, que a lo menos estaria veinte y cinco leguas no se percibia bien. Por el N. parecia ser tierra baja y al contrario por el N. E. se dejaba ver muy alta y un mogote en ella todo nevado: aunque algo abrió el dia con que pudimos ver la tierra, pero no se dejó ver el sol para poder observar: como a las cuatro de la tarde cambió el viento al O. S. O. y con el se andaban dos millas y media; y poco despues de las cinco se cambió otra vez al N. O. muy suave, al principio algo anduvo con él, pero por la noche calmó totalmente.

Martes diez y nueve amaneció el dia nublado pero con los orizontes claros, con que se divisaba bien la tierra distante de siete a ocho leguas, pero nos hallamos con la misma calma que hemos tenido toda la noche. Vimos bien la costa y a todos nos pareció que la que teniamos a la vista corre del N. N. O. al S. S. E. y que remataba su curso al N. N. E. en donde hace un cabo y desde alli parece que tuerce al mismo N. N. E. ó hasta el N. E. Antes de las siete se cerró el dia de tal neblina que apenas se veia la costa y prosiguiendo la calma: a las once se nos cambió el viento al S. E. del segundo cuadrante algo fresco y empezamos a andar hacia el cabo de la costa que habiamos visto por la mañana a fin de ver el curso de la costa del otro lado de la costa hacia el N.; cerca de las once se descubrió el sol y se dejó ver bien a las doce, con esto pudieron los señores observar y segun nos dijo el señor capitan nos hallamos en 53 grados y 58 minutos: por la tarde refrescó mas el viento y como a las cinco estabamos ya como tres leguas de la tierra y vimos que despues del cabo que habiamos visto seguia la costa baja hacia el N.: como era tarde viraron de bordo para apartarnos algo de la costa poniendo la proa al N. y a las seis nos pusimos a la capa, en la que hemos estado toda esta noche con una gran marejada y con una continua llovisna.

Miercoles veinte de Julio amaneció el dia muy cerrado de neblina

part and, along the body of the cross between the arms and the foot, the words *Carolus tertius: Rex Hispaniarum:** and on the arms *año* 1774, so that, on landing in a country where we have made no discoveries as yet, it may be planted there.†

Sunday, the 17th, dawned cloudy, with some fog. It was almost calm, with a southwest wind which during the night had become less. We both celebrated the mass; at his mass my father companion preached a sermon—as he has done every Sunday when the weather permitted. Although during the morning there was some fog and a brief shower it cleared later, so that an observation could be obtained. The Captain told us that we were in 53° 13'. In this latitude the sun sets, at this season of the year, at eight o'clock and rises about four in the morning; so that at nine at night it is still light, while at three in the morning the dawn begins. Had we arrived a month earlier, it is said, we should have seen the sun set at nine o'clock.

Monday, the 18th, dawned very foggy, and there was a drizzling rain. At five in the morning there was a squall, followed by light winds from the south and southeast—so that the ship made but little way. About half past eleven it was said that land was seen, and so it was we began to get sight of the coast. The nearest point was on the bow to the northeastward, about sixteen leagues away. It seemed to end at a point bearing northwest ¼ north; but, as it was very hazy and the land distant, being at least twenty-five leagues away, this could not be made out clearly. In the north the land seemed to be low; but, on the contrary, in the northeast it appeared to be very high and there was a high cliff, or peak, with a flat top covered with snow. Although the weather lightened so that we could see the land, the sun did not shine out so that an observation could be obtained. At four o'clock in the afternoon the wind hauled to west-southwest and the ship made two miles and a half an hour. Shortly after five o'clock the wind went to the northwest; it was very light, and, although at first we made some progress, by night there was a dead calm.

Tuesday, the 19th, dawned cloudy, but the horizon was clear, so that the land was seen clearly, seven or eight leagues away. But then it was calm, as it had been all night. We had a good view of the coast, and it seemed to all that the portion we saw trended north-northwest

---

* Charles III, King of Spain.

† For a consideration of the act of possession, see Manuel Servin, "Religious Aspects of Symbolic Acts of Sovereignty," in *The Americas*, Vol. XIII, 1957.

que a muy corta distancia nada se veia y lluvisnando con viento E. bastante fuerte y con mucha marejada con un continuo balance: soltaron las velas y la proa al N. ¼ al N. E.: antes de las nueve abrió algo el dia y se vió bien la tierra, viraron de bordo y se puso la proa al N. E. para hacer la diligencia de arrimarnos a una punta de tierra: a las diez estavamos como cuatro leguas de dicha punta que a todos nos parecieron tres islas: al medio dia no se pudo observar por estar nublado y tapado el sol: como a las tres de la tarde estavamos como dos leguas de tierra y la que antes nos habia parecido ser tres islas ya parecia una y no muy apartada de la costa: vimos muchas humaderas de los habitantes en ella y que era tierra muy poblada de arboleda que parecian pinos y que con la dicha punta formaba la tierra una buena ensenada ó baia.

Y reparamos que de una bocana que formaba la tierra salia una canoa que a fuerza de remo venia para la fragata; de bien apartados del barco los oiamos cantar y en el tono conocimos ser gentiles, pues es el mismo que usan en sus mitoles los gentiles desde San Diego a Monte-Rey: llegaron ya cerca de la fragata y vimos eran ocho hombres y un muchacho los siete remando, el otro que venia algo envijado, parado y con ademanes de bailar, y tirando a la mar varias plumas dieron una vuelta a la fragata; desde el balcon de la camara los llamamos que se arrimasen y aunque al principio no se atrevian por algun recelo que tendrian enseñandoles pañuelos, avalorios y galleta se arrimaron a la popa y recibieron todo lo que se les tiró; les hecharon un mecate para que subiesen y aunque se agarraron de él no se atrevieron a subir pero asidos de él nos siguieron bastante trecho.

Cuando dicha canoa llegó a bordo ya eran como las cuatro de la tarde y se habia cerrado de espesa neblina y viento contrario, por estos motivos habia mandado el señor capitan virar de bordo reservando el arrimarnos mas a la tierra y desembarcar para el dia siguiente, y viendo los gentiles que nos apartavamos de su tierra nos convidaban con ella y conocimos ó entendimos por señas que nos decian que alli tenian que comer y mucha agua y lugar para estar el barco, y respondiendoles por señas que el dia siguiente iriamos, se fueron.

Estos gentiles son bien corpulentos y gordos, de buen semblante y de color blanco y vermejo, con pelo largo y cubiertos con cueros de nutria y de lobos marinos segun nos parecia y todos ó lo mas con sus sombreros de junco bien tejido, con la copa punteaguda: no son nada

and south-southeast, and that this direction was changed to north-northeast at a point where there was a cape, whence it seemed to trend to the north-northeast or northeast. Before seven o'clock the fog had thickened so that we were barely able to make out the coast, the calm still continuing. At eleven o'clock the wind came from the southeast rather fresh, and we began to move toward the cape we had seen in the morning, in order to discover the lay of the land beyond the coast seen to the northward. About eleven the sun shone out and was clearly seen at twelve, so that an observation was obtained. The Captain said we were in 53° 58′. During the afternoon the wind freshened, and about five o'clock we were some three leagues from land. We saw that, beyond the cape we had seen, a low coast stretched toward the north. As it was late we went about in order to get away from the land, the ship's head being put to the northward. At six the ship was hove to, and so we remained all night, during which there was a high sea and a drizzling rain.

At daybreak on Wednesday, the 20th, there was a very thick fog, so that at a short distance nothing could be seen. There was a drizzling rain and an east wind so strong that the ship was tossed about continually. The sails were loosed and the ship's head put to northeast ¼ east. Before nine o'clock the weather lightened, so that we made out the land very well. We went about and stood northeast, in order to make a point of the land. At ten we were about four leagues from this point, which to all seemed to consist of three islands. At midday no observation could be obtained, for it was cloudy and the sun was hidden. About three in the afternoon we were some two leagues from the land, and what had appeared to us to be three islands now seemed to be one, not very distant from the land. We saw many bonfires of its inhabitants, and that it was a land densely covered with trees, apparently pines, and that behind said point was a good bight or bay.

And we noticed that a canoe came out from a break in the land like the mouth of a river and was paddled toward the ship. While it was still distant from the vessel we heard the people in it singing, and by the intonation we knew that they were pagans, for it was the same sung at the dances of pagans from San Diego to Monterey. Presently they drew near to the ship and we saw that they were eight men and a boy. Seven of them were paddling; the other, who was advanced in years, was upright and making dancing movements. Throwing sev-

boruquientos y a todos nos parecieron ser mansos y de buena indole.

Como a la media hora de haberse apartado de nosotros dicha canoa, oimos otra vez cantar y vimos venir otra canoa mas chica y juntandose con la primera se arrimaron las dos a la fragata: en esta segunda venian seis gentiles, arrimandose ambas a la popa se les regalaron varias cositas y diciendoles que el dia siguiente iriamos a su tierra se fueron todos contentos despues de habernos seguido bastante trecho.

Nos parecieron dichas canoas todas de una pieza salvo la borda de arriba, bien labradas con sus quillas formadas casi de la misma manera que las que usan en la canal de Santa Barbara, salvo que estas tienen su popa y la proa no la tienen abierta como las de la canal y usan sus remos bien labrados: vimos en estas canoas dos fisgas bien largas para pescar y dos achas; la una de ellos por lo reluciente de la punta nos pareció seria de fierro aunque no me pude cerciorar de ello. La punta de una de las fisgas, si vimos era de fierro, y nos parecia como un chuso.

Despues de idas dichas dos canoas siendo ya entrada la noche, estando todos resando la corona a nuestra señora la purisima concepcion oimos otra vez cantar y fué otra canoa que se arrimó con las mismas ceremonias que las antecedentes, y reparando ellos que no se les hacia caso, a causa de estar el rezo, empezaron a gritar y continuaron voceando hasta tanto que se concluyó el rezo cuotiano de corona y rezos particulares a algunos santos, y cantado el alabado que les causó bastante admiracion concluido el rezo por estar ya oscuro mandó el señor capitan sacar luces a la borda de la fragata y vimos arrimada otra canoa con siete gentiles, se les convidó a que subiesen a bordo pero ellos ó no lo quisieron ó no entendieron las señas con que se les hablaba se les regaló algunas cositas y ellos correspondieron con algo de pescado seco que parecia bacalao aunque mas blanco.

Un marinero consiguió por un belduque que les dió, un sombrero de junco bien tejido y de varios colores, la hechura de la copa piramidal de como una tercia de alto y las alas del sombrero no pasaban de sesma de ancho: otro marinero por otro belduque les compró un pedacito de como una vara en cuadro bien vistoso tejido de palma fina, al parecer, de colores blanco y negro, que tejido en cuadritos hace muy buena y vistosa labor. Esta canoa estuvo arrimada como una hora, y diciendoles por señas que se fuesen por ser ya muy noche, y que el dia siguiente iriamos a su tierra se fueron contentos y tenian que desandar como seis leguas pues tanto distariamos ya de la tierra.

eral feathers into the sea, they made a turn about the ship. From the gallery of the cabin we called out to them that they should draw near; and, although at first they did not venture to do this because of some fear they entertained, after showing them handkerchiefs, beads and biscuit, they came near to the stern of the ship and took all that was thrown to them. A rope was thrown to them, that they might come on board; although they took hold of it they did not venture to ascend it, but, keeping hold of it, they went on with us to a considerable distance.

When this canoe reached the ship it was about four in the afternoon, and a dense fog had come on, while the wind was not favorable. For these reasons it was ordered that the ship be put about, farther approach to the coast and a landing being put off till tomorrow. The pagans, seeing that we were going away from their country, invited us thither, and we knew, or understood from their signs, that they told us there were provisions and abundant water there and a place where the ship might anchor; and, we replying by signs that on the following day we would go thither, they went away.

These pagans are corpulent and fat, having good features with a red and white complexion and long hair. They were clothed in skins of the otter and the seawolf, as it seemed to us, and all, or most of them, wore well woven hats of rushes, the crown running up to a point. They are not noisy brawlers, all appearing to us to be of a mild and gentle disposition.

About half an hour after the departure of the canoe we heard singing again and we saw another canoe, smaller than the first, which joined the other, and the two came together to the ship. In the second canoe came six pagans. Both canoes drew near to the stern of the ship and we gave these people various trifles, telling them that on the day following we would visit their country. After having followed us for some time they went away, all very content.

These canoes seemed to us to be of a single piece of wood except the gunwale. They are well made, their keels being fashioned almost like those used by the natives of the Channel of Santa Barbara,* except that these have a poop and the prow is not open like those of the channel, and their paddles are well made. In these canoes we saw

* From the beginning of contact with the Spaniards, the Chumash Indians were considered to be culturally advanced, particularly in navigation and associated arts.

Jueves veinte y uno de Julio amaneció no tan cerrado de neblina como los antecedentes aunque llovisnando y soplando el sueste fuerte con una buena marejada: a las ocho de la mañana viraron de bordo poniendo la proa para la punta que ayer vimos y que se nombró por el señor capitan la punta de Santa Margarita por haberse divisado ayer dia de la gloriosa santa: caminamos a la bolina con la proa al E. ¼ al N. E. Como a las doce (que no se pudo observar por estar el sol tapado con nublados) estavamos como un cuarto de legua cerca la punta de Santa Margarita la que fuimos costeando hacia el E. S. E. en donde nos parecia hacer recodo, con el fin de registrar y sondear para dar fondo y saltar a tierra y plantar en ella el estandarte de la santa cruz; pero no fué posible montar dicha punta ni cerciorarnos si era isla ó punta de la tierra firme por la fuerza de las corrientes que nos rechaza- ban al S. por cuyo motivo mandó el señor capitan virar de bordo, y hallandonos ya apartados de la tierra como una legua hacia el S. O. se calmó el viento que toda la mañana se habia mantenido y habia causado grande marejada, asi nos mantuvimos en calma sin poder dar fondo porque no lo habia por lo apartado que nos hallavamos.

La punta dicha Santa Margarita es una loma medianamente alta y tajada a la mar muy poblada de arboleda hasta pegada a la mar, de arboles que nos parecieron a todos cipreses de todos tamaños. Tiene dicha loma como una legua de largo haciendo dos puntas la una al S. O. ¼ al S. en donde intentamos fondear y no se encontró fondo, como media legua poco mas ó menos apartada de ella, y la otra punta al E. S. E. de dicha loma a donde ibamos costeando por hacer en esta punta un recodo con playage al parecer, y no pudimos acabar de montar por habernos rechasado las corrientes como ya dije arriba: desde esta dicha punta del E. S. E. sigue tierra baja como diez leguas ó mas que corre hasta el E. y aí vimos rematar la costa que es lo que pudimos divisar y vimos estaba tan poblada como la punta de la misma arboleda de ciprezes.

Al N. de la punta del S. O. de Santa Margarita como diez y seis leguas distante de ella divisamos un cabo muy alto de la misma manera poblado de arboleda, que llamó el señor capitan el cabo de Santa Maria Magdalena. Desde el dicho cabo sigue la costa de tierra muy alta y tambien poblada de arboleda que corre del E. a O. todo lo que pudimos alcanzar con la vista y al N. O. ¼ al O. de dicha costa divisamos un islote que se llamó de Santa Cristina, su curso de N. O.,

two very large harpoons for fishing and two axes. One of these seemed, on account of the shining appearance of the edge, to be of iron; but I could not verify this. We saw that the head of one of the harpoons was of iron, and it looked like that of a boarding-pike.

After the canoes had gone away and night had fallen, and we were all reciting the rosary of Our Lady of the Immaculate Conception, we again heard singing. This proceeded from another canoe, which drew near with the same ceremonies observed by the others. Seeing that no attention was paid to them, because we were at prayers, the people in the canoe began to cry out, and they continued shouting until such time as the daily recital of the rosary and special prayers to some saints were concluded and the hymn of praise, which caused great admiration on their part, was sung. As it was now dark the Captain ordered lights to the side of the frigate, and we saw that another canoe, containing seven pagans, had arrived. They were asked to come aboard the ship, but either they did not wish to do so or they did not understand the signs made to them. They were given some little things of trifling value, and gave us in return some dried fish which seemed to be cod, although it was whiter.

A sailor obtained in exchange for a large knife he gave them, a hat of rushes, well woven of several colors. The crown was conical and about a third of a *vara* in height, while the brim was not more than a sixth of a *vara* in its breadth.* For a large knife, also, another sailor obtained a piece of stuff about a square *vara* in size; it was very showy, apparently woven of fine palm leaves. The colors were black and white, and woven in little checks; it was a very good and showy piece of work. This canoe remained alongside about an hour, when, on our telling them by signs that they should go away, for it was very late, and that on the following day we would go to their land, they went away content. They had to go six leagues, for we were already at that distance from land.

The dawn of Thursday, the 21st, was not so foggy as that of the preceding days, although there was a drizzling rain and it blew strong from the southeast, with a heavy sea running. At eight o'clock we went about with the ship's head toward the point we saw yesterday, which the Captain named Point Santa Margarita, because it was seen

* The various styles of Pacific Northwest Culture whaling hats, which here caught the attention of the Spaniards for the first time, were depicted by many later explorers of the coast. The Pérez expedition was here dealing with the Haida Indians.

S. E. a distancia de unas diez y seis leguas de la dicha punta de Santa Margarita del S. O. aunque no pudimos certificarnos si era isla porque puede tener tierra baja con que comunique con tierra firme que como la vimos de lejos no pudimos salir de la duda: mas desde el dicho cabo de Santa Maria Magdalena corre costa mas mediana hasta el N. E. y por el E. N. E. ya no se veia correr tierra hasta el E. en donde remata la tierra baja que llevo espresada arriba y empieza desde la punta de Santa Margarita del E. S. E. y rematan sus diez leguas de largor al dicho E.

El cabo de Santa Maria Magdalena que está N. S. con la punta de Santa Margarita del S. O. entre el dicho cabo y el E. hace una abra de como diez leguas en donde hace como una ensenada muy grande ó bolson que la violencia de las corrientes (que de ella venian nos rechazavan al S.) no nos dejaron registrar ni entrar en ella y así no pudimos saber de cierto si es ensenada, bolson ó estrecho, que si no es estrecho sino ensenada puede ser que en ella puede ser que desemboque algun caudaloso rio que causase aquella fuerza de corrientes que no permitió entrasemos a registrar. El cabo de Santa Maria Magdalena dista como diez leguas hasta la punta de tierra baja que se empieza a formar ó a correr desde la segunda punta del E. S. E. de Santa Margarita y remata en el mismo E. y esto es lo que tiene de ancho la boca ó entrada de dicha ensenada, estrecho, ó golfo, ó bolson. El cabo de Santa Maria Magdalena sale mar a fuera del E. al O. y cerca la punta que hace al O. es la dicha isla de Santa Cristina que no está muy apartada de la punta y puede ser que no sea isla sino punta de la tierra firme como ya dije.

A las doce horas de estar en calma y apartados de la tierra como una legua enfrente de la punta ó loma de Santa Margarita del S. O. empezaron a salir canoas asi de la primera punta del S. O. como de la segunda punta que mira al E. S. E. y en breve tiempo se arrimaron veinte y una canoas algunas bien grandes otras medianas y otras chicas; entre ellas habia dos que cada una de ellas no bajaria de doce varas de quilla, en la una venian veinte hombres y en la otra diez y nueve; en las medianas venian diez ó doce personas, y en las mas chicas no bajaban de seis a siete: en breve nos vimos cercados de las veinte y una canoas y de mas de doscientas almas entre hombres, mugeres, niños y niñas, pues en las mas habia algunas mugeres; entre las dichas canoas vino una solo de mugeres que serian unas doce, ellas

yesterday which was the day of that glorious saint. We sailed with a side wind, headed east ¼ northeast. About twelve—when no observation could be taken because the sun was obscured by clouds—we were about a quarter of a league from Point Santa Margarita, along which we ran to the east-southeast, towards where there appeared to be an elbow in the land, intending to examine the same and to sound for the purpose of finding an anchorage, so that we might land in order to plant there the standard of the holy cross. But it was not possible to make that point, nor to make sure whether it were an island or a point of the mainland, for the force of the current threw us to the southward, on which account the Captain ordered the ship to be put about. When we were about a league away from the land toward the southwest the wind which had held all morning, and which had caused a very high sea, died away entirely. So we remained becalmed, and were unable to anchor because, as we were so far from the land, there was no anchorage ground.

Point Santa Margarita is a hill of medium height close to the seaside and is very thickly covered with a growth of trees to the water's edge, seemingly cypresses of all sizes. This hill is about a league long and has two points, one to the southwest ¼ south, where we tried to anchor and found no bottom at a distance of about a half a league from the land, and the other to the east-southeastward of the hill, and thither we were going along the coast because at this point there was an elbow in the land and apparently a beach. But as I have said, we could not reach this place for the current carried us away from it. Beyond this east-southeast point of the hill the land is low and trends to the eastward for ten leagues, or more, where it ended so far as we could see. We saw that this land was as covered with cypresses as the point was.

North of the southwest point of Santa Margarita, and about sixteen leagues from it, we saw a very high cape, also covered with trees. This the Captain named Cape Santa María Magdalena. Beyond this cape the coast consists of very high land covered with timber and trending east and west as far as we could distinguish it. On this coast, and bearing northwest ¼ west, we made out an island which was named Santa Cristina. It lies northwest and southeast, and is about sixteen leagues southwest of Point Santa Margarita.* But we were uncertain

---

* For identification of these names see notes to document No. 18, pages 157, 165.

solas remando y governando la canoa como los mas diestros marineros. Venian las canoas hacia bordo sin el menor recelo, cantando y tocando unos instrumentos de palo como atambor ó pandero y algunos con ademanes de bailar, arrimaronse a la fragata cercandola por todos lados y luego se abrió entre ellos y los nuestros una feria que luego conocimos venian a tratar y feriar sus trastes con otros de los nuestros; estos les dieron algunos belduques, trapos y avalorios y ellos correspondieron dando cueros de nutria y de otros animales no conocidos, bien curtidos y agamuzados, colchas de nutria, tambien cocidas unas con otras que ni el mejor sastre la haria mejor; otras colchas ó fresadas de lana fina ó de pelo de animales que parece lana fina, tejida y laboreada de hilo del mismo pelo de varios colores principalmente de blanco, negro y amarillo, un tejido tan tupido que parece ser hecho en telares.

Y todas las colchas tienen al rededor sus flecos del mismo hilo torcido, de modo que para una sobre mesa ó carpeta es al proposito, y como si para dicho fin estuviesen hechas. Dieron tambien algunos petatillos al parecer de palma fina con labores de varios colores; algunos sombreros de junco, algunos ordinarios otros mas finos y los mas de ellos pintados, la figura de ellos como ya dije de copa piramidal y de alas angostas, con su hilo para asegurarlo en la barba que no lo lleve el viento. Tambien se consiguió de ellos algunas bateas de madera chicas, bien labradas y laboreadas, como de escultura ó talla en la misma madera, de figuras de hombres animales y pajaros, y algunas cucharas tambien de madera con labores por la parte de afuera y lizas por adentro y una de ellas bastante grande toda de cuerno que no pudimos saver de que animal seria.

Se consiguieron dos cajas de pino de como una vara en cuadro bien labradas de tablas y en lugar de clavason cocido con hilo en las cuatro esquinas; no tienen goznes ni chapas, sino que las tapas son como las de las petacas con el ajuste segun y como las cajas de polvos por dentro algo toscas pero por afuera muy bien labradas y lisas y en la delantera con labores a modo de talla con varias figuras y ramos y embutidas conchas y caracolitos de la mar con tan buen encaje que no pudimos conocer como estan embutidas, y algunas de ellas estan pintadas de varios colores, principalmente de colorado y amarillo: en todas las canoas vimos de estas cajas y algunas habia de cerca de vara y media de largo, con su anchor correspondiente, se sirven de ellas para guardar

whether it was an island, or not, because there may be some low land connecting it with the main. As it was so far off we could not resolve this doubtful point. But from Cape Santa María Magdalena the land, of medium height, trends northeast. In the east-northeast no land was in sight; nor was any seen between that point and the east, where the low land which I mentioned as beginning at the east-southeast point of Santa Margarita and running ten leagues to the eastward ends.

Cape Santa María Magdalena lies north and south with the south-west point of Santa Margarita. Between this cape and the land to the eastward of it there is an opening about ten leagues in width, where there is a great bay, or gulf, whence came the said current which carried us to the southward. Because of the strength of this current we could not examine nor enter it; therefore we do not know whether it be bay or gulf or strait. If it is not a strait and is a bay, it may be that some great river empties into it, and that this is the cause of the strong current which prevented our entrance and examination. Cape Santa María Magdalena is distant about ten leagues from the point of the low land which begins at the second or east-southeast point of Santa Margarita and ends at the place mentioned lying to the eastward. This intermediate distance is the width of the mouth or the entrance of this bay, strait, gulf, or pocket. Cape Santa María Magdalena runs from east to west into the sea. At its western extremity lies the island of Santa Cristina. It is not very far away from the end of the cape; it may be, as I have said, that it is not an island but a point of the mainland. After the calm had lasted twelve hours and the ship was about a league from land, off the southwest point or hill of Santa Margarita, canoes began to put out, both from this southwest point and that running to the east-southeast; and, in a short time twenty-one canoes had come near to us. Some were very large; others of medium size; others small. Among them were two, neither of which would measure less than twelve *varas* along the keel; in one of these were twenty men and in the other nineteen. In the canoes of medium size there were ten or twelve persons, and in the smallest not less than six or seven. In a short time we saw ourselves surrounded by these twenty-one canoes, which contained more than two hundred persons, between men, women, boys and girls—for in the greater number of the canoes there were some women. Among the canoes was one con-

sus trastecitos como tambien para sentarse en ellas para remar: dieron tambien algunos señidores de hilo de lana, ó pelo, tejidos y bien tupidos y algun pescado seco del mismo que dije ayer. Se les conoció grande aficion a las cosas de hierro y de corte, pero que no sean piezas chicas: a los avalorios no se les conoció particular aficion, recibieron alguna galleta y sin el menor reparo comieron de ella.

Ya dije que son indios bien formados y de buenas caras algo blancos y vermejos con pelo largo y algunos de ellos barbados todos vinieron vestidos en todo el cuerpo; unos de pieles de nutria y otros animales, y otros de mantas tejidas de lana ó de pelo que parecia fina lana y una pieza a modo de esclavina con que se tapan hasta la cintura y los demas del cuerpo se tapan con pieles agamuzadas y con dichos tejidos de lana de varios colores que hace hermosas labores, unos con mangas y otros sin ellas: trahian los mas sus sombreros de junco como llevo expresado. Las mugeres andan de la misma manera vestidas, estas traen en el labio de abajo que tienen agujereado colgada una rodeta pintada de colores que parecia de tabla delgada curba, que les afea mucho pues de algo apartadas parecen que traen sacada y colgada la lengua; con facilidad y con solo el movimiento del labio se levanta dicha tablita y les tapa la boca y parte de la nariz, dijeron de los nuestros, los que las vieron mas de cerca que tienen taladrado el labio de abajo y de él cuelgan dicha rodeta, no sabemos que fin tendran en esto si será para afearse como algunos asi lo entienden, ó para en-galanarse, y a esto me inclino pues en la gentilidad descubierta desde San Diego a Monte Rey, hemos observado que cuando van de visita a otra rancheria se embijan de varios colores que se ponen feisimos; de los hombres vimos algunos embijados de almagre con un color bien fino.

Aunque combidamos a dichos indios subiesen a bordo no se atrevieron, solo dos se arrimaron y se les enseñó todo y quedaron ad-mirados de cuanto veian en la fragata: los entraron en la camera y nosotros les enseñamos la imagen de nuestra señora y despues de haberla mirado con admiracion la tocaron con la mano y entendimos provaban si era verdadera y viva; se les regaló y se les dijo por señas que iriamos a su tierra a hacer agua. Mientras estos estaban en la fragata dos de nuestros marineros saltaron a las canoas de que se alegraron mucho los indios é hicieron grande fiesta, los embijaron y bailaron con ellos con tales espresiones de contento que no harian si

taining only women, some twelve in number, and they alone paddled and managed the canoe as well as the most expert sailors could.

These canoes came alongside without their occupants manifesting the least distrust, they singing and playing instruments of wood fashioned like drums or timbrels, and some making movements like dancing. They drew close to the ship, surrounding her on all sides, and presently there began between them and our people a traffic, and we soon knew that they had come for the purpose of bartering their effects for ours. The sailors gave them knives, old clothing and beads, and they in return gave skins of the otter and other animals unknown, very well tanned and dressed; coverlets of otter skins sewn together so well that the best tailor could not sew them better; other coverlets, or blankets of fine wool, or the hair of animals that seemed like wool, finely woven and ornamented with the same hair of various colors, principally white, black and yellow, the weaving being so close that it appeared as though done on a loom.

All these coverlets have around the edge a fringe of some thread twisted, so that they are very fit for tablecloths, or covers, as if they had been made for that purpose. They gave us, also, some little mats, seemingly made of fine palm leaves, wrought in different colors; some hats made of reeds, some coarse and others of better quality, most of them painted, their shape being, as I have said, conical with a narrow brim, and having a string which passing under the chin keeps the hat from being carried away by the wind. There were obtained from them, also, some small wooden platters, well made and ornamented, the figures of men, animals and birds being executed, in relief or by incising, in the wood; also some wooden spoons, carved on the outside and smooth within the bowl, and one rather large spoon made of a horn, though we could not tell from what animal it came.

There were obtained from them two boxes made of pine, each about a *vara* square, of boards well wrought and instead of being fastened together by nails, they were sewed with thread at all the corners. They have neither hinges nor locks, but the cover comes down like that of a trunk with a fastening like that of a powder chest; and they are rather roughly fashioned within, but outside are well made and smooth, the front being carved with various figures and branches, and inlaid with marine shells in a manner so admirable that we could not

hubiese sido gente conocida, dando a entender con la seña de poner la mano en el pecho que los querian mucho.

De que inferimos todos ser esta gente de paz y muy docil; los de las canoas convidaron a los dos marineros que si querian los llevarian en las canoas a su tierra; pero no quisieron sino que les dijeron que irian con el barco y con la demas gente; pero no fué dable por la calma el arrimarnos porque prosiguió toda la tarde y las corrientes nos apartaron de la tierra y las canoas se despidieron convidandonos con su tierra, y entendimos por señas que nos decian no fueramos mas arriba porque la gente que habia era belicosa y matadora, ordinario encargo de casi todos los gentiles para dar a entender que ellos son buenos y los demas malos. Nos llevó la atencion, asi su aspecto de bien carados hombres y mugeres con su pelo largo bien peinado y hecha trenza, particularmente las mugeres llevaban la cabeza muy compuesta y como el usar vestido casi talar, los tejidos tan buenos y tan bien fabricados y demas obritas de manos que de ellos consiguieron los nuestros asi de madera, de palma, junco y tambien de marfil.

El ver que las mugeres usan de anillos en los dedos y de brazaletes de hierro y cobre, estos yo los vi en diferentes mugeres y nuestros marineros que las vieron de cerca aseguraron que habia muger que llevaba cinco ó seis anillos de hierro y cobre en los dedos de las manos; y de estos metales algo se vió aunque poco y conocimos el aprecio que de ellos hacen, principalmente de piezas grandes y de corte. El señor capitan que ha estado bastante tiempo en China y Philipinas dice que mucho se asemejan a los sangleyes de Philipinas; lo cierto es que el tejido de los petatillos finos se asemeja a los que vienen de china. Aunque la noche es bien corta pues nos sale el sol antes de las cuatro se nos hizo larga por los deseos que teniamos de saltar a tierra. Algunos de los marineros de los que compraron mantas la pasaron mala, porque habiendose arropado con ellas tuvieron que rascar por los piquetes que les dieron los animalitos que tambien crian estos gentiles en sus ropas.

Viernes veinte y dos de Julio, como a las dos de la mañana se levantó el viento S. O. aunque muy lento, y como a las cinco distavamos como cuatro leguas de la tierra. Caminavamos cerca de ella con la proa al E. ¼ al N. E. con el fin de montar la segunda punta del E. S. E. de Santa Margarita y registrar si ai fondeaderos en el recodo que hace tras de dicha punta, pero las corrientes que mucho nos sotaventavan

discover how the inlay was made. Some of these figures are painted in various colors, chiefly red and yellow. In all the canoes we saw these boxes and some of them were nearly a yard and a half long and of a proportionate width. They use them for guarding their little possessions and as seats when paddling. They gave us, also, some belts very closely woven of threads of wool or hair, and some dried fish of the kind I mentioned yesterday. It is apparent that they have a great liking for articles made of iron for cutting, if they be not small. For beads they did not show a great liking. They accepted biscuit and ate it without the least examination of it.

As I have said, these Indians are well built; their faces are good and rather fair and rosy; their hair is long, and some of them were bearded. All appeared with the body completely covered, some with skins of otter and other animals, others with cloaks woven of wool, or hair which looked like fine wool, and a garment like a cape and covering them to the waist, the rest of the person being clothed in dressed skins or the woven woolen cloths of different colors in handsome patterns. Some of these garments have sleeves; others have not. Most of them wore hats of reeds, such as I have described. The women are clothed in the same manner. They wear pendent from the lower lip, which is pierced, a disk painted in colors, which appeared to be of wood, slight and curved, which makes them seem very ugly, and, at a little distance they appear as if the tongue were hanging out of the mouth. Easily, and with only a movement of the lip, they raise it so that it covers the mouth and part of the nose. Those of our people who saw them from a short distance said that a hole was pierced in the lower lip and the disk hung therefrom. We do not know the object of this; whether it be done to make themselves ugly, as some think, or for the purpose of ornament. I incline to the latter opinion; for, among the heathen found from San Diego to Monterey, we have noted that, when they go to visit a neighboring village, they paint themselves in such a manner as to make themselves most ugly. We saw that some of the men were painted with red ochre of a fine tint.

Although we invited these Indians to come aboard ship they did not venture to do so, except two of them, who were shown everything and who were astonished at all they saw in the vessel. They entered the cabin and we showed them the image of Our Lady. After looking at it with astonishment, they touched it with the hand and we under-

no nos dieron lugar a llegar a dicha punta, antes se vieron precisados a virar de bordo con la proa al S. S. E. Al medio dia que nos hallavamos en el paralelo de la punta de Santa Margarita del S. O. en donde aviamos querido fondear el dia veinte y uno y no hallaron fondo: pudieron los señores observar y nos dijo el señor capitan que nos hallavamos en la altura de cincuenta y cinco grados cabales, y asi en esta altura se halla la punta de Santa Margarita. Cerca de la una de de la tarde viraron poniendo la proa acia tierra, pero a las dos horas poco mas se llamó el viento al O. S. O. y viraron poniendo la proa al S. y poco despues cambió al S. O. y se puso la proa al S. S. E.: esta tarde ha estado el viento muy fresco con grande neblina muy espesa que nada se veia y tan humeda que parece estar lloviendo, por este motivo y ser el viento contrario y grande la marejada con la fuerza de las corrientes que nos echavan sobre la tierra, se caminó para fuera y se perdió de vista la tierra.

Sabado veinte y tres de Julio amanecimos con una gran marejada por la proa que llevamos toda la noche para fuera apartandonos de la tierra; sigue el mismo viento, neblina, y agua que la noche antecedente, de modo que en todo el dia no se ha dejado ver el sol. Antes de medio dia se mudó el viento al O. S. O. y caminamos al S. a tres millas y a dos y media por hora: viendo los tiempos tan contrarios para conseguir el deseado fin de saltar en tierra y registrar la costa determinamos hacer una novena a San Juan Nepomuceno para que nos alcance del señor con su soberano patrocinio los tiempos favorables, la que se empezó esta tarde luego de concluido el cuotidiano rezo de la corona a Maria Santisima nuestra señora.

Domingo veinte y cuatro de Julio dia de San Francisco Solano Apostol del Perú y patron de estos mares del sur; nos amaneció el dia claro y con viento fresco O. S. O.; el padre compañero dijo misa y en ella hizo su platica como en todos los domingos, pero antes de acabar la misa refresco demasiadamente y amenazando chubascos y algo llovió por cuyo motivo no pudo haver segunda misa aunque yo ya havia logrado asistir a la del padre Fray Tomas. Poco despues de las ocho de la mañana volvió a abrir siguió el dia muy claro y hermoso sol, qual no hemos logrado desde que subimos de 40 grados por arriba. A las doce observaron los señores a toda satisfacion y nos dijo el señor capitan nos hallavamos en la altura de cincuenta y tres grados y cuarenta y ocho minutos; el viento se iva manteniendo fresco y

stood that they were examining it in order to learn whether it were alive. We made presents to them, and told them by signs that we were going to their land in order to obtain water. While these two were on board the frigate two of our sailors went down into the canoes, whereat the Indians rejoiced greatly, and made a great to-do. They painted them and danced with them with such expressions of content that they could not have done more had they been well known to them, giving it to be understood by the sign of placing the hand on the breast that they loved them dearly.

From this we all inferred that this is a peaceable and very docile people. Those in the canoes invited the two sailors to their land, telling them that, if they wished, they would take them thither in their canoes; but they did not wish to go, telling them that they would go in the vessel with the rest of the people. But this was not possible, on account of the calm which lasted all the afternoon and the currents which bore us away from the land. So the canoes went away, the Indians inviting us to visit their country, and we understood them to say by signs that we should not go farther up the coast because the people there were warlike and slayers of men, this being the customary warning of almost all pagans, in order to make it understood that they are good men and the rest bad. Our attention was drawn to the pleasant faces of both men and women and their long hair well combed and braided, the women particularly keeping the head in good condition, to their using clothing almost like woven stuffs, the fabric being as good and as well made, and to the manufactured articles of wood, palm, reeds and ivory which our people got from them.

It astonished us, also, to find that the women wore rings on their fingers and bracelets, of iron and of copper. These things I saw on several women, and the sailors who saw them nearer assured me that there was a woman who had five or six rings of iron and of copper on the fingers of her hands. We saw these metals, though not to any great amount, in their possession, and we noted their appreciation of these metals, especially for large articles and those meant for cutting. The Captain, who spent a great deal of time in China and the Philippines, says that they greatly resemble the Sangleyes of the Philippines. It is certain that the weaving of the fine little mats resemble those that come from China. Although the night is very short, for the sun rises before four o'clock, yet this night was long for

bueno del O. S. O. hasta el O. y andavamos bien, poco despues de medio dia se puso la proa al E. aunque desde las seis de la mañana hasta esta tarde se ha andado a cuatro millas no podemos divisar tierra; siendo asi que logramos los orizontes muy claros. Antes de meterse el sol se calmó el viento y se divisó la tierra y segun dicen es la misma que divisamos el dia diez y ocho.

Cuya costa desde la punta de Santa Margarita corre tierra baja Norte Sur como siete leguas y desde dicha tierra baja que está en cincuenta y cuatro grados y cuarenta y cuatro minutos, comienzan unas sierras muy altas y gruesas con diferentes picachos muy elevados y nevados que nos parecieron estar muy poblados de arboledas que aunque no podiamos distinguir que arboles serian hicimos juicio que serian cipreses, pinos, fresnos y ayas; pues de todas estas maderas y aun ramas se vieron en las canoas que se nos arrimaron en frente de la punta de Santa Margarita. Dichas sierras altas que llamó el señor capitan las sierras de San Cristoval, corren desde la altura de cincuenta y cuatro grados y cuarenta y cuatro minutos hasta cincuenta y tres grados y ocho minutos de N. O.; S. E. para el S., miradas de la mar, y desde tierra parece que tienen su curso N. N. O.; S. S. E.

Lunes veinte y cinco de Julio dia de nuestro patron Santiago el mayor, amaneció el dia bien claro y con buen sol: digimos ambos misa; en la mia comulgaron el cirujano y dos de los marineros, y en la misa del padre compañero, se administró el viatico al marinero enfermo, que quince dias antes haviamos oleado por el peligro que entonces vió. Aunque amanecimos con la misma calma que hemos tenido la noche pasada; pero a las seis de la mañana nos entró el viento E. de la costa contrario para podernos arrimar a la tierra que tenemos a la vista y solo distante como ocho leguas que es la sierra de San Cristoval que ya dije ayer, y segun la observacion que oy ha hecho el señor capitan se halla en la altura de cincuenta y tres grados y veinte y un minutos. Tiene de largo dicha sierra alta como treinta y seis leguas al parecer desde dos picachos el uno que está al S. y otro al N.

Despues de medio dia se volvió a cerrar de espesa neblina y como a las seis de la tarde empezó a llover y arreció mas a entrada de noche; todo el dia se mantuvo el viento E. contrario para arrimarnos a la tierra y por la noche se fué alargando hasta el S. S. E. y S. Poco antes de las siete murió el marinero que haviamos sacramentado llamado Salvador Antonio, natural del pueblo de Guainamota. *Anima ejus requiescat in pace Amen.*

us, on account of the desire we had to go ashore. Some of the sailors who bought cloaks passed a bad night, for, having put them on, they found themselves obliged to take to scratching, on account of the bites they suffered from the little animals these pagans breed in their clothing.

Friday, the 22d of July. About two o'clock in the morning the wind came from the southwest, although light, and at five we were some four leagues from land. We drew near to it, with the ship's head east ¼ northeast, with the intention of doubling the second point, that to the east-southeast of Santa Margarita, in order to examine the elbow behind it for anchorage ground; but the current set us to leeward so fast that we could not make the point and found ourselves obliged to go about to the south-southeastward. At midday we were off the southwest point of Santa Margarita, where we had wished to anchor on the twenty-first but found no bottom. An observation was obtained and the Captain said that we were in latitude of just 55°. So this is the latitude of Point Santa Margarita. It was nearly one in the afternoon when we tacked toward land; but, in about two hours, the wind went to west-southwest, and we tacked to the southward. Shortly afterward the wind went to southwest and our course was made south-southeast. This afternoon the wind has been very fresh, and a good deal of very thick fog, as wet as though it were raining, prevented our seeing anything. For this reason, and because the wind was unfavorable and a high sea running, while the current was forcing us landward, we stood out to sea and the land was lost to our sight.

On Saturday, the 23d, at dawn, there was a high head sea running, as had been the case all night, which forced us from the land; the same wind, fog and rain continued, so that, all day long, the sun was invisible. Before midday the wind hauled to west-southwest, and we went to the southward, at the rate of two and a half or three miles an hour. As the weather was so unfavorable for our design of going ashore in order to make an examination of the coast, we determined on a novena to San Juan Nepomuceno, to the end that, through the merit of his sovereign patronage, he might obtain for us favorable weather from the Lord; it was begun this evening, on the conclusion of the daily recital of the rosary of Our Lady, Most Holy Mary.

Sunday, the 24th, day of San Francisco Solano, Apostle of Peru and patron of the South Sea, dawned fair with a brisk wind from the

Martes veinte y seis de Julio, dia de la señora Santa Ana, amaneció llovisnando y el dia cerrado de espesa neblina, por cuyo motivo solo se pudo decir una misa que la celebró el padre compañero, la que dijo de cuerpo presente para el difunto, el qual se hechó a la agua con las ceremonias eclesiasticas luego de concluida la misa. Fué poco a poco reciando el viento S., de modo que a las diez del dia era tan fuerte que nos iba a hechar sobre la costa, la que no nos dejava ver la espesa neblina y receloso el señor capitan nos diesemos a peñas en una costa no conocida mandó virir de bordo poniendo la proa al O. y nos quedamos a la bolina forzada con solo el velacho del palo mayor, porque el viento por instantes se ponia mas fuerte, y por no perder altura, y no apartarnos mucho de la costa; apretó mas el viento y movió grande marejada de tal manera que ya no podiamos aguantar los balances: asi pasamos todo el dia con dicho viento y lluvia hasta las once de la noche que se cambió al S. O. y luego viraron de bordo poniendo la proa a la costa haciendo todas las diligencias posibles para conseguir el saltar a tierra.

Miercoles veinte y siete de Julio amaneció muy cerrado el dia de espesa neblina y lloviendo, soplando el S. O. que nos entró a las once de la noche antecedente, con que caminamos para la costa con la proa al S. S. E. con bastante marejada que nos dejó el viento S. de ayer. Antes de las diez abrió el dia y se descubrió bien el sol que dió lugar a la observacion, y nos dijo el señor capitan que nos hallavamos en cincuenta y dos grados y cincuenta y nueve minutos. El viento despues de medio dia abrió una quarta mas y se puso la proa al S. E. ¼ al S., y como a las tres fué aflojando de modo que al entrar la noche nos quedamos en calma: aunque por la tarde tuvimos buen sol y el dia claro no divisamos la costa: al meterse el sol estavan los orizontes cerrados no sé si por esto ó por estar muy apartados no divisamos la costa.

Jueves veinte y ocho de Julio amanecimos con la misma calma que nos entró anoche, pero con el dia muy claro y divisamos la tierra como seis ó siete leguas distante, y se mira una cordillera de sierra muy alta y gruesa. Demarcó el señor capitan los dos estremos de ella que se

---

[8] Santiago, the patron saint of Spain, whose name was the Spanish war-cry— "Santiago y a ellos!" The surgeon communed again this day. It is evident that devout officers and men of the expedition received the sacrament on occasions other than their birthdays.

west-southwest. My father companion said mass and preached, as on all Sundays; but, before the mass came to an end, the wind strengthened too much, with squalls threatening and some rain falling, for a second mass, though I managed to attend that celebrated by Father Fray Tomás. Shortly after eight o'clock in the morning the weather cleared again and the day was fine with bright sunshine, which we have not had since coming to the northward of forty degrees of latitude. At twelve o'clock a perfectly satisfactory observation was obtained, and the Captain told us that we were in 53° 48′. The wind continued to blow fresh and favorable from west-southwest to west and our progress was good. Soon after noon the ship's head was put to the eastward. Although since six in the morning until after noon we had made four miles an hour, we could not make out the land, and this although the horizon was very clear. Before sunset the wind died away and we saw land, said to be the same seen on the eighteenth instant.

This coast from Point Santa Margarita, is low lying and trends from north to south for about seven leagues; and, after this low land ends, in 54° 44′, very high and broad mountain ranges begin, with detached peaks which are very lofty and snowy. These mountains seemed thickly clothed with timber; and, although we could not determine the kinds of trees of which these forests consist, we took them to be cypresses, pines, beeches and ashes, for, in the canoes which came out to us off Point Santa Margarita, we saw wood of all these kinds, and even branches of the trees. These ranges of lofty mountains, which the Captain named the Sierra of San Cristóbal, run from latitude 54° 44′ to latitude 53° 08′, in a northwesterly and southeasterly direction. From the south, seen from the sea and near to the land, their course seems to be from north-northwest to southsoutheast.

Monday, the 25th, day of our patron, Santiago,[8] dawned clear and the sun shone. Both of us celebrated the mass. At mine the Surgeon and two sailors communed; during that of my father companion the viaticum was administered to the sick sailor to whom, a fortnight ago, the holy oil was administered because of the dangerous condition in which he then was. At dawn the calm which had lasted all night was still present, but the wind sprang up from the east, from the land which is in sight about eight leagues distant, but contrary for our being

veian bien claro uno al N. y otro al S.: el del N. le demoró al N. N. O. y el del S. al E., y la distancia de estremo a estremo de como 18 leguas, y segun la dicha demarcacion corre esta costa de N. O., S. E., aunque puede haber alguna variacion, por estar apartados de la costa quando se demarcó: vimos bien claros los picachos nevados que descubrimos el dia 18 de este mes, y ya los miramos bien apartados de nosotros acia el N.; esta costa de donde la miramos parece estar acantilada a la mar aunque puede tener playa baja que la distancia no nos deje verla, no tuvimos mas que unas ventolinas calmosas que no nos dieron lugar a arrimarnos. Al medio dia observaron y nos dijo el señor capitan que nos hallavamos en la altura de cincuenta y dos grados cuarenta y un minutos. Demarcó de nuevo la tierra y sierras altas de San Cristoval; y lo que se veia de ellas mas al N. le demoraron al N. N. O. a distancia de como 18 leguas y el otro estremo mas al S. le demoró al E. S. E., siguieron toda la tarde y noche ventolinas calmosas.

Viernes veinte y nueve de Julio, amaneció el dia muy nublado aunque sin neblina y asi miramos bien la costa que dista de nosotros de siete a ocho leguas, dejando ya atras la sierra de San Cristoval que segun el parecer del señor capitan tienen las dichas como cincuenta y cinco leguas de largo empezando desde la punta de Santa Margarita. Esta otra costa que oy tenemos a la vista es tambien sierra medianamente alta con algunos mogotes, aunque no tanto como la dicha de San Cristoval y aunque la miramos algo apartados della nos ha parecido que es acantilada a la mar y que tiene algunas quebradas, aunque si se logra el verla mas de cerca y registrarla se podra saber lo cierto de ello, como tambien si contiene puertos, ensenadas, bahias, o radas que por lo que hasta oy hemos visto no podemos dar mas razon que la dicha y que tiene su curso de N. O., S. E., y segun la demarcacion que se ha hecho nos demora al E. N. E.; para notar en la altura que se halla faltó el sol para la observacion, pues en todo el dia no le hemos visto a causa del mucho nublado: como a las diez poco mas de la mañana se cambió el viento al S. S. E. y luego pusieron la proa al S. O. aunque en breve aflojó y poco a poco nos quedamos en calma que continuó toda la noche.

Sabado treinta de Julio aunque amaneció el dia bien nublado, estava claro y sin neblina; amanecimos bastante apartados de la costa que apenas se veia porque a la madrugada refrescó algo el viento S. E. ¼ al S., a las once y media se llamó algo el viento al S. y viraron para la

able to draw near. It is the Sierra of San Cristóbal, of which I made mention yesterday; and, according to an observation obtained today by the Captain, it is in latitude 53° 21'. This high sierra appears to be about thirty-six leagues in length between two peaks, one at the southern end and one at the northern.

After midday a dense fog arose; at six o'clock it began to rain and the fall was greater as the night came on. All day the wind was east, unfavorable for our drawing near land. During the night it hauled to the south-southeast and south. Shortly before seven o'clock the sailor to whom we had administered the sacrament died; his name was Salvador Antonio, and he was a native of the town of Guaina-mota. *Anima ejus requiescat in pace. Amen.**

At dawn on Tuesday, the 26th, day of Santa Ana, there was a drizzling rain falling and a thick fog, so that only one mass could be celebrated, and this was said by my father companion. It was a funeral mass for the deceased, and the body was committed to the deep with ecclesiastical ceremonies as soon as the mass was finished. Little by little the south wind went on increasing, so that, at ten o'clock, it was so strong that it was forcing us on shore, which we could not make out because of the thick fog; and the Captain, fearing lest we might go on the rocks of an unknown coast, ordered the ship to be put about with her head to the west, close-hauled with only the main-topsail set, for the wind grew stronger continually, and he did not wish to lose any northing nor to get very far off the coast. The wind freshened more, and a heavy sea was running, so that we could not stand the tossing of the ship. So, the wind and rain continuing, we passed the day until at eleven o'clock at night, when the wind shifted to southwest. Presently we went about with the ship's head toward the coast, being anxious to do everything possible in order to make a landing.

Wednesday, the 27th, began much obscured by thick fog, and it was raining. The southwest wind had been blowing since eleven o'clock last night, and we were approaching the coast with the ship's head to the south-southeast, through a heavy sea left by the south wind of yesterday. Before ten o'clock the weather cleared and the sun shone out well, so that an observation was obtained. The Captain said we were in 52° 59'. After noon the wind shifted another quarter, and the

* May his soul rest in peace.

costa con el fin de registrar dos abras que ayer se divisaron en la costa, pero no fué dable el conseguir dicho registro porque a las doce y media volvió a llamarse el viento al S. E. y viraron otra vez poniendo la proa al S. O.: fué por instantes refrescando dicho viento y causando bastante marejada que entrava por la proa cabeceando mucho la fragata y dando continuos balances que no podiamos estar en pié: así duró toda la noche que fué bien pesada así por lo dicho como por lo que llovió, y se pasó pasando el temporal con solo el trinquete y la mayor.

Domingo treinta y uno de Julio, amaneció el dia muy cerrado y lloviendo, aunque el viento algo havia aflojado. No ha sido posible decir misa este dia asi por la agua como por los grandes balances y marejada: continua el viento S. S. E., aunque no tan fuerte como por la noche, llevamos la proa al S. O. y ya sin ver tierra: abrió algo el sol y dió lugar a poder observar y segun nos dijo el señor capitan nos hallamos en la altura de cincuenta y un grados y cincuenta y ocho minutos; por la tarde y parte de la noche continuó el mismo viento y marejada. Esta tarde concluimos la novena a San Juan Nepomuceno para la felicidad del viaje.

Agosto: Lunes primero de Agusto amaneció el dia muy nublado con viento S. O. que nos entró a la una de la noche y desde dicha hora llevamos la proa al S. S. E. a fin de arrimarnos otra vez a la costa; a las ocho abrio bien el sol, con que pudieron observar y nos dijo el señor capitan que nos hallamos en la altura de cincuenta y un grados y treinta y cinco minutos: despues de las doce calmó algo el viento variando desde el S. al S. O.: a las seis de la tarde se fué alargando el viento hasta el O. y duró así toda la noche y nos dejó la marejada que nos molestó estos dias.

Martes dos de Agosto amaneció nublado pero en breve desterró el sol las nubes y se descubrió: el viento O. nos duró hasta las quatro de la mañana que se alargó mas cambiandose al O. N. O. del quarto quadrante, viento a Dios gracias favorable para arrimarnos a la costa, para cuyo fin pusieron en dicha hora la proa al S. E. y para ella se camina. Al medio dia se observó y nos dijo el señor capitan nos hallamos en cincuenta grados y veinte minutos: acabado de observar viendo lo que hemos bajado mandó el señor capitan poner la proa al E. ¼ al S. E. y va manteniendose el mismo viento fresco y ha seguido toda la tarde y noche siguiente. Como a las seis de la tarde se cerró de una espesa neblina.

ship's head was put southeast ¼ south. About three o'clock the wind began to die away; and, when the night came, we were becalmed. Although there was a clear sun in the afternoon, and the weather was fair, we could not see the coast. At sunset the horizon was obscured; I do not know whether it was for this reason, or because we were so far away from it, that we could not make out the land.

At dawn on Thursday, the 28th, the calm continued. But the day was fair, and we saw the land some six or seven leagues distant. It was a chain of mountains very broad and high. The Captain took the bearing of the two extremities, which were seen very plainly, one in a northerly and the other in a southerly direction. The northerly extremity bore north-northwest; the southerly, east. The distance between them was about eighteen leagues; and, according to this demarcation, the coast trends northwest and southeast, although in this there may be some variation because of our distance from land when the bearings were taken. We saw very clearly the snowy peaks discovered on the 18th of this month, and now we saw them far away toward the north. From where we saw it this stretch of coast appeared to be of high land immediately on the seaboard, though there may be some low land which, on account of the distance, we could not see. There were only light puffs of shifting wind, so that we could get no farther in. At midday an observation was made, and the Captain said we were in 52° 41′. He took the bearings of the land and of the high ranges of San Cristóbal. The bearing of what was seen of the range farther to the northward was north-northwest, the distance being about eighteen leagues; the southerly extremity bore east-southeast. The shifting, light winds continued during the afternoon and night.

Friday, the 29th, dawned very cloudy, although there was no fog, and we saw the coast plainly. It was distant from us some seven or eight leagues, the range of San Cristóbal being now left behind us. According to the Captain's belief, this range, beginning at Point Santa Margarita, is about fifty-five leagues long. The other stretch of coast, in sight today, is also a range moderately high with some peaks, although not so many as in the range of San Cristóbal; and, though our observation of it has been at some distance, it seems to us to rise abruptly from the seaside and that there are some gaps in it. But, if we can manage to get a nearer view of it and examine it, this can be

Miercoles tres de Agosto amaneció con el mismo viento O. N. O. y con la misma neblina que nos entró ayer tarde y tan espesa que nada se puede ver aun de popa a proa: poco antes de la nueve nos entró el viento N. O. muy deseado por ser el mas favorable para poder costear y registrar la costa; con el se va con la proa al E. ¼ al S. E., por instantes ha ido refrescando de modo que a las once y doce del dia se andavan cinco millas. Se a mantenido la espesa neblina y solo al medio dia abrió algo por la parte del S. con que se pudo observar y nos dijo el señor capitan nos hallamos en la altura de cuarenta y nueve grados y veinte y cuatro minutos. Oy reparó el señor capitan que la aguja varia como dos quartas, atendiendo a esto y a lo muy cerrado que estan los orizontes con la dicha neblina y que la costa no puede estar muy apartada, receloso de no dar a ella impensadamente, mandó poco antes de las tres aferrar dos andanas de rizos y poner la proa al S. E. ¼ al S. A las cinco de la tarde aclaró bien el dia, de modo que salió el sol y se abrieron los orizontes, y por ninguna parte se vió tierra que imaginavamos ya cerca, y por esto mandó luego el señor capitan poner la proa al E., y por instantes iba refrescando mas el N. O. de manera que con solo el trinquete y vela de gabia con solo un rizo andavamos quatro millas y media y por la noche refrescó mucho mas de manera que obligó a ponernos a la capa; y a las diez de la noche volvió a cerrarse de espesa neblina.

Jueves cuatro de Agosto, cerca de las quatro de la madrugada se levantó un N. muy fuerte, de modo que con solo el trinquete y velacho de gabia con solo un rizo andavamos como cinco millas y con una neblina tan espesa que no veiamos de popa a proa: el mar se fué alborotando y el N. por instantes apretando mas de modo que a las ocho ya no podia la fragata aguantar y viendo esto el señor capitan mandó aferrar todas las velas quedandonos en palo seco con solo el velacho del trinquete y se puso la proa al S. E.: como a las once fué aclarando el dia y salió el sol que desterró la neblina y hubo lugar para observar y nos hallamos en cuarenta y ocho grados y cincuenta y dos minutos: hasta despues de comer andavamos con solo el velacho de trinquete y andavamos tres millas por hora: habiendo abierto los orizontes y no descubriendose la costa y aflojado algo el viento mandó el señor capitan soltar todas las velas y poner la proa al E. N. E. para probar si por alguna parte se divisaba la costa; siguió el mismo viento aunque mas tarde fué minorando, y con él en todas las horas andava-

determined precisely; also whether there be harbors, gulfs, bays or roadsteads. From what we have seen today no better account can be given. The trend of this stretch of coast is northwest and southeast, and, according to the bearings taken, it is east-northeast of our position. There was no sun to get our latitude as it was not visible but hidden all day by the heavy clouds. Shortly after ten o'clock in the morning the wind went to south-southeast and the ship's head was put to southwest, although the wind gradually died away to a dead calm which lasted all night.

Although Saturday, the 30th, dawned cloudy, the weather was fair and there was no fog. We were at a considerable distance from the coast, which we could scarcely make out. In the early morning the wind from the southeast ¼ south freshened somewhat, and at half past eleven, it went toward the south. We went about and stood for the coast, with intent to examine two breaks we saw in it yesterday; but it was not possible to make such examination, because at half past twelve, the wind went back to the southeast, and we went about again, with the ship's head to the southwest. The wind freshened constantly, causing a heavy sea which was on our bow and made the frigate pitch and toss so that we could not keep our feet. So it went on all night, which was uncomfortable enough, on this account and because it rained. We weathered the storm with only the fore and main sails.

Sunday, the 31st, dawned very dark and rainy, though the wind was rather less strong. Today it was impossible to celebrate the mass on account of rain, heavy sea and great pitching and tossing of the ship. The wind remained in the south-southeast, although it was not so strong as during the night. Our course is southwest, and we no longer see the land. The sun shone out so that an observation could be had, and the Captain said we were in 51° 58′. The same wind and sea continued during the afternoon and part of the night. This afternoon we finished the novena to San Juan Nepomuceno for the success of the voyage.

August. Monday, the 1st, began very cloudy, with a southwest wind which began to blow at one o'clock in the morning. From that hour our course has been south-southeast, in order to draw near to the coast again. At eight o'clock the sun shone out clear. An observation was obtained and the Captain told us that our position was 51° 35′.

mos quatro millas y de la misma manera se pasó la noche. Esta tarde despues del cuotidiano rezo de la corona a nuestra señora y devociones de algunos particulares santos dimos principio a una novena a la Señora Santa Clara poniendo por intercesora a esta gloriosa santa para alcanzar del Señor el tiempo favorable y dias claros para poder registrar la costa.

Viernes cinco de Agosto amaneció el dia muy claro y sin neblina y abiertos los orizontes y por ninguna parte se divisó tierra; prosiguiendo el mismo viento de ayer norte aunque no tan fresco y llevamos la proa la N. E., aflojó antes de las doce algo el N. de modo que ya no andavamos mas que dos millas y media y por la tarde solas dos. Oy observaron a toda satisfaccion por estar el dia bien claro y nos hallamos en 48 grados cabales.

Sabado seis de Agosto amanecimos con el viento N. O. fresco con la proa al N. E. ¼ al N., con el dia muy claro sin nubes ni neblina y con buen sol cual ningun dia lo hemos logrado tan bueno. Como a las once se divisó tierra aunque á lo lejos y nos pareció tierra muy alta y nevada: a las doce observaron y nos hallamos segun nos dijo el segundo piloto Don Estevan en 48 grados y 52 minutos, y el señor capitan dijo que en la misma altura que ayer de 48 grados cabales: por la tarde se cerró de espesa neblina por la costa de modo que apenas se divisaba la costa al ponerse el sol, y fué calmando el viento de tal manera que al anochecer estavamos en calma que duró toda la noche.

Domingo siete de Agosto amanecimos con la misma calma que hubo de noche y cerrado de una espesa neblina que nada se veia ni aun de popa a proa; digimos ambos misa y en la del padre compañero (en que huvo su platica de doctrina) comulgó el contramaestre. En todo el dia y noche duró la calma y la neblina que no dejó oy observar; esta tarde se vieron algunos peces grandes que parecian taurones, pero dijeron que no lo eran y son los primeros peces que en la navegacion hemos visto.

Lunes ocho de Agosto, amaneció el dia nublado con ademanes de querer llover; como a las quatro de la mañana empezó a soplar al E. y salimos de la calma y empezamos a andar con la proa al N. y N. N. E., antes de las ocho se cambió el viento al S. E. del segundo cuadrante y se puso la proa al N. E. ¼ al N. para arrimarnos a la costa, aunque el dia ha estado algo cerrado no dejaron de observar aunque con trabajo y nos dijo el segundo piloto D. Estevan que nos hallamos en la altura

After midday the wind died away, and shifted about between south and southwest. At six in the evening the wind went hauling to the west, where it remained all night. During the night the sea that had been annoying us all these days went down.

Tuesday, the 2d, dawned cloudy, but the sun soon dispelled the clouds and shone out. The west wind held until four in the morning, when it went back to the west-northwest—a wind, thanks be to God, favorable for our drawing near to the coast and for traveling along it. To this end at that hour the ship's head was put to the southeast. At midday an observation was obtained, and the Captain said we were in 50° 20'. After getting this result, and noting the southing we had made, the Captain ordered the ship's head to be put to east ¼ southeast. The same wind held fresh during the afternoon and the following night. About six o'clock in the evening a dense fog came on.

At dawn on Wednesday, the 3d, the same west-northwest wind held. The fog of yesterday continued, so dense that nothing could be seen, even for the ship's length. Shortly before nine o'clock the wind came from the northwest. This wind is very desirable, that we may run along the coast and examine it, and our course is east ¼ southeast. The wind freshened continually, and by noon we were making five miles an hour. The dense fog continued and only at midday cleared away a little to the southward, so that an observation could be had. The Captain informed us that we were in 49° 24'. Today the Captain noticed that the needle varies about two points. Noting this and that the fog kept the horizon very obscure and that the coast can not be very far away, anxious lest we might strike it unexpectedly, shortly before three o'clock he ordered the sails to be double-reefed and the course to be made southeast ¼ south. At five o'clock in the afternoon the sky cleared so that the sun shone out and the horizon was unobscured; yet nowhere could we see the land we thought to be already near. For this reason the Captain soon ordered the ship's head put to the east. The northwest wind increased constantly, and, with the foresail and the fore-topsail single-reefed, we made four miles and a half an hour. During the night the wind freshened to such an extent that the ship was hove to. At ten o'clock at night a thick fog came on.

At four o'clock in the morning of Thursday, the 4th, the wind came, very strong from the north, so that, under the foresail and the

de 49 grados y 5 minutos: antes de comer divisamos la tierra y pareció ser tierra baja la que no estaba muy retirada pero por el mucho nublado no se podia divisar bien: como a las quatro de la tarde estavamos de ella como quatro leguas y aunque el viento era lento poco a poco nos pudimos arrimar y estando como dos leguas, y aqui sondearon varias veces y se encontró fondo en 24 y en 22 brazas: como a las quatro vinieron de tierra tres canoas chicas, en la una venian quatro hombres en la otra tres y en otra dos, y antes de llegar a nosotros empezaron a gritar con ademanes y señas que nos fuesemos; los nuestros les hicieron señas que se arrimasen sin miedo y les dieron a entender que buscabamos agua, pero ellos ó no entendieron ó no hicieron caso y se fueron para tierra y con el poco viento que soplava nos ivamos arrimando y a las seis de la tarde estando como una legua de tierra sondearon de nuevo y se halló buen fondo en 25 brazas y se dejó caer una ancla con que se dió fondo en dicha hora y se paró del todo el viento y nos quedamos en calma reservando para el dia siguiente el saltar en tierra y plantar en ella el estandarte de la Santa Cruz y tomar posesion de dicha tierra en nombre de nuestro catolico monarca que Dios guarde.

Divisamos bien la tierra que es una rada que se nombró por el señor capitan la rada de San Lorenzo que tiene figura de una C, tierra baja muy poblada de arboleda que no pudimos distinguir que arboleda seria. Este surgidero está muy poco resguardado de los vientos, hace dos puntas la una al S. E. que se llamó la punta de San Estevan a contemplacion del segundo piloto; y desde esta punta empieza la tierra baja muy poblada de arboleda, y corre de la misma manera de quatro ó cinco leguas hasta el N. O. que ya es tierra alta en donde tiene la otra punta que se llamó de Santa Clara a cuya santa estamos haciendo su novena para prevenirnos para su dia.

Como a una legua de la tierra muy baja de dicha rada de San Lorenzo, vimos una sierra muy alta igualmente poblada de arboleda que la tierra baja y tras de dicha sierra divisamos acia el N. otra sierra mas alta con diferentes picachos cubiertos de nieve; me pareció que esta rada ay solo resguardo; desde el N. O. al S. E. y todos demas vientos están abiertos.

Estando dando fondo en esta rada como a las ocho de la noche, vinieron otras tres canoas mas grandes con quince hombres y se estuvieron apartados de la fragata dandonos gritos a modo de lloros,

fore-topsail, single-reefed, we made about five miles an hour. The fog was so dense that it was impossible to see more than the ship's length. There was a high sea running and the north wind became stronger every instant, so that, at eight o'clock, the ship was unable to stand the stress of weather. The Captain, seeing this, ordered the canvas to be reduced to the fore-topsail and the ship's head to be put to the southeast. About eleven o'clock the weather cleared and the sun drove the fog away, so that an observation was obtained and it was found that we were in latitude 48° 52′. Until after dinner the only sail set was the fore-topsail and we made three miles an hour. As the horizon was clear and we saw no land and as the wind was not so strong, the Captain ordered all sail to be made and that the ship's head should be put east-northeast, so that it might be determined whether the coast could be made out. The wind held, although later it was not so strong; yet, all this time, we made four miles an hour. Thus the night passed. This evening, after the daily orison of the rosary of Our Lady and the devotions of some saints in particular, we began a novena to Santa Clara, asking that glorious saint to intercede with the Lord, so that we might have good weather and clear days for examination of the coast.

Friday, the 5th, dawned very fair; there was no fog and the horizon was clear. No land was seen. The wind held from the north, although not so strong, and our course was northeast. Before noon the wind died away, so that we made only two miles and a half an hour, and, during the afternoon, only two. Today a very satisfactory observation was obtained, for the weather was very fair, and our position was exactly 48°.

On Saturday, the 6th, the wind was fresh from the northwest, the course being northwest ¼ north, and the day was very fair, without clouds or fog, and with a clearer sun than so far we have had. About eleven o'clock we saw the land, though it was far away, and it appeared to be very high and snow-crowned. At noon an observation was obtained, and, as we were told by the second navigating officer, Don Esteban, our position was 48° 52′; but the Captain said that we were in the same latitude as we were yesterday—48°. During the afternoon a dense fog hid the land, so that at sunset the coast was barely discernible; and the wind decreased so that at nightfall there was a calm, which continued all night.

los llamamos y se acercaron algo y les preguntamos por señas si tenian agua, no lo entendieron ó no atendieron y se fueron para tierra, pero encontrando en el camino con otras dos volvieron las cinco y se arrimaron como a tiro de fusil del barco y por muchas señas y gritos que les dieron de abordo no se quisieron arrimar y se estuvieron hasta cerca de las once de la noche hablando entre sí, y de tanto en tanto davan sus gritos.

Estas canoas no son tan grandes como las que vimos en la punta de Santa Margarita, pues la mayor de estas no pasaria de ocho varas, ni son de la misma figura pues tienen la proa larga en canal y son mas chatas de la popa: los remos de estas son mas curiosos que los de aquellas pues están bien labrados y pintados de varios colores y forman una paleta que en ella remata una punta de cerca de una quarta de largo; las mas de estas canoas son de una pieza aunque tambien vimos algunas de piezas bien cocidas.

Martes nueve de Agosto amaneció el dia en calma como toda la noche, el dia algo claro por el N. O. aunque por los demas rumbos cerrado de espesa neblina. En quanto amaneció se dió mano a hechar la lancha al agua a fin de ir a tierra y clavar la Santa Cruz, y estando en esta maniobra vimos salir de tierra 15 canoas, y en breve rato estuvieron cerca nosotros y vimos venian en ellas como cien hombres y algunas mugeres aunque no muchas. Se les dió a entender se arrimasen sin miedo, y se acercaron y comenzaron a comerciar con nosotros quanto traian en sus canoas que todo ello se reducia a pieles de nutria y de otros animales no conocidos, a unos sombreros de junco pintados como los de la punta de Santa Margarita salvo que en estos vimos que la copa piramidal remata con una bola a modo de perilla y algunos tegidos de un hilo muy semejante al cañamo con sus flecos del mismo hilo. Los nuestros les compraron algunas pieles y algunos de dichos tegidos y sombreros a trueque de ropa, de belduques y de conchas de lapa que havian los marineros recogido en las playas de Monte-Rey y del Carmelo y conocimos en estos indios grande aficion a dichas conchas y a los belduques. No se vieron en estos indios tegidos de lana ó pelo como en Santa Margarita; se les vieron algunos pedazos de fierro y de cobre y algunas pedazos de cuchillo.

Observamos que estos indios son tan bien formados como los de Santa Margarita pero no tan bien tapados ó vestidos como aquellos; se cubren estos con dichas pieles de nutria y otros animales y de dichos

The same calm continued at daybreak on Sunday, the 7th, and the fog was so thick that we could not see the ship's length. Both of us said mass; and, in that of my father companion, he preached a sermon on doctrine and the boatswain communed. Day and night the calm continued, and there was a fog which did not permit any observation today. This afternoon some great fishes were seen; they seemed to be *taurones*, but it was said that they were not. These are the first fish we have seen during the voyage.

Monday, the 8th, dawned cloudy, and it threatened to rain. About four o'clock in the morning the wind began to come from the east; the calm came to an end, and the course was north and north-northeast. Before eight o'clock the wind hauled to the southeast, and the ship's head was put to the northeast ¼ north so that we might get nearer to the coast. Although the day was rather obscure, the officers did not fail, with some difficulty, to take an observation, and the second navigating officer, Don Esteban, told us that our position was 49° 05′. Before dinner we made out the land, which appeared to be low and not very distant; though, as it was very cloudy, we could not see it very well. About four in the afternoon we were some four leagues from it. Although the wind was light we approached it gradually, and, being about two leagues away from shore, we sounded several times in from twenty-two to twenty-four fathoms. About four o'clock three small canoes came off to us; in one there were four men, in another three, in the third two. Before reaching us they began to cry out, making gestures and signs that we should go away. Our people made signs to them that they should draw near without fear, and gave them to understand that we were seeking water; but either they did not understand our meaning, or they gave no heed to it, for they went back to the shore. With the light wind that was blowing we drew near to the land, and, at six o'clock, being about a league from it, the lead was cast again; and, good holding ground being found, we came to anchor in twenty-five fathoms at that hour. The wind died away to a dead calm, and thus we remained, waiting till the morrow to land for the purpose of setting up in the land the standard of the holy cross and taking possession of it in the name of Our Catholic Monarch, whom God guard.

We made out the land very well, it being a roadstead which has the shape of a C, and which the Captain named San Lorenzo. The

tegidos de hilo y trahen su esclavina que es de hilo de corteza de arbol; usan su pelo largo. Las mugeres que vimos no traen en el labio la rodeta que las de Santa Margarita por lo que no son tan mal parecidas como aquellas.

Como a las seis de la mañana estando ya la lancha a la agua y prompta para ir a tierra se levantó el viento O. y se reparó que nos hechava a tierra arrastrando la ancla; luego mandó el señor capitan levar la dicha ancla para ponernos a la vela é ir bordeando mientras iva la lancha a tierra y volvia, pero el mucho viento y marejada por instantes nos hechava sobre la tierra: y visto y el evidente peligro en que estavamos de perdernos, tomó a buen partido el señor capitan el perder la ancla y calabrote y asi mandó cortar este y luego se hizo a la vela poniendo la proa al S. O. ¼ S. y con mucho trabajo pudimos montar una punta de piedra que sale una legua a la mar; rebasada la punta y apartados ya de la tierra como tres leguas fué tanto el viento y marejada que fué preciso aferrar todas las velas y quedarnos con sola la trinquetilla para poder subir a bordo la lancha y estando en esta faena vino un golpe de mar que dió a la lancha, que de milagro no la perdimos y con ella algunos marineros que estaban en ella. En quanto estuvo la lancha arriba alargaron las velas y se puso la proa al S. S. O., por instantes soplava mas fuerte el viento y era mayor la marejada. Al medio dia pudieron observar y nos dijo el señor capitan que nos hallamos en 49 grados y 12 minutos: por la tarde fué aflojando el viento de modo que por la noche ya calmó.

Miercoles diez de Agosto amanecimos con la misma calma que tuvimos toda la noche con el dia toldado aunque sin la acostumbrada neblina, con que pudimos divisar la costa aunque muy apartada cerca de quince leguas. Pudimos ambos celebrar el santo sacrificio de la misa al glorioso San Lorenzo; todo el dia se mantuvo nublado, sin dejarse ver el sol, por lo que no se pudo observar y siguió la calma todo el dia y noche.

Jueves once de Agosto amaneció con la misma calma y el dia tambien nublado; como a las nueve de la mañana abrió el dia y salió el sol y divisamos por el E. un cerro muy alto distante de donde estavamos como 18 leguas y nos parecia tenia manchones colorados que parecen barrancas y dijeron algunos si seria nieve ó algun cerro pegado a la playa con grande meganos de arena: a dicha hora nos entró algo de viento N. O.; a las doce observaron y nos dijo el señor

land was low and heavily covered with timber, though of what kind we could not distinguish. This anchorage is but little protected against winds. There are two points. That to the southeast was called Point San Esteban, out of regard for the second navigating officer. At this point the low land, thickly covered with timber, begins, and it stretches away to the northwest for a distance of four or five leagues to the other point, where the land becomes higher. This point was named Point Santa Clara, to which saint we are now making a novena, in anticipation of her day.

At a distance of about a league from the very low land of the Roadstead of San Lorenzo, we saw there was a very high range of mountains, also covered with timber, and behind this range, to the northward, was another still higher, having many peaks covered with snow. It seemed to me that this roadstead is sheltered from the northwest and southeast winds only, and is open to all others.

Having anchored in this roadstead at eight o'clock at night, three canoes of larger size, with fifteen men in them, came out, and remained at some distance from the ship, their occupants crying out in a mournful tone. We called out to them and they came nearer; whereupon we asked them by signs whether water was to be had. They did not understand or paid no attention, and went toward the land; but, on the way thither, meeting with two other canoes, all five came on together to about a musket shot's distance from the ship. Although from on board we made many signs to them and cried out to them, they would come no nearer, but remained where they were until about eleven o'clock, talking one with another, and from time to time crying out.

These canoes are not as large as those we saw at Point Santa Margarita, the longest of these not being more than eight *varas* in length; nor are they of the same build, the bow being larger and hollowed out and the stern bluffer. The paddles used in these canoes attract attention more than those others; they are well made and painted in various colors, and are shaped like a spade ending in a point about a quarter of a *vara* in length. These canoes are almost all of a single piece, though we saw some which were made of several pieces fastened together with cords.

At dawn on Tuesday, the ninth, the calm continued still. In the northwest the sky was clear; in all other quarters there was a dense

capitan que nos hallamos en 48 grados y 9 minutos: por la tarde refrescó algo el viento y en todas las horas andamos tres millas y con esto nos vamos otra vez arrimando a la costa y vemos claramente que dicho cerro alto está todo nevado y por los lados de él al N. E. y E. S. E., tierra mas adento que dicho serro se ven tambien buenos manchones de tierra nevada; por ser serro tan elevado y tan señalado por la figura que hace de mar adentro no quiso el señor capitan se quedase sin nombre y asi le llamó *el serro alto nevado de Santa Rosalia*: como el viento era N. O. tan favorable todo el dia vamos con la proa al E. con los deseos de ver si podemos estar mañana cerca la tierra para saltar y fijar en ella la Santa Cruz; prosiguió dicho viento hasta la media noche que se cambió al S. S. E.

Viernes doce de Agosto, amaneció este dia lloviendo y tan cerrado de espesa neblina que a quatro pasos no nos veiamos unos a otros: despues de media noche nos entró el S. S. E. bien fuerte y con marejada del S. O. corriendo con la proa al E. para el serro alto nevado de Santa Rosalia: en quanto amaneció ya estabamos muy cerca pero por la neblina y agua nada se veia. Receloso el señor capitan de no dar impensadamente a tierra mando virar de bordo y poner la proa al S. O. para apartarnos del peligro hasta tanto que abriese algo el tiempo: aunque ambos estavamos con vivos deseos de celebrar oy misa y todos de oirla por ser el dia de la gloriosa Santa Clara a quien concluimos este dia su novenario, pero no fué dable ni siquiera decir una por la agua, viento y marejada fuerte y estraordinarios balances por lo que nos conformamos con la voluntad de Dios ofreciendoles nuestros buenos deseos. A las once del dia cambió el viento al O. S. O. y volvieron a virar poniendo la proa hacia la costa, continuando el dia cerrado sin dejarse ver el sol en todo él; y gastaron la tarde y noche en dar bordos para no apartarnos mucho de la costa.

Sabado trece de Agosto amaneció el dia bien nublado aunque sin la neblina baja nos hallamos a la vista de la costa como unas tres ó quatro leguas de la tierra que algo se dejava ver aunque no del todo porque a tierra adentro estaba muy nublada. La costa que estavamos mirando es tierra baja y alguna de ella medianamente alta muy poblada de arboleda desde el serro nevado de Santa Rosalia que ya queda atras hacia el N.: por todo la costa estamos divisiando varias y grandes humaderas en que conocimos estar poblada. Amanecimos con el viento O. que nos entró anoche llevando la proa al S. E. ¼ al S.

fog. At daybreak we set about getting the longboat into the water, in order to go ashore to plant the holy cross. While thus engaged we saw fifteen canoes leaving the land; in a short time they had come near to us, and we saw that there were about a hundred men, and some, though not many, women in them. They were given to understand that they might draw near without fear, and they came near and began to trade with what they had in their canoes, which consisted only of skins of otters and other animals unknown to us, and some hats made of reeds and painted like those seen at Point Santa Margarita, except, we noticed, that in these the conical crown ends in a ball like a little pear,* and some cloths woven of a material very like hemp, and with a fringe of the same thread. Our people bought some skins and some cloths and hats in exchange for clothing, knives and shells which the men had picked up on the beach at Monterey and Carmelo,† and we noted that these Indians had a great liking for the shells and knives. Among these Indians no cloths woven of wool or hair, like those seen at Santa Margarita, were met with. Some pieces of iron and of copper and of knives were seen in their possession.

We observed that these Indians are as well built as those of Santa Margarita, but they are not as well covered or clothed. These cover themselves with skins of otter and other animals and the woven cloths mentioned, and they have capes made of fiber of the bark of trees. Their hair is long. The women we saw did not have a disk pendent from the lip as those of Santa Margarita do, and, therefore, did not appear to be as ugly as those others.‡

About six in the morning, the longboat being in the water and all in readiness for going ashore, the wind came from the west and it was noticed that we were being forced ashore, the anchor dragging. The Captain immediately ordered the anchor to be weighed, so that we might get under way and remain tacking off and on while the longboat went to land and returned, but the strong wind and the sea were forcing us toward the shore constantly. Seeing the evident danger there was that we should be cast away, the Captain very properly re-

---

* There exist several drawings of the Nootka whaling hat as it is described here.
† On this trade which developed to some proportion, see Robert F. Heizer, "The Introduction of Monterey Shells to the Indians of the Northwest Coast," in *Pacific Northwest Quarterly*, Vol. XXXI (1940).
‡ For additional information on the Nootkans, see Philip Drucker, *The Northern and Central Nootkan Tribes.*

aunque despues se pasó al S. E. para ir costeando á ver si se puede divisar alguna ensenada para fondear pero el viento fué poco a poco aflojando: como a las diez se mudó el viento al S. O. y empezó a reciar siendo contrario para costear y por estar sobre la costa y poder evitar el peligro se puso la proa al S. y S. S. O.: no dió lugar lo muy nublado del dia á observar, poco despues de las doce ya no veiamos la tierra por lo mucho que nos hemos apartado. Esta madrugada que se descubrió bien el N., demarcó el señor capitan bien la tierra y me dice que segun su observacion viene a correr la costa desde el serro nevado de Santa Rosalia hasta San Blas ochocientas leguas rumbo del N. O. ¼ al N. y S. E. ¼ al S.

Domingo catorce de Agosto amaneció el dia muy nublado de gruesas nubes y de tanto en tanto entravan sus chuvascos con sus aguaceritos, la marejada que nos venia del O. causaba bastantes balances y tales que no podiamos tenernos en pié por cuyo motivo no fué dable decir misa: como a las siete de la mañana abrieron algo las nubes y pudimos ver algo de la costa que estariamos della como siete ó ocho leguas. A las ocho se llamó el viento al N. O. muy lento y variable: poco antes de las doce salió el sol y pudieron observar aunque no a toda satisfaccion porque estando en ello vino un chuvasco y se tapó el sol, pero por lo poco que lo divisaron nos dijo el señor capitan que nos hallamos en 46 grados y 8 minutos: aunque por la tarde se aclaró algo el dia ya no pudimos divisar la costa: al anochecer se llamó el viento al N. y andavamos tres millas y media por hora llevando la proa al S. S. O.

Lunes quince de Agosto, amaneció el dia bien claro saliendo el sol con el mismo viento N. fresco con bastante marejada del O. que causaba continuos balances de modo que juzgamos quedarnos sin misa; se animó mi Padre compañero y la dijo y la oimos los demas; en ella comulgaron el señor capitan, el cirujano y tres marineros. Al salir el sol se divisó bien clara la costa de la que distavamos quatro ó cinco leguas de la que divisamos bastante tramo que demarcó el señor capitan y le demoro el curso de ella del N. N. O. al S. S. E.; es tierra baja y en partes levanta algo toda poblada de arboleda que nos parecian pinos pero no se diviso nieve: desde las tres de la mañana que se divisó la tierra hasta las ocho se llevó la proa al S. ¼ al S. O. y a las ocho se governó al S. S. O. A las doce observaron los señores y nos dijo el señor capitan que nos hallamos en 44 grados y 35 minutos.

solved to lose the anchor and cable in preference, and ordered the latter to be cut forthwith. Sail was made and the ship's head was put to the southwest ¼ south and with great difficulty we were able to double a point of rocks running out about a league into the sea. Having weathered this point, and being about three leagues off land, the wind and sea were so high that it was necessary to take in all sail, except the fore stay-sail, so that the longboat could be got on board. While doing this a heavy sea struck the boat, so that it was by a miracle we did not lose it and some sailors who were in it. The longboat once aboard, the sails were loosed and the course was made south-southeast. The wind and sea were still increasing. At midday an observation was obtained and the Captain told us that we were in 49° 12′. During the afternoon the wind died away gradually and by nightfall it was calm.

At dawn, on Wednesday, the 10th, this same calm continued, and the day was cloudy, though the usual fog was lacking. Thus we were able to see the coast, though it was distant, being nearly fifteen leagues away. Both were able to celebrate the mass in honor of the glorious San Lorenzo. It was cloudy all day, the sun not being seen, and no observation was obtained. The calm continued all day and the following night.

Thursday, the 11th, dawned calm and cloudy. About nine o'clock in the morning the weather cleared and the sun shone out. To the eastward we saw a very high peak, distant about eighteen leagues from where we were. It seemed to us that there were great red spots on the peak, as though they were ravines; some said that there might be snow there, or that a hill was close to the shore and these were great banks of sand. At this hour the wind blew rather fresh from the northwest. At noon an observation was obtained, and the Captain told us we were in latitude 48° 09′. During the afternoon the wind freshened and all the time we made three miles an hour. In this way we approached land again, and we saw clearly that the peak mentioned was entirely covered with snow, and that on its flanks, to the northeast and the east-southeast, farther inland were seen other goodly stretches of land covered with snow. As this peak was so high and so marked by its shape as seen from the sea, the Captain did not wish that it should remain without a name, and so called it the Cerro Alto Nevado de Santa Rosalía. The northwest wind being so favorable all

Toda la mañana hemos estado costeando como tres leguas distante de la costa y por la tarde hicimos lo mismo, viendo con mas claridad la costa porque no estuvo tan ahumada quanto mas bajavamos al S. era la tierra mas baja en la playa vimos algunas mesas sin arboleda pero con mucho sacate al parecer; vimos varias barrancas blancas tajadas a la mar y algunas cañadas ó abras que corren N. O., S. E.: como a las seis se repararon que la tierra salia por la proa al S. y luego mandó el señor capitan poner la proa al S. S. O., hasta las ocho que ya se governó al S. y se llevó este rumbo toda la noche con viento tan fresco que al anochecer caminavamos cinco y media millas por hora.

Martes diez y seis de Agosto amaneció el dia bien claro pero los orizontes totalmente cerrados de espesa neblina, y asi no se divisó tierra en todo el dia, aora sea por lo dicho que se mantuvieron cerrados los orizontes, aora sea porque estemos apartados de ella. Amanecimos con el mismo viento N. fresco, aunque en quanto subió el sol calmó algo; por la mañanita se puso la proa al S. S. E. que habiamos llevado toda la noche al S.: como a las nueve estavamos quasi en calma y asi estuvimos quasi todo el dia con tal qual ventolina, en dicha hora se levantó la espesa neblina que por la mañana estava por los orizontes y nos serró de tal manera que a pocos pasos nada veiamos. A las doce se dejó ver el sol entre la neblina lo muy preciso para la observacion que segun nos dijo el señor capitan le salió la latitud del N. de 42 grados y 38 minutos: y atendiendo a esta observacion y lo que se refiere en el viaje del general Don Sebastian Vizcaino, conjeturamos que por aqui viene a estar el cabo blanco de San Sebastian y aquel famoso rio que descubrió Martin de Aguilar, porque aunque este lo ponen aquellos antiguos diarios en la altura de 43 grados pero como se ha observado que en los mismos parajes donde entonces observaron se ha hallado menor latitud, por los nuevos y mas arreglados instrumentos, se debe creer que el cabo blanco y dicho rio han de estar en menor altura que la que señalaban los antiguos, y asi puede ser estemos al paralelo de dicho cabo aunque las neblinas no dan lugar a divisar la tierra. Poco antes de media noche nos entró N. bien recio que nos duró toda la noche y con él se puso la proa al S. ¼ al S. O. y fué apretando de tal manera que solo se pudo mantener la fragata con solo el trinquete y se andava bastante.

Miercoles diez y siete de Agosto amaneció el dia muy cerrado de neblina como los antecedentes y con el N. bien fuerte con la proa al

day long the course was eastward, we being desirous of seeing whether by tomorrow we might not be near land—so that we may land and plant the holy cross there. The wind continued to blow from that quarter until midnight, when it hauled to south-southeast.

At dawn on Friday, the 12th, it was raining, and there was so thick a fog that we could not see one another when at a distance of four paces apart. After midnight the wind blew strong from the south-southeast and the sea came from the southwest. Our course was eastward, toward the snowy peak of Santa Rosalía. By the time it was fairly day we were very near to it, but the fog and the rain prevented our seeing anything of it. The Captain, fearing lest we might strike the land unexpectedly, ordered the ship to be put about with her head to the southwest, so as to carry us out of danger until such time as the weather should be clearer. Although both of us were as desirous of celebrating mass today as all were of hearing it, because it was the day of the glorious Santa Clara and our novena in her honor came to an end, nevertheless we were unable to say even one mass, for the rain and wind, the high sea that was running and the extraordinary tossing about of the ship prevented our doing so. So we conformed to the will of God, assuring the people of our strong desire in the matter. At eleven in the morning the wind went to the west-southwest, and the ship was put about with her head toward the coast, the day remaining overcast so that at no time could we see the sun. The afternoon and night were spent in standing off and on, so as not to go too far away from the land.

Saturday, the 13th, dawned very cloudy, although there was no low lying fog, and we found that we were about three or four leagues from shore. We had a partial view of the land; far inland the clouds hung over it. The coast we saw consists of low land, though a portion of it is of medium altitude, thickly covered with timber, stretching down from the snowy peak of Santa Rosalía, which we have left behind toward the north. All along the coast we saw the smokes of many great fires, so that we know this coast to be inhabited. At dawn the wind was in the west, having begun to blow from that quarter during the night, and our course was southeast ¼ south and afterward southeast—so that we might run along the coast in search of some bay in which to come to anchor; but gradually the wind died away. About ten o'clock the wind came from the southwest and began to freshen.

S.: así como empezó a levantar el sol fué abriendo la neblina y se dejó ver este mayor luminar; siguió la neblina en los orizontes hasta cerca medio dia que se aclararon, pero no vimos tierra en todo el dia y asi sin duda estaremos muy apartados della. Al medio dia se hizo la observacion y segun nos dijo el señor capitan nos hallamos en la latitud de 41 grados y 27 minutos: hasta esta hora siendo asi que andamos con solo el velacho de trinquete caminamos mas de quatro millas por hora. Despues de las doce mandó el señor capitan poner la proa al S. S. E. para la costa: el viento N. se mantuvo (aunque no con tanta fuerza como por la mañana) esta tarde, la noche en que llevamos la proa para la costa.

Jueves diez y ocho de Agosto amanecimos con el dia bien cerrado de neblina que a pocos pasos no nos veiamos unos a otros: bastante trabajo para una navegacion en costas no conocidas, que si hubiere yslas ó bajos, no quedara quien diera razon de nosotros: esta madrugada calmó algo el N. y asi se mantuvo todo el dia aunque no dejamos de andar algo con la proa al S. E.: se mantuvo el dia cerrado de neblina por lo que no se pudo observar ni divisar la tierra.

Viernes diez y nueve de Agosto amaneció con la misma neblina de los dias antecedentes y con tal rocio que parecia haber llovido y con la calma de toda la noche y asi se ha mantenido todo el dia con tal qual ventolina y con la obscuridad que por la mañana sin dejarse ver el sol en todo el dia.

Sabado veinte de Agosto amaneció con la misma neblina y rocio, con la calma y se mantuvo asi todo el dia con tal qual ventolina aunque estuvo todo el dia cerrado de neblina, poco antes de las doce entre la misma neblina se dejó ver el sol y aunque con trabajo observó el señor capitan y nos dijo nos hallavamos en la altura de 39 grados y 48 minutos.

Domingo veinte y uno de Agosto amaneció el dia con la misma neblina que los antecedentes con buenos rocios que parecen aguaceros y con demasiado frio de lo que ha resultado de las mojadas antecedentes y frios que la mayor parte de la tripulacion se halla imposibilitada por el accidente del escorbuto de que se hallan quasi todos picados y algunos bien agravados: yo tambien me he sentido malo de la boca que no he podido oy celebrar pero mi Padre compañero dijo misa é hizo su platica: hasta las once del dia estuvimos en calma y dicha hora nos entró un poco de viento S. E. aunque suave y contrario

This wind being unfavorable for coasting, as it blew towards the shore, and in order to avoid danger, the ship's head was put south and later south-southwest. As the day was very cloudy no observation could be obtained. By a short time after twelve o'clock we had lost sight of the land, being far from it. At dawn, when it was clear to the northward, the Captain took the bearings of the land carefully, and told me that, according to his calculations, the coast ran from the snowy peak of Santa Rosalía to San Blas for eight hundred leagues, with a general trend of northwest ¼ north and southeast ¼ south.

At dawn, on Sunday, the 14th, the day was very cloudy, the clouds being very heavy, and, from time to time there were squalls of wind accompanied by showers. The sea, which came from the west, tossed the ship about so that we could not keep our footing. For this reason it was impossible to say mass. About seven o'clock in the morning the clouds rolled away partially, so that we were able to see something of the coast, from which we were distant some seven or eight leagues. At eight the wind went to the northwest, very light and variable. Shortly before twelve the sun shone out and an observation was obtained, although it was not entirely satisfactory, because while the officers were taking it a squall came on and the sun was hidden; but, according to what was made out, the Captain told us that we were in 46° 08'. Although the weather cleared a little in the afternoon we could see the land no longer. At nightfall the wind went to north, and we made three miles and a half an hour with the ship's head to south-southwest.

Monday, the 15th, dawned very clear, the sun shining out well and the wind still blowing fresh from the north. There was a good deal of sea from the west which caused considerable rolling so that we thought that we should be obliged to go without mass, but my father companion took heart and said one, the rest of us hearing it, the Captain, the Surgeon and three sailors communing. When the sun shone out we saw the coast clearly, being four or five leagues from it. We saw a considerable stretch of it, of which the Captain took the bearings and which trended north-northwest and south-southeast. It is low land, which rises, however, in places, and is covered with a thick growth of trees which appeared to us to be pines. We saw no snow. From three o'clock in the morning, when we saw the land, until eight our course was south ¼ southwest, at eight o'clock it was made south-

no obstante pusieron la proa al E. N. E. para la costa. A las doce se descubrió algo el sol y pudieron aunque con trabajo observar y segun nos dijo el señor capitan nos hallamos en la latitud del N. de 39 grados y 30 minutos; el dicho viento fué tan lento que por la tarde ya estavamos en calma y la misma tuvimos toda la noche.

Lunes veinte y dos de Agosto amaneció con la misma calma de anoche, el dia algo nublado pero sin la neblina ordinaria: al salir el sol vimos la costa que estavamos de ella como seis ó siete leguas y divisamos la cumbre de la sierra entre la neblina hacia al N. como diez leguas de distancia se divisaba un cabo alto y del cabo para arriba no veiamos tierra por lo que hicimos juicio que tuerce alli la costa para otro rumbo. Este cabo segun el sentir del señor capitan es el Cabo Mendozino el qual demarcó al N. N. O. cinco grados para el N. Desde dicho cabo rumbo al S. como diez leguas es toda tierra alta con diferentes abras que nos parecian ser cañadas, toda la tierra muy poblada de arboleda que nos parecian pinos. Despues de dicha tierra alta hacia al S. divisamos como cinco leguas de costa no tan alta y la demas que se sigue ya parecia tierra mas baja y toda poblada de arboleda: poco despues de estar mirando dicha costa se levantó la espesa neblina que la cubrió y ya no la pudimos ver mas. Antes de las siete de la mañana empezó a soplar el S. E. y se vieron precisados a poner la proa al S. S. O. desviandonos otra vez de la costa, porque dicho viento no daba lugar a otra cosa: a las nueve abrió algo el dia y a las doce pudieron observar y segun nos dijo el señor capitan nos hallamos en la altura de 39 grados y 46 minutos.

Y asi hemos subido desde ayer 16 minutos y esto ha sido porque ayer tarde y por la noche llevamos la proa al E. N. E. y con las ventolinas aunque suaves algunas leguas andariamos y asi viene a resultar esta mayor altura. Despues de la observacion de este dia nos dijo el señor capitan que segun sus cuentas y computo que hacia el cabo Mendocino que dejamos arriba está en la latitud de 40 grados con la diferencia de pocos minutos: las ventolinas de la mañana han continuado todo el dia con la misma lentitud hasta ponerse el sol que nos quedamos en calma y lo mismo por la noche.

Martes veinte y tres de Agosto amaneció el dia tapado con la neblina no obstante dijeron algunos que a lo lejos entre la neblina que por aquel lado no estava tan cerrado divisavan la tierra. Despues de las seis volvió a levantarse la ventolina del S. S. E. y se hubo de poner

southwest. At twelve the officers obtained an observation, and the Captain told us that the latitude was 44° 35′.

All morning we were running along the coast at a distance from it of about three leagues, and we did the same thing during the afternoon; but we saw it more distinctly as there was not so much haze. The farther south we advanced the lower the land immediately on the coast was. We saw some tableland where there was no timber, but seemingly a great deal of grass. We saw several white cliffs near to the sea, and some ravines, or openings, which ran northwest and southeast. About six o'clock it was noticed that the land stretched out past our bow to the southward, and the Captain at once ordered the ship's head to be put to the south-southwest. This was our course until eight o'clock, when it was made south. And this was our course all night, the wind being so fresh that we made five miles and a half an hour.

At dawn, on Tuesday, the 16th, the day was fair, but the horizon was entirely hidden by a thick fog. During the whole day we did not see the land, because of this fog that kept the horizon obscured or because we were so far away from it. At daybreak the wind was still blowing fresh from the north, although it became calmer as the sun rose higher. Early in the morning the course was made south-southeast, it having been south all night. At nine o'clock it was almost calm, and so it continued to be almost all day long, except for an occasional puff of light wind. At the hour last mentioned the thick fog, which earlier had been confined to the horizon, so enveloped us that at the distance of a few paces nothing could be seen. At noon the sun shone out through the fog just long enough for an observation to be obtained. According to the Captain the latitude was 42° 38′. This being the latitude, and considering what is related of the voyage of General Don Sebastián Vizcaíno, we conjecture that hereabout must be the Cape Blanco of San Sebastián and that large river discovered by Martín de Aguilar; for, although in the old journals he locates it in latitude 43°, it is noticeable that the latitude of other places where observations were had at that same time has been found to be less by the new and more serviceable instruments. Therefore it may be concluded that Cape Blanco and the river mentioned are in a lower latitude than that given to them by those ancient observers; and it may be that we are in the parallel of that cape, although, by reason of the fog,

la proa al S. O.; fué poco a poco refrescando y se llamó al S. E. ¼ al S.; poco se ha dejado ver el sol y al medio dia estuvo mas tapado que no se pudo observar: la ventolina ceso al ponerse el sol y nos quedamos en calma. Viendo que estas calmas van continuando y que el tiempo nos es tan contrario y que los enfermos van empeorando y aumentandose el numero de ellos se determino hacer una novena a Nuestra Señora de Talpa implorando su patrocinio, despues de concluida su sacratisima corona dimos principio a ella. En breve esperimentamos su soberano patrocinio, pues poco a poco despues de las ocho empezó a soplar el E. aunque suave y duro hasta despues de media noche que se cambió al N. O. bien fresco que duró hasta las tres de la madrugada que se llamó al N. bastante fresco y se llevó toda la noche la proa al S. E. ¼ al E. con la que anduvimos bien gracias a Dios y a la Virgen Santisima a quien se le ofreció cantar una misa, el dia de su natividad si nos deja llegar con bien.

Miercoles veinte y cuatro de Agosto amaneció con el mismo viento N. y el dia algo claro que por la mañanita se dejó ver el sol. Pudimos ambos celebrar el santo sacrificio de la misa y estando en la segunda misa se empezó a nublar amenazando llover, como en efecto a lo lejos se veia estar lloviendo, aunque no llegó a nosotros la agua, con el nublado calmó algo el viento y nos entró una gran marejada que nos balanceó bien. Al medio dia no se pudo observar por lo muy nublado que no se dejó ver el sol, siguió la tarde y noche la calma y marejada.

Jueves veinte y cinco de Agosto amaneció con la misma calma y marejada y continuos balances que hemos tenido toda la noche y cerrado el dia con espesa neblina: a las once de la mañana nos entró la ventolina calmosa del E. S. E. ó S. E., y por ella pusieron la proa al N. E. para no apartarnos mucho de la costa que no sabemos que tan lejos la tenemos. Al medio dia se descubrió algo el sol y aunque con trabajo observó el señor capitan y nos dijo nos hallamos en la altura de 38 grados y 32 minutos. La ventolina del E. S. E. nos duró, y nos tuvo en calma hasta las siete de la noche que nos entró N. N. O. fresco, con el que empezamos a andar y antes de las nueve ya se cambió al N. O. que duró hasta por la mañana y asi con este viento en popa se anduvo bien con la proa al S. E. ¼ al E. a fin de arrimarnos a la costa.

Viernes veinte y seis de Agosto amaneció muy nublado y cerrado de espesa neblina que a un tiro de fusil nada se veia. Como a las cuatro de la mañana se cambió el viento que tuvimos anoche al O. N.

we cannot see the land. Shortly before midnight the wind began to blow very strong from the north and so continued to blow all night, during which time our course was south ¼ southwest. The wind increased so that sail was taken in until only the foresail remained set; even thus the ship made way enough.

The dawn of Wednesday, the 17th, was obscured by a thick fog, as former dawns had been, the north wind still blowing strong and our course being south. As the sun rose the fog lifted and allowed that luminary to become visible. But the fog remained on the horizon until about noon, when it cleared away. During the day no land was seen; undoubtedly we must be very far away from it. At midday an observation was obtained and, as the Captain told us, our position was in 41° 27′. Until this hour, under the fore-topsail alone, we made more than four miles an hour. After noon the Captain ordered the ship's head to be put to the south-southeast, toward land. The wind was still in the north during the afternoon and night, though not so strong as it had been. During this time our course was landward.

At dawn on Thursday, the 18th, there was so thick a fog that, at the distance of a few paces, we could not see one another. This is troublesome enough for navigating on an unknown coast; for, if there be islands or shoals, there would be no one to give an account of us. In the early morning the north wind became lighter and so continued all day, although we made considerable progress on a southeast course. The fog continued all day so that no observation could be had; nor was the land seen.

At dawn on Friday, the 19th, the fog of the preceding days was still present, and the dew had been so heavy that it seemed to have been raining. There had been a calm all night long and it continued all day, except that there was an occasional light puff of wind. All day long the obscurity continued and the sun was not seen.

The same fog, dew and calm were present at dawn on Saturday, the 20th. They continued all day, except that there was, once in a while, a puff of wind, and that, shortly before twelve o'clock, the fog lifted so that the sun could be seen and the Captain managed with difficulty to get an observation. He said that our latitude was 39° 48′.

At dawn on Sunday, the 21st, the same fog continued and the moisture from it was like a shower, and it was very cold. From this and previous wettings and cold it has resulted that the greater part

O. y se puso la proa al E. S. E.: esta mañana vimos muchos pajaros chicos y grandes y patos y muchas ballenas no muy apartadas de la fragata, señales todas de no estar muy apartados de la costa y segun la observacion de ayer y lo mucho que esta noche hemos andado hacemos juicio que no estamos muy lejos del puerto de San Francisco: por la mañanita nos calmó el O. N. O. y como a las nueve nos entró el N. O. bien fresco; como a las diez dijeron se divisava la tierra por la proa no muy lejos, la que pude divisar con algun trabajo por causa de la espesa neblina, y el señor capitan dijo que eran los Farallones de San Francisco, los primeros bajando de N., S., y dice ay dos ringleras de ellos como cinco leguas apartados de la costa ó tierra firme, tendidas las dos ringleras de N. O., S. E., como a legua y media a dos de distancia la una ringlera de la otra.

La primera ringlera que vimos bien clara y pasamos como una legua de ellos que son los que estan hacia el N., son siete faralloncitos no muy grandes ni iguales; el de en medio es algo mas elevado que no demas, pero todos entre si están segregados; de estos parece que no hacen mencion las historias ni el viaje del general Don Sebastian Vizcaino. Para desviarnos de estos pusieron la proa al S. ¼ al S. E.: al medio dia los dejamos ya por la popa que si se hubiera descubierto el sol, era buena ocasion de notar de fijo su latitud. A la misma hora del medio dia empezamos a divisar los segundos, son tambien siete bien altos, que al parecer estan contiguos y vistos de lejos parecen una isla con siete picachos, unos mas altos que otros y cojen el tramo de como una legua de circumferencia. De estos parece que habla el Almirante Cabrera Bueno, que de ellos dice: son buena señal para conocer el puerto de San Francisco, pues estos siete segun me dice el señor capitan Don Juan Perez estan tendidos enfrente la punta de Reyes y al N. de ella, en la encenada que dicha punta empieza a formar, está el dicho puerto.

Los Farallones que en la espedicion de tierra en la que yo iba el año pasado de 1769, y los divisamos el dia 31 de Octubre, como digo en mi diario son distintos de todos estos que ahora he visto, pues estos no era dable el verlos del paraje de donde lo divisó la espedicion de tierra que fué la playa de la encenada del otro lado quasi opuesto a dicha punta de Reyes; pues desde dicha playa los demarcamos y nos demoraban los Farallones que nosotros entonces vimos al O. ¼ S. O. y la punta de Reyes nos demoraba al O. ¼ al N. O., que van a decir dos

of the crew is unfit for duty on account of scurvy. Almost all are affected by it, some quite seriously. I, myself, have a sore mouth, so that I have been unable to celebrate the mass. But my father companion said mass and preached a sermon. Until eleven o'clock in the morning the calm lasted; at that hour a little wind came from the southeast. Although it was light and unfavorable, the ship's head was put to the east-northeast, toward the coast. At noon the sun shone out so that, although with difficulty, the officers got an observation. The Captain told us that we were in latitude 39° 30'. The wind was so light during the afternoon that we were virtually becalmed. This condition lasted all night.

The same calm continued at dawn on Monday, the 22d; the day was cloudy, but the customary fog was absent. As the sun rose we made out the coast, from which we were six or seven leagues distant, and we saw the crest of the sierra looming out of the fog, about ten leagues to the northward. This was a high cape and beyond this cape no land was seen, and we concluded that beyond this point the coast trended in another direction. In the opinion of the Captain this is Cape Mendocino; it bore five degrees to the northward of north-northwest. From this cape the coast trends south for about ten leagues. It is all high land with several breaks in it, apparently ravines. All this land is thickly covered with trees which seemed to be pines. To the southward of this high land we saw about five leagues of coast not so high, and that which appeared beyond that seemed to be lower. All was thickly covered with timber. Shortly after we had this view of the coast a thick fog settled down and hid it, so that we saw it no more. Before seven o'clock in the morning the wind began to blow from the southeast, and it was necessary to put the ship's head to south-southwest; this was going away from the coast again, this wind making it impossible to do anything else. At nine o'clock the weather cleared so that at noon an observation could be had; according to what the Captain said we were in latitude 39° 46'.

And so we have made sixteen minutes of northing since yesterday. This is owing to the fact that during the afternoon and night our course was east-northeast and that, although the puffs of wind were light, we made several leagues in distance, with this result. After the observation of today the Captain told us that, according to his reckoning, the latitude of Cape Mendocino, which we had left behind us, is

quartas; y estos que ahora hemos visto, corren ó estan tendidos de N. O., S. E. Mas: en la espedicion de tierra quando demarcamos los Farallones estavamos dentro de la encenada ó bolson, solo distantes de la bocana de los dos grandes esteros como tres leguas y teniamos a la vista los siete Farallones que distaban de nosotros como legua y media y la punta de Reyes distava por el ayre como diez y ocho leguas, y distando estas dos cordilleras de Farallones segun el sentir del señor capitan Don Juan Perez como cinco leguas de la costa y punta de Reyes se sigue que la espedicion de tierra quando descubrió en la grande encenada los siete Farallones de que hablan los diarios habian de estar distantes de estos que hoy hemos visto veinte y tres leguas y de consiguiente no pueden ser los mismos, sino otros distintos y que entonces no pudieron ser vistos estos de la espedicion de tierra. Noto esto para evitar toda equivocacion.

Sabado veinte y siete de Agosto amanecimos con el mismo viento favorable N. O. bien fresco que logramos toda la noche pasada: como a la seis de la mañana estavamos enfrente de le punta de año nuevo y luego empezamos a entrar a la encenada de Monte-Rey en cuyo puerto dimos fondo como a las quatro de la tarde, aunque no desembarcamos hasta el dia siguiente despues de haber dicho ambos misa: gracias a Dios y a su Purisima Madre que nos ha dejado llegar con toda felicidad a este puerto aunque con la pena de no haberse logrado el principal fin de llegar hasta los sesenta grados de altura y de saltar a tierra y plantar en ella el estandarte de la Santa Cruz: quiera su divina Magestad que este viaje sirva a lo menos para mover el corazon de nuestro Catolico Monarca y el cristiano celo del Excelentisimo Señor Virrey, para que con la mayor luz que ahora se tendrá de estas costas y de la buena gente de que están pobladas, envien de nuevo otra espedicion y evangelicos operarios para plantar en ella nuestra santa fé y convertir aquella gentilidad al gremio de la santa yglesia; asi se lo pido a Dios a quien sea toda honra y gloria. Amen.

Este diario segun va espresado forme yo el sobre dicho Fray Juan Crespi de dia a dia en el discurso de la navegacion, escriviendolo en un libro segun ofrecian los eventos ocurentes, pero como a veces el mal recado de escribir, a veces los balances del barco, y otras el mareo ocasionaban alguna diformidad en la letra y en el estilo, despues de llegado a esta mision lo he sacado en limpio, procurando abreviar de palabras donde buenamente se podia, pero sin variar, ni alterar a la

40°, within a few minutes of difference. The light morning puffs of wind continued all day and at sunset we were becalmed. The calm continued all night.

Tuesday, the 23d, dawned with the day obscured by fog, notwithstanding which there were those who said that, far away amid the fog on the side where it was not so thick, they made out land. After six o'clock light puffs of wind came from the south-southeast, and it was necessary to put the ship's head to the southwest. Little by little the wind freshened and went to southeast ¼ south. The sun had been seen but little and at midday was so hidden that no observation was possible. At sunset the light winds ceased and we were becalmed. Inasmuch as these calms continue and the weather is so unfavorable, and as the sick become sicker while the number of them increases, it was resolved to make a novena to Our Lady of Talpa* beseeching her patronage; and, after finishing the most holy rosary, we began it. Very soon we had evidence of her sovereign patronage; for, after eight o'clock, little by little the wind began to blow from the east, although gently, and it held in that quarter until after midnight, when it hauled to northwest and blew fresh until three in the morning, when it went to the north and blew rather strong. All night our course was southeast ¼ east, and we went well on our way—thanks be to God and to the Most Holy Virgin, to whom we offered to sing a mass on the day of her nativity if she permit us to reach home in safety.

At dawn on Wednesday, the 24th, the same north wind was blowing and the day was so clear that during the earlier part of the morning the sun was seen. Both of us were able to celebrate the holy sacrifice of the mass. While we were engaged in celebrating the second mass, clouds began to form and rain threatened, though no rain reached us. As the clouds formed the wind fell and a high sea began to run which tossed us about well. At midday it was impossible to get an observation, for it was so cloudy that the sun could not be seen. During the afternoon and night the calm and high sea continued.

---

* The reference is to Nuestra Señora del Rosario de Talpa. The ancient statue of Nuestra Señora was miraculously renewed on September 19, 1644, when plans to retire it from worship because of its dilapidated condition were issued by the responsible curate. José Ignacio Dávila Garibi, *Apuntes para la Historia de la Iglesia en Guadalajara*, (Guadalajara, 3 Tomos), Tomo II, 370–73. Talpa is situated in inaccessible western Jalisco about 40 miles east and slightly south of Puerto Vallarta on Bahía Banderas.

substancia de él cosa alguna: y asi lo certifico y para que conste lo firmé en esta mision de San Carlos de Monte-Rey al Rio Carmelo en 5 Octubre de 1774.

Fray Juan Crespi
(rúbrica)

This same calm and high sea continued at dawn on Thursday, the 25th, as well as the tossing about we had experienced during the night, and a thick fog obscured the day. At eleven o'clock in the morning light puffs of wind began to come from the east-southeast or southeast, and the ship's head was put northeast, so that we might not go too far away from the coast, though we do not know how far away it is. At midday the sun came out so that with difficulty the Captain got an observation, and told us that our position was latitude 38° 32′. The light wind from the east-southeast continued, and we were in effect becalmed until seven at night, when a fresh northwest wind set in and we began to make some progress. Before nine the wind hauled to the northwest and so held until morning; and, this being a stern wind, we made good progress on a course southeast ¼ east, with intent to draw near to the coast.

Friday, the 26th, dawned with the sky overcast, and the fog was so thick that at the distance of a musket-shot nothing could be seen. About four o'clock in the morning the wind which we had had during the night shifted to the west-northwest, and the ship's head was put to east-southeast. This morning we saw many birds, both great and small, and ducks and many whales, not very far away from the ship. All this indicates that we are not very far from the coast; and, according to yesterday's observation and the considerable distance we have sailed during the night, we opine that we are not very distant from the port of San Francisco.[9] During the early morning the west-northwest wind ceased and, at about nine o'clock, it began to blow very strong from the northwest. About ten o'clock it was said that land was in sight on the bow and not very distant, although I was able to make it out with difficulty because of the thick fog. The Captain said that these were the *farallones* of San Francisco, the first to be met with in going from north to south; and he says that there are two groups of them, about five leagues distant from the coast or mainland, both groups stretching from northwest to southeast, distant about a league and a half, or two leagues, one group from the other.

The first group, which we saw very plainly as we passed it about a league away, is that toward the north, and consists of seven small rocky crags, not very large nor equal in size. That in the middle is

9 As has been mentioned elsewhere, this was the original San Francisco Bay, or Port, and is now know as Francis Drake's Bay, or Drake's Bay.

somewhat higher; and all are separated, one from the other. Of these, it appears, the histories and the records of the voyage of General Don Sebastián Vizcaíno make no mention. In order to pass by them the ship's head was put south ¼ southeast. By midday they were astern; and, had there been a clear sun, this would have been a good opportunity for the determination of their latitude. At this same hour of noon we began to make out the second group. They also are seven in number, and are very lofty. They seemed to be contiguous, and, seen from afar, appeared to form an island with seven peaks, some higher than others, with a circumference of about a league. Of these, it would appear, Admiral Cabrera Bueno* speaks, when he notes that they make a good landmark for finding Port San Francisco; for these seven, as Captain Don Juan Pérez tells me, stretch out in front of Point Reyes, and to the northward of this point, in the bay which begins to be formed there, that port is situated.

The *farallones* which, during the expedition by land of the year 1769, in which I took part, we saw on the 31st of October—as I relate in my diary†—are distinct from all these I have seen now; for it was not possible to see these from the place where the land expedition saw those, which was the shore of the bay on the other side of and almost opposite to Point Reyes. From that beach we took the bearings of those we saw then, and they were west ¼ southwest, and Point Reyes bore west ¼ northwest—that is to say, the bearings were two quarter points apart. Those which we have seen now lie northwest and southeast. Moreover: when, on that expedition, we took the bearings of the *farallones* we then saw, we were within the bay, or pocket, distant only about three leagues from the outlet of the two great lagoons, and had in full view the seven *farallones* which were distant only about a league and a half from us, while Point Reyes was distant, as the crow flies, about eighteen leagues. And as, according to the opinion of Captain Don Juan Pérez, these two chains of *farallones* are distant only about five leagues from the coast and from Point Reyes, it follows that, when the land expedition, being within the great bay, discovered the seven *farallones* of which the journals of the expedition tell, its

---

* An old time pilot who left sailing directions concerning the West Coast. See Joseph González Cabrera Bueno, *Navegación Especúlativa y Práctica*, 1734.

† See Bolton, *Fray Juan Crespi, Missionary Explorer on the Pacific Coast, 1769–1774,* 223, 227–28, and 250.

islands must have been twenty-three leagues away from those we have seen today. Consequently they can not be the same, but others which could not have been seen by the land expedition. I make a note of this so that all error may be avoided.[10]

At dawn on Saturday, the 27th, the same favorable and very fresh northwest wind which we had enjoyed during the night still held. About six in the morning we were off Point Año Nuevo, and presently began to enter the bay of Monterey. We came to anchor in that port about four in the afternoon, although we did not go ashore until the following day, after both of us had said mass. Thanks be to God, and to His mother most pure who has permitted us to arrive most happily at this port, although we suffer the disappointment of not having gained our chief end, which was to go as far north as sixty degrees of latitude, there to go ashore and to raise the standard of the holy cross.* May the Divine Majesty design that this voyage shall serve, at least, to move the heart of Our Catholic Monarch, and increase the christian zeal of the Most Excellent Viceroy, so that, by reason of the greater knowledge now acquired concerning this coast, and the good people dwelling there, they may send forth another expedition, and evangelical laborers who shall plant our holy faith among them and bring that pagandom into the fold of our holy church. Thus I beseech God, to whom be all honor and glory. Amen.

This diary, as has been stated, I, the above mentioned Fray Juan Crespi, kept from day to day during the voyage, writing the same in a book as occasion served and the events occurred. But, as at times poor facilities for writing, at others the tossing about of the ship, and at others still seasickness, had occasioned some error in handwriting and in style, after my arrival at this mission I have made a clean copy, making it a point to abbreviate where this could be done with propriety, yet without varying or substantially altering anything. And

---

10 Father Crespi's statement is very explicit. The opinion of the Bancroftian writer concerning that statement has already been noticed. Any one who chooses to compare Father Crespi's diary of the land expedition of 1769 and his diary given here will not find it difficult to understand what he says about *farallones*. Mr. Bancroft's writer (*History of the Pacific States*, vol. XIII, p. 146 et seq.) gives Crespi's diary of the expedition of 1769 to the 31st October, but does not give the entry made on the 31st. The account of what the explorers did see on the 31st, given on p. 156 of the same volume, appears to be what is termed "fine writing," but does not appear to be what Father Crespi, or any one else who took part in the expedition, did say.

thus I certify. In witness whereof I sign, at this mission of San Carlos de Monterey, at Río Carmelo, this 5th day of October, 1774.[11]

Fray Juan Crespi
(rubric)

[11] It will be interesting for the general reader to read what Mr. Bancroft's writers say concerning the voyage of the *Santiago*, in connection with these very minute diaries of Fathers de la Peña and Crespi. If, in addition, he will refer to any good map of the coast of Oregon and Washington, he may find that he will be unable to agree with those writers in the identification of points on that coast. The Bancroftian account of the voyage of the *Santiago* will be found, principally, in the *History of the Pacific States*, vol. XIII, 227–29, and vol. XXVII, 150–58.

* In addition to the four diaries of the expedition, a list of items picked up from the natives of the Northwest Coast was compiled. It appears in A. G. N., Historia 61; "Inventario de las Prendas combalachadas con los Yndios descubiertos a la altura de 55 grados y 49 minutos por los individuos de la Fragata Santiago destinada a explorar la costa septentrional de Californias que se remiten a S. M. por el virrey de Nueva España," Mexico, December 27, 1774.

A cloak that appears to be of coconut burlap.

Another of the same made with greater ability and bordered on one side with white and black, with little pieces of sea-otter skin in the form of little squares on both sides like a checker board.

A belt or sash that looks like wool and well-woven with the edges bordered with black.

A skin cap that looks like a he-goat with a sort of vizor of black seal skin adorned with two rows of teeth alongside, which appear to be those of a fish.

A hat woven with a great deal of ability which appears to be of fine basketry.

Another of the same, of Chinese style and much more beautiful because of its weaving and because it has depicted thereon the canoes which they use, and made of basketry material dyed black.

A quadrangular pouch also of basketry and without any stitching, with 24 little sticks of wood, well-carved and delicate, which they use for playing music during their dances.

A pouch or bag of very delicate basketry, very beautifully made, and on it, a species of bird made of bone with its upper beak broken, acquired from an Indian woman who wore it around her neck along with a number of little teeth, which looked like those of small alligators.